Motor Transport

Studies in Transport History

Series Editor: John Armstrong

Coastal and Short Sea Shipping
John Armstrong

Railways (volume I)
Terry Gourvish

Railways (volume II)
Geoffrey Channon

Road Transport in the Horse-Drawn Era
Dorian Gerhold

Air Transport
Peter J. Lyth

Canals and Inland Navigation
Gerald Crompton

Motor Transport
Margaret Walsh

The World of Shipping
David M. Williams

Motor Transport

Edited by

MARGARET WALSH

Routledge
Taylor & Francis Group
LONDON AND NEW YORK

First published 1997 by Ashgate Publishing

Reissued 2018 by Routledge
2 Park Square, Milton Park, Abingdon, Oxon, OX14 4RN
711 Third Avenue, New York, NY 10017, USA

Routledge is an imprint of the Taylor & Francis Group, an informa business

A Library of Congress record exists under LC control number: 97032125

ISBN 13: 978-1-138-32286-8 (hbk)
ISBN 13: 978-1-138-32289-9 (pbk)
ISBN 13: 978-0-429-45176-8 (ebk)

Contents

Studies in Transport History

Series Editor's Preface

The idea for this series originated in a meeting of the Editorial Board of *The Journal of Transport History*. As part of the celebrations to mark the fortieth anniversary of the founding of the journal, a classified index of the articles appearing in each of the series was compiled by Julie Stevenson and published in the September 1993 number of the journal. This exercise revealed the wealth of material that lay in the journal but which was largely forgotten and relatively inaccessible, unless a full run of the journal was close to hand. The index took the first step in making it simpler to determine what was in the journal. The Editorial Board decided it should continue this process by making the best of the essays more readily available.

Hence it is proposed to issue a series of volumes, each containing a number of articles reprinted from *The Journal of Transport History*, dealing with a particular mode of transport. As initially planned there are eight volumes in this series, each covering one form of transport and edited by a different member of the Editorial Board. Each volume contains about ten articles, reprinted from *The Journal of Transport History*. The articles have been selected because they were seminal at the date of their publication and have stood the test of time. Hence they are still important contributions to the state of our knowledge on the topic.

Each volume also contains an introduction by the editor of the volume, which seeks to contextualise the articles selected; that is, to show how each contribution fitted into the state of knowledge at the time of its publication, to explain its importance, to indicate any more-recent literature on the topic that might moderate its findings, and suggest how the debate has moved since the initial publication. Each article retains its original pagination, as in the journal. This will allow citations to be made to the original source.

Thus this series aims to make easily available the most important essays which have appeared in *The Journal of Transport History* over the last forty years, collected together on a thematic basis. It is hoped that this will encourage and provoke further research into transport history, in order to carry the debates into the twenty-first century.

John Armstrong
1996

Thames Valley University

Introduction: mass motoring, missing from history

MARGARET WALSH

In an era of mass motoring in Western economies, motor transport had eluded most historians, leaving it, like women until recently, almost invisible in history. Indeed, missing from history has been the well-known clarion call of women's historians in the quarter century since 1965 as they searched for the female past. Now women's history has become one of the most dynamic and prolific branches of history. Thousands of academics have become involved in producing not only scholarly monographs and general surveys, but numerous articles on more specialised areas such as women and labour, women and social reform, and immigrant women.[1]

Motor transport history has not seen a fraction of such activity. Missing from history remains the most appropriate expression to use when describing scholarly research on what has become the dominant form of transport in the twentieth century.[2] Why has there been such a paucity of interest and work? Part of the neglect stems from the reluctance, until recently, of European historians to examine events and issues in contemporary history. The mass of data to be sifted, the difficulties of being objective about recent events, the governmental caution about revealing official documents and the more appropriate skills of social scientists for current analysis have all been offered as rationales for scarcity of certain types of modern historical work. North Americans, however, have not been so cautious about undertaking recent twentieth-century history. Yet they, too, have undervalued motor transport, despite taking to the road to such an extent that they have coined terms like automobility, autopia and motorisation.

Other explanations for historical indifference to motor transport can be offered. Transport historians have generally favoured one mode, the railways, and have encouraged their research students to follow in their footsteps. There may well be only one journal worldwide, devoted to all of transport history, namely *The Journal of Transport History*, but historians have promoted significant specialised research on trains and rail companies, especially when examining nineteenth-century transport. Among transport enthusiasts, too, there is a greater knowledge and awareness of trains and their technologies than there is about cars, motor-cycles, lorries (trucks) and buses. Particularly in the United States, where rail service is now geographically limited, an ethos of wistfulness, if not romance, is associated with the 'Iron Horse' and there seems to be an inverse relationship between the extent of academic knowledge and the popular use of modes of transport.

Perhaps of equal practical importance in encouraging rail research and writing, rail companies, especially in their post-pioneering days, often retained their records. These materials have been made available to historians in either public or company depositories and, indeed, have provided ample evidence to suggest that railways were the pioneers of modern business format and behaviour.[3] Motor vehicles, by contrast, have generally been owned by individuals and have been run privately for their convenience. It is thus more difficult to examine motor vehicle patterns and systems. Furthermore, when used commercially, such vehicles have frequently been operated by small firms, whose records have been either destroyed or, as apparently unimportant family ventures, not sought out by archivists and librarians. Lacking access to a compact and easily identifiable body of primary sources, historians have turned elsewhere for their research interests.

Yet there is no direct correlation between the availability of business records and the significance of past events and issues. Much historical knowledge depends on the decisions of entrepreneurs, civil servants and bureaucrats to keep records, and on chance. Historians may need to be less traditional and more creative in discovering information about motor vehicles on the road and about roads and their use by vehicles. Significant sources exist, some of which belong peculiarly to the twentieth century. Government reports, hearings, debates, plans and statistics, trade journals, the records of trade and motoring associations and newspapers need to be exploited more fully. Media sources like photographs, documentary and popular films, oral interviews, social surveys and information from advertising agencies, the tourist trade and auxiliary services, like garages, restaurants, service stations and motels, offer both direct and indirect evidence of the rise and continued growth of motor transport. Theoretical frameworks for analysing motor transport problems and possibilities are available in a variety of social science literature. Much research and writing remains to be done in a post-modern age when historians have the advantages of using diverse sources alongside the more conventional tools of the profession.

This collection of motor transport articles was selected by Theo Barker, the doyen of the field. He was unable to write the introduction. The selection, however, does include his own recent excellent observations on the state and historiography of motoring research.[4] In order to avoid duplication, this introduction draws on my experience as a European historian of the United States and one whose research interests in transport history have focused on long-distance buses (as distinct from urban bus transit).[5] It also suggests a different generational view of the subject drawing on American research and an awareness of post-structural methodologies and ideas. Both articles, Theo Barker's and mine, show that there is plenty of room for new work in the field.

I

The Journal of Transport History has in some ways fallen victim to what Theo Barker has called the history of the motor industry masquerading as motor transport history.[6] Research and writing on the manufacture of motor vehicles, particularly cars, has taken the place of studies of the actual use of modern road vehicles. In macro-economic terms the motor industry, with its backward and forward linkages, has been the engine of growth for many twentieth-century economies, similar to the role played by the railway in the mid-to-late nineteenth century.[7] The motor industry has also developed new styles of business management, whether of the Ford or General Motors type. These have been central to the analysis of patterns of business behaviour and administration in the twentieth century.[8] With these foci, most academics who have written about the motor industry have been business and economic historians or economists applying theoretical frameworks to case studies. John B. Rae, who had a world-wide reputation as a transport historian, was one of a select few who wrote on the car manufacturing industry and also on the car as a mode of transport.[9]

The majority of articles in this collection are concerned with British motor transport and many deal with the motor industry. Roy Church's article of 1982 examines the growth of the motor industry before the First World War and compares its progress with that of its French counterpart.[10] In looking at sales policies in the pioneering years he found that firms and entrepreneurs in both countries failed to realise that the future of the industry lay in producing low-priced cars for a sizeable market. Both engineers and retail managers were wedded to the traditional and European concepts of luxury and sporting vehicles rather than adopting the more democratic American notion of a car for every family. Motor transport was, in this sense, limited by the producers.[11]

Twelve years later, in 1994, Timothy Whisler also analysed the British motor industry from a producing and retailing viewpoint.[12] Looking at the European market after the Second World War, he suggested that British companies captured only a small proportion of European sales. Once again producers were at fault. Using a Chandlerian approach Whisler found that automobile companies required a three-pronged investment in management, production and distribution if they were to expand their business in a mature or a post-industrial economy. British firms lacked the long-term vision to change established routines. Clinging to outmoded distribution networks in particular, they maintained only haphazard product channels. Certainly political issues connected to the European Free Trade Association and the European Economic Community complicated market arrangements, but firms did not appreciate the need to co-ordinate their product, the manufacturing process and the shipping of vehicles.[13]

The 'missing link' between the pioneer and mature British motor industry, namely the inter-war years, is the concern of the article written in 1976 by D. G. Rhys, who is interested in industrial concentration.[14] Writing within a framework of economics rather than of business history, he suggests that concentration in the industry was a result of severe price competition between manufacturers rather than of economies of scale. The concentration which developed in these years was not enough. There would have to be a further shake out after the Second World War. Yet again British managers displayed shortcomings in their operations. They preferred the 'fuddy-duddy' style of the entrepreneurial enthusiast rather than the progressive style of the professional manager.[15]

Production of cars depends not only on entrepreneurial and managerial decisions, but also on the physical layout of plants and the organisation and treatment of the labour force. Paul Collins and Michael Stratton, writing in 1988, discuss the importance of the design and layout of buildings in the manufacture of British cars before the Second World War.[16] As industrial archaeologists, they bring a different set of criteria to an understanding of the motor industry. Using engineering and popular journals, press clippings, photographs and building plans, they trace the transition from 'trestles to tracks'. Before the First World War a variety of buildings housed car firms. With increased demand for cars after the war, plants were reorganised, yet without undertaking any substantial new building. From the mid-1920s it was increasingly necessary to move from fixed to flexible shops with linear production arrangements in order to gain the full economic benefit of tracked assembly lines fed by overhead conveyors.[17] In considering the structure and shape of the British motor industry from its early days, these articles leave the reader to make judgements about how firms and their actions had an impact on the flow of motor vehicles on roads, whether in Britain or more distant export markets like Australia. Output figures and prices of vehicles are reported by firm and by industry but these say little about actual registrations, ownership of second-hand as well as new vehicles, usage in terms of length of journeys, seasonality, speed or ease of travel. Early ownership in Britain was limited and did not become widespread until the 1960s,[18] but the authors are more concerned with business behaviour than vehicle usage.

British motor transport was not solely concerned with cars. In his 1995 article on the motor-cycle industry in the 1930s Steve Koerner examines the potential of an alternative motor vehicle.[19] At the start of the 1930s Britain was the world's leading motor-cycle producer. This situation, however, did not continue. The preference for larger capacity motor-cycles, for sporting use or capable of drawing sidecars, may well have provided an alternative to the car for less well-off consumers in the 1920s. It also meant, however, that British manufacturers failed to develop the small-capacity cycle which might have been a rival to the bicycle for short-distance commuting. When the price of new and second-hand cars started to fall in comparison to the sidecar combination the British motor-cycle industry suffered. Lagging in technological improvements the industry could only find a niche market for sports use. Again British manufacturers' assessment of the potential popular market was deficient, or at least it was deficient by later standards.

Looking beyond the British producer's view of motor vehicles, Corinne Mulley probes the role of government intervention in influencing the development and use of commercial motor passenger transport in Britain in the 1920s.[20] Initially consideration of legislation stemmed from a concern for public safety on the highways. This examination of safety led to a substantive review of the economic conditions of operation, particularly competition. Issues of balancing the elimination of wasteful competition and protecting the travelling public from potentially oppressive monopolies demonstrated not only the mechanisms of public policy, but also the growth of the omnibus and the concern of trams and railways about their future passenger traffic.[21]

In this volume North American contributions to an understanding of the growth of motor transport reflect both the British emphasis on production of the motor vehicle and a wider perspective incorporating the consumer and the socio-economic environment. In analysing the Locomobile Company of America and its production of small steam cars at the turn of the twentieth century, L. J. Andrew Villalon and James M. Laux demonstrate that a market for lightweight and inexpensive cars existed before it was established by petrol cars.[22] Between 1899 and 1903 Locomobile sold some 5,200 vehicles, in the \$600-\$850 range, accessible to those in the professions and more generally the middle class. That these vehicles did not retain their initial lead stemmed from weaknesses in design which demanded regular refilling with water and which did not resolve the dangers of the boiler burning out. Technical and financial difficulties prompted the company to adopt petrol cars designed to appeal to the wealthy. The origins of the world-famous American automobile industry are more diverse, both technically and locationally than many historians have recognised.[23]

Travel patterns are central to Rod Bantjes's discussion of road transport in the Canadian province of Saskatchewan in the second quarter of the twentieth century.[24] Eschewing the standard interpretation advanced by rural sociologists and historians of the United States that the car was adopted quickly in rural areas and had a marked impact on social patterns of behaviour, he advocates a much slower take-up of cars. The predominance of dirt roads, constructed and improved by farmers as part-payment of their taxes, the length of these roads built in accordance with the Dominion Land Survey rather than taking the shortest and geographically easiest route, winter weather conditions and poor speed performance by cars, persuaded prairie farmers to retain proven modes of transport. Buggies, farm carts and cabooses provided a reasonable, albeit relatively slow, service. These conveyances helped retain older ways of rural living, like self-provisioning, health care as a family responsibility, local market exchanges and mail order. These ways persisted until the 1950s. In some locations in North America, there were significant environmental and technical limits to car use.[25]

Like Rod Bantjes, Margaret Walsh is also interested in consumers' responses to and perception of motor transport in the first half of the twentieth century.[26] In considering the advertising of major bus companies in the United States she tried to ascertain the demand for bus travel and to see how effective the efforts of bus operators were in stimulating that demand in a competitive environment. In the early years of their commercial development in the 1920s and 1930s buses were popular because they facilitated mobility along routes which were not fixed by rails. Given the existence of, and familiarity with, trains and the growing availability of cars which could satisfy individual needs, bus operators soon turned to advertising to promote their endeavours. Here they moved from informational text to imagery and slogans to encourage actual and potential customers to travel by bus. How successful their advertising was remains unknown because of the lack of independent survey data. Their perception of the best selling points of bus travel, namely, price, dependability, convenience and comfort, both for business and leisure use, demonstrated the nature and extent of travel patterns in a competitive era.

II

The ten articles in this volume offer an instructive portrait of the style of motor transport history available in recent years. Though concentrating on Britain, which is not the country where modern road transport has developed most intensively,[27] the selection points to the range of published materials which are available. What emerges from the articles is an emphasis on production and sales of motor vehicles, particularly cars. What is missing are analyses of traffic use, consumer choices, intermodal competition or co-operation and the relationship between motor vehicles and the social and physical environment. At the end of the twentieth century motor transport has stimulated as much, if not more, economic and social development and political debate than rail transport, yet historians have been reluctant to investigate either commercial or individual usage. In 1972 Derek Aldcroft remarked that a definitive study on the economic and social repercussions of motor transport still had to be written. He then added that it would be a brave person who undertook the task.[28] That person so far has not emerged. Writing in 1987, Theo Barker commented that little had been written in any systematic manner about the effects of motor vehicles on the road.[29] The session on the economic and social effects of the spread of motor vehicles which he organised for the International Historical Congress in Stuttgart in August 1985 clearly demonstrated an available expertise in motor vehicles and an interest in the subject in a wide range of countries.[30] Yet there have been only a few subsequent non-American academic publications which attempt a broader, perhaps multi-thematic history of motor transport or an aspect of it.[31]

In the United States, where the twentieth century has been recognised as 'the automobile age', transport historians have not always been trained as either economic or business historians. Political, social, cultural and urban historians and geographers have also written diverse contributions which involve discussing a range of activities focusing on motor vehicle ownership, road development and patterns of government involvement in the transport sector. 'Autopia' or 'automobility' recognises that the car, at least, has been of paramount importance in influencing American lifestyle as well as American development.[32]

The two motor transport historians of the United States, with world-wide reputations, John B. Rae and James J. Flink, have both recognised the centrality of the car as a privately owned and individually operated vehicle which must be placed in contexts relating to everyday experiences as well as to industrial production and distribution, the dynamics of regional and national growth and political influences. They have thus tackled issues like highway policy, relocation of business, leisure pursuits, freight carriage, car culture, inter-modal competition and the role of the State through regulation and taxation. Production of vehicles has remained at the heart of their work, but they discuss travel, individual and family mobility, the state of the roads, support systems like garages, filling stations, restaurants, fast-food chains, motels and recreational facilities, and problems associated with cars, like pollution, urban blight, accidents, speed, and supply of fuel. Their analyses may not be as rigorous as those of their railroad or canal counterparts but they have not neglected motor transport. Thanks to their work some discussion of motor vehicles can be found in mainline American history textbooks, as well as economic or business history texts.[33]

Though transport historians have emphasised the growth of car production and ownership, much more remains to be ascertained about vehicle usage while in private ownership. Clearly historians face considerable problems in finding sufficient data, even in social surveys, to build a composite picture of usage at the local level, let alone the regional or national level. Yet much information can be gained from examining the archival or statistical records of activities necessary to, or auxiliary to, motoring. Garages have retained records of sales and servicing. Urban planning authorities have often conducted inquiries about traffic flows in order to establish priorities for improving or changing road functions in cities, for establishing restricted zones and for building car parks. Use of cars for leisure pursuits has contributed to the growth of camping facilities, caravan parks, drive-ins, fast-food stops and the relocation and redesignation of hotels into motels. American historians have examined some of these aspects of motorisation in greater detail;[34] more remains to be done in both North America and Europe. Certainly Europeans, until recently, have not taken to the road in their own vehicles to the same extent as their counterparts across the Atlantic, but the growing impact of American cultural influences world-wide, has already stimulated American patterns of automobility elsewhere.

In developing countries where privately owned cars still are for many, luxury items, historians could usefully explore the ways in which these vehicles have been received officially and individually. Colonial administrators understood that road-building, however primitive, was an important means of control and economic development. The relatively few vehicles used in the colonial era were either owned by the state or by business companies and were often heavier vehicles used for haulage. Colonial records can provide useful insights into the reception and perception of motor transport.[35] Since independence motorisation has played a significant part in economic development, but its extent has been shaped by purchasing power, by foreign investments and by the policies favouring public rather than private forms of travel. In socialist countries where central planning has governed development, motorisation often became part of Soviet national plans. A vigorous road-building programme, the necessity of motor freight transport, bus routes, especially in rural areas, taxis in urban areas and the growth of privately owned cars all need exploration as well as the changes which have taken place since 1989.[36]

In developing countries large-scale people and goods movers have often been more important than cars; but the reverse seems true for 'first world' economies. The history of buses and trucks has been practically ignored in the United States and in Britain. American buses, now typecast as a 'poor person's vehicle' and a minor segment of the transport industry, have also been deemed unworthy of serious attention by either historians or analysts, unless the government or some private agency commissions specific reports. This neglect is compounded by a paucity of readily available and identifiable sources. Numerically bus companies have been, and remain, predominantly family enterprises which have not retained their records. Two large bus operations have dominated the industry since the 1930s, but their archives are either partial or unavailable. Other public sources are scattered, non-professional and time-consuming to use. Yet there is an important and relevant history which needs to be reclaimed both on the bus as a means of transport in its own right and as a competitor with other modes of transport.[37]

In Britain the history of buses has also been neglected by academics. The little information which is cited in general volumes on transport comes primarily from John Hibbs's long-standing association with bus operations.[38] Yet much more has been written about companies and regions in popular histories aimed primarily at the enthusiast audience and the general reading public. This type of contribution, however, has often been treated as peripheral to scholarly research. The scarcity of indicators, like bibliography, endnotes and archival evidence, the author's personal involvement with the industry and their oft-times dominant interest in design of vehicle, technology of engine, and photographic evidence all seem to render the volumes less than 'professional'.[39] Certainly the quality of this material varies; yet authors like Doug Jack who has written on Leyland and Volvo buses and who contributes regularly to *Bus Ride*, one of the leading journals world-wide for those in the bus business, has expertise in the field which is of use to the scholarly historian.[40] Academics need to interact more often with those in the trade and with enthusiasts to exchange information, and they need to make better and more use of visual evidence.

Lorries and the road haulage business, like buses, have been overlooked by historians. Again family firms using one or two vehicles, have until recently dominated the industry numerically and have thus been difficult to document.[41] Yet some academics have recovered a considerable amount of information about an activity which began in the early years of the century and expanded noticeably after the Second World War with the advent of high-quality, long-distance roads, capable of carrying heavy loads at speed. In the United States an interest in the role of the government and regulation has provided useful, albeit preliminary knowledge about 'trucking'. Bill Childs, for example, contributed insights into the origins, growth and management of truck companies in the inter-war years when they first became subject to federal government regulation. Donald Harper concentrated on regulation at the state level for a longer time period. For more recent years discussions of deregulation have offered a starting point.[42] Otherwise historians need to consult textbooks in transport economics, trade journals, government hearings, trade association records and business reports. The major monographs on motor freight companies still have to be written, as they do in Britain.[43]

Some further material on commercial motor transport has been accessible through work on inter-modal competition or co-operation. This research has focused primarily on the railways, their struggle to maintain routes and business from the 1920s and government transport policy. Some rail companies bought into both existing bus and truck operations or set up their own motor subsidiaries as feeders into their main lines. In the United States railroads were not restricted from such ventures in the early years of commercial motor transport. The regulatory community, however, soon treated buses and trucks as competition to railroads and enforced rules about the independence of each mode of transport.[44] Until the 1950s many government officials and professional economists, although not necessarily all transport operators, believed that each mode of transport had its 'natural advantages'. It took the deregulatory movement of the 1970s and 1980s to redesign the shape of the transport industry. Such changes in public policy on transport have not been decided in a vacuum. Government inquiries have been held to ascertain the nature and degree of competition within and between the different modes of transport. These hearings offer significant evidence of motor use and their potential has yet to be exploited.[45]

Yet another area in need of more research is that of the development and improvement of roads, at both the local and national level. John Rae was fond of remarking that the United States may have had the highest per capita ratio of cars in the world, but until recently it also had the worst roads in the world. His observation is also applicable to the history of American roads. Little published work is available. Official reports exist at the local, state and federal level, but the most coherent, albeit brief surveys, are located in textbooks on transport economics and their regularly revised editions.[46] There have been some policy studies on building major roads which add some evidence on the flow of motor transport, but these are few and far between.[47]

In his article surveying motor transport research Theo Barker suggested that work on roads in Europe was also negligible. The standard histories of transport in Britain say little about roads themselves.[48] Perhaps the undertaking is much more complicated than examining the history of building a canal or constructing a stretch of rail line and may be considered a subject more suited to civil engineering. Perhaps, too, the history of transport which is not generated from specific company records will need to be bequeathed to a future generation of academics who are better equipped to deal with a variety of diverse information, ranging from government policy through engineering decisions, to traffic counters on roads measuring flows and visual records. Certainly the twentieth century has seen the creation of substantial data, some of which is available electronically. What is needed are professional historians eager to examine physical communications and lateral mobility. They also require time and opportunity to work in the area themselves and to encourage postgraduate students to follow their example.

The rapid expansion of motor vehicles in the world, particularly in the advanced world, and the growth of roads upon which to run these vehicles suggests that there should be a flood of historical works on motor transport and its effects. We may well be living in the automobile age, the motorway age or the interstate highway age, but the extent of general knowledge is often limited to bare-bone statistics or scraps of information pieced together. Forecasts suggest that the car, motor-cycle, bus and lorry will remain with us for years to come and all will have major effects on their socio-economic hinterland. Perhaps the 'green' lobby or the cost of fuel will promote more interest in commercial motor passenger transport. Or perhaps an alterative fuel to petrol will emerge and will encourage even more small vehicles on the roads. Certainly past experiences will have some part to play in the shaping of future motor transport policy and historians will be failing in their role if they do not provide the public and governments with more information about what actually happened 'on the roads'.

Notes

Acknowledgements

I am very grateful to John Armstrong, Philip Bagwell and Chris Wrigley for reading and much improving an earlier version of this introduction. All mistakes and omissions remain my responsibility.

1 Most major academic presses and commercial presses which sell in the general as well as academic market have either a series in Women's History or Gender History. Articles are published not only in the three specialist journals, *Gender and History, Journal of Women's History* and *Women's History Review* but also in periodicals ranging from *History* to *Economic History Review.*

2 See also T. C. Barker, 'Slow progress: forty years of motoring research', *The Journal of Transport History*, 3rd series, vol. XIII, no. 2 (1992), pp. 142-3, reprinted as Chapter 1 in this volume and T. Barker and D. Gerhold, *The Rise and Rise of Road Transport, 1700-1990* (London, 1993), pp. 74-100.

3 This idea was advocated by A. D. Chandler Jr (ed.), *The Railroads: the Nation's First Big Business* (New York, 1965) and was made more popular in his article, 'The beginnings of big business in American industry', *Business History Review*, vol. XXXIII, no. 1 (1959), pp. 1-31 and his book, *The Visible Hand: the Managerial Revolution in American Business* (Cambridge, Mass., 1977), part II. Much of the academic work on railways is written within a Chandlerian framework.

4 Barker, 'Slow progress', pp. 142-3, reprinted as Chapter 1 in this volume.

5 In the United States 'transit' means a system of urban public transport. In the mid and late nineteenth century and early years of this century, transit applied to horse-drawn trolleys, electric streetcars, whether trams or trolleys, underground and overground railways and buses when they displaced streetcars. Though most systems were road transport, only buses strictly speaking were motor transport. Transit is distinct from urban transport which refers to all movement within an urban area by public and private means. In many statistics it is not always possible to distinguish between buses in urban transport and those in intercity movement.

6 Barker, 'Slow progress', p. 142, reprinted as Chapter 1 in this volume.

7 W. E. Leuchtenberg, *The Perils of Prosperity, 1914-1932* (Chicago, 1958), pp. 184-8 ; K. T. Jackson, *Crabgrass Frontier. The Suburbanization of the United States* (New York, 1985), pp. 157-89, 246-71.

8 A. D. Chandler Jr, *Strategy and Structure. Chapters in the History of Industrial Enterprise* (Cambridge, Mass., 1962), part III; *idem*, (ed.), *Giant Enterprise. Ford, General Motors and the Automobile Industry* (New York, 1964).

9 J. B. Rae, *American Automobile Manufacturers: the First Forty Years* (Philadelphia, 1959); *idem, The American Automobile. A Brief History* (Chicago, 1965); *idem, The Road and the Car in American Life* (Boston, 1971); *idem, Nissan/Datsun: a History of the Nissan Motor Corporation in U.S.A., 1960-1980* (New York, 1982); and *idem, The American Automobile Industry* (Boston, 1984).

10 R. Church, 'Markets and marketing in the British motor industry before 1914 with some French comparisons', *The Journal of Transport History*, 3rd series, vol. III, no. 1 (1982), pp. 1-20, reprinted as Chapter 2 in this volume.

11 Roy Church has recently produced a historiographical overview of the industry in *The Rise and Decline of the British Motor Industry* (London, 1994). For a detailed account of the French car industry in these years, see J. M. Laux, *In First Gear: the French Automobile Industry to 1914* (Montreal, 1976). A more recent and shorter description which includes other European pioneers, can be found in *idem, The European Automobile Industry* (New York, 1992), pp. 1-60.

12 T. R. Whisler, 'The outstanding potential market: the British motor industry and Europe, 1945-75', *The Journal of Transport History*, 3rd series, vol. XV, no. 1 (1994), pp. 1-20, reprinted as Chapter 3 in this volume.

13 For discussion of when and whether the British car industry was rising or falling in the post-war years see P. J. S. Dunnett, *The Decline of the British Motor Car Industry: the Effects of Government Policy, 1945-1979* (London, 1980); Church, *The Rise and Decline,* and J. Foreman-Peck, S. Bowden and A. McKinley, *The British Motor Industry* (Manchester, 1995).

14 D. G. Rhys. 'Concentration in the interwar motor industry', *The Journal of Transport History*, 2nd series, vol. III, no. 4 (1976), pp. 241-64, reprinted as Chapter 4 in this volume.

15 For a more recent analysis of the inter-war car industry which addresses the post-war debate about nationalisation see S. Bowden, 'The motor vehicle industry', in R. Millward and J. Singleton (eds), *The Political Economy of Nationalisation in Britain, 1920-1950* (Cambridge, 1995), pp. 88-115.

16 P. Collins and M. Stratton, 'From trestles to tracks: the influence of the motor car manufacturing process on the design of British car factories', *The Journal of Transport History*, 3rd series, vol. IX, no. 2 (1988), pp. 198-208, reprinted as Chapter 5 in this volume.

17 P. Collins and M. Stratton, *British Car Factories from 1896* (Goldmanstone, 1993), provides a fuller survey of the historical, geographical and architectural development of the industry.

18 D. H. Aldcroft, *British Transport since 1914. An Economic History* (Newton Abbot, 1975), pp. 164-8; D. Dorling, *A New Social Atlas of Britain* (Chichester, 1995), pp. 82, 196.

19 S. Koerner, 'The British motor-cycle industry during the 1930s', *The Journal of Transport History*, 3rd series, vol. XVI, no. 1 (1995), pp. 55-76, reprinted as Chapter 6 in this volume.

20 C. Mulley, 'The background to bus regulation in the 1930 Road Traffic Act: economic, political and personal influences in the 1920s', *The Journal of Transport History*, 3rd series, vol. IV, no. 2 (1983), pp. 1-19, reprinted as Chapter 7 in this volume.

21 For a further critique on government policy, both in relation to the 1930 Road Traffic Act and later legislation see S. Glaister and C. Mulley, *Public Control of the British Bus Industry* (London, 1983). Much more information has become available on the thorny issue of bus regulation since the advent of deregulation in 1985. P. Mackie, J. Preston and C. Nash, 'Bus deregulation: ten years on', *Transport Reviews*, vol. XV, no. 3 (1995), pp. 245-51 briefly surveys the domain and provides references for those who wish to follow the debate.

22 L. J. A. Villalon and J. Laux, 'Steaming through New England with Locomobile', *The Journal of Transport History*, 2nd series, vol. V, no. 2, (1979), pp. 65-82, reprinted as Chapter 8 in this volume.

23 For a broader perspective on early road vehicles in the United States see J. J. Flink, *The Automobile Age* (Cambridge, Mass., 1988), pp. 1-14.

24 R. Bantjes, 'Improved earth: travel on the Canadian prairies, 1920-50', *The Journal of Transport History*, 3rd series, vol. XIII, no. 2 (1992), pp. 115-40, reprinted as Chapter 9 in this volume.

25 Bjantes is at odds with the Canadian geographer G. Bloomfield on the issue of whether the car brought major changes in travel patterns in Saskatchewan before the Second World War. See G. T. Bloomfield, 'Motorisation on the new frontier: the case of Saskatchewan,

Canada, 1906-34', in T. Barker (ed.), *The Economic and Social Effects of the Spread of Motor Vehicles* (London, 1987), pp. 165-93.

26 M. Walsh, '"See this amazing America": the long-distance bus industry's use of advertising in its first quarter century', *The Journal of Transport History*, 3rd series, vol. XI, no. 1 (1990), pp. 61-88, reprinted as Chapter 10 in this volume.

27 In 1994 there were 2.7 persons per car and 2.3 persons per motor vehicle in the United Kingdom. In the United States the respective figures were 1.8 and 1.3. The figures for France and Germany, other early pioneers of motor vehicles, were respectively 2.3 persons per car and 2.0 persons per motor vehicle and 2.0 persons per car and 1.9 persons per motor vehicle. These figures are calculated from United Nations, *Statistical Yearbook*, 41 (New York, 1996), tables 8 and 62, pp. 35-48 and 534-9.

28 D. H. Aldcroft reviewing W. Plowden, *The Motor Car and Politics* in *The Journal of Transport History*, 2nd series, vol. I, no. 3 (1972), p. 192.

29 Barker, *The Economic and Social Effects*, p. ix.

30 The papers from this conference are printed in ibid.

31 An earlier exception was H. Perkin, *The Age of the Automobile* (London, 1976) whose social history of Britain in the twentieth century placed transport at its centre. In the past decade the interest of British economists and historians in consumerism has produced some information on the impact of the car in British society. See, for example, S. M. Bowden and P. M. Turner, 'Some cross-section evidence on the determinants of the diffusion of car ownership in the interwar UK economy', *Business History*, vol. XXXV, no. 1 (1993), pp. 55-69; S. M. Bowden and P. M. Turner, 'The UK market and the market for consumer durables', *Journal of Economic History*, vol. LIII, no. 2 (1993), pp. 244-58; S. O'Connell, 'The social and cultural impact of the motor car in Britain, 1918-39', PhD thesis, University of Warwick, 1996. A. Offer, has recently commented on the American car in 'The American automobile frenzy of the 1950s', in K. Bruland and P. K. O'Brien (eds), *From Family Firms to Corporate Capitalism: Essays in Business Industrial History in Honour of Peter Mathias* (forthcoming, Oxford, 1998), pp. 315-53.

32 Both of these words are American in parentage and are used to describe the central role of the automobile in American life in the twentieth century. Automobility received its most important usage in J. J. Flink, *The Car Culture* (Cambridge, Mass., 1975). Autopia, describing the continuing American love affair with the car, was used by J. Interante, 'The road to autopia: the automobile and the spatial transformation of American culture', *The Michigan Quarterly Review*, vol. XIX-XX (1980-81), pp. 502-17. This double issue of the journal, when over thirty authors contributed to a broad discussion of the car was subsequently published as D. L. Lewis and L. Goldstein (eds), *The Automobile and the American Car Culture* (Ann Arbor, Michigan, 1983).

33 Rae, *The American Automobile*; *idem*, *The Road and the Car*; *idem*, *The American Automobile Industry*; Flink, *The Car Culture; idem*, *The Automobile Age*.

34 For example, see W. J. Belasco, *Americans on the Road. From Autocamp to Motel, 1910-1945* (Cambridge, Mass., 1979); M. Berger, *The Devil's Wagon in God's Country - the Automobile and Social Change in Rural America* (Hamden, Conn., 1979); J. A. Jackle and K. A. Sculle, *The Gas Station in America* (Baltimore, Md, 1994); J. A. Jackle, K. A. Sculle and J. S. Rogers, *The Motel in America* (Baltimore, Md, 1996); P. J. Ling, *America and the Automobile. Technology, Reform and Social Change, 1893-1923* (Manchester, 1990); H. L. Preston, *Automobile Atlanta: the Making of a Southern Metropolis, 1900-1935* (Athens, Ga, 1979); S. L. Bottles, *Los Angeles and the Automobile* (Berkeley, Ca, 1987) and D. R. Goldfield and B. A. Brownell, 'The automobile and the city in the American South', in Barker, *The Economic and Social Effects*, pp. 115-29. For examples of this type of work on Europe see D. F. Dixon, 'Petrol distribution in the United Kingdom, 1900-50', *Business History*, vol. VI, no. 1, (1963), pp. 1-19; R. Brown, 'Cultivating a "green" image: oil companies and outdoor publicity in Britain and Europe, 1920-36', *Journal of European Economic History*, vol. XXII, no. 2 (1993), pp. 347-65; J. Foreman-Peck, 'Death on the roads: changing responses to motor accidents', in Barker, *The Economic and Social Effects*, pp. 264-90 and P. S. Bagwell, *The Transport Crisis in Britain* (Nottingham, 1996), pp. 28-36.

35 E. Sh. Tshund'olela, 'Motor transport in a developing area. (i) Zaire, 1903-59', in Barker, *The Economic and Social Effects*, pp. 236-55; S. Heap, 'The development of motor transport in the Gold Coast, 1900-39', *The Journal of Transport History*, 3rd series, vol. XI, no. 2 (1990), pp. 19-37; O. Oshin, 'Road transport and the declining fortunes of the Nigerian Railway, 1901-50', *The Journal of Transport History*, 3rd series, vol. XII, no. 1 (1991), pp. 1-36; P. Drummond-Thompson, 'The rise of entrepreneurs in Nigerian motor transport', *The Journal of Transport History*, 3rd series, vol. XIV, no. 1 (1993), pp. 46-63; B. J. Turton, 'The road motor services of Rhodesia, 1927-38', *The Journal of Transport History*, 3rd series, vol. XVIII, no. 1 (1997), pp. 1-15.

36 M. A. Akhunova, B. A. Tulepbaev and J. S. Borisov, 'Motor transport in a developing area. (ii) Soviet Central Asia', in Barker, *The Economic and Social Effects*, pp. 256-63; J. N. Westwood, 'Transport', in R. W. Davies, M. Harrison and S. G. Wheatcroft (eds), *The Economic Transformation of the Soviet Union, 1913-45* (Cambridge, 1994), pp. 179-80, suggests that little has been written on road transport in this period.

37 M. Walsh, *Making Connections. The Long-Distance Bus Industry in the United States* (Aldershot, forthcoming, 1998).

38 Among J. Hibbs's many publications are *The Omnibus. Readings in the History of Road Passenger Transport* (Newton Abbot, 1971); *The History of British Bus Services*, (Newton Abbot, 1st edn, 1968; 2nd edn, 1989); *The Bus and Coach Industry: Its Economics and Organization* (London, 1975) and 'The history of the motor bus industry. A bibliographical survey', *The Journal of Transport History*, 2nd series, vol. II, no. 1 (1973), pp. 41-55. See also J. Singleton, 'Ribble Motor Services and co-operation in the interwar bus industry', *The Journal of Transport History*, 3rd series, vol. XVI, no. 2 (1995), pp. 117-33. Researchers can find more information in the records of such organisations as the Society of Motor Manufacturers and Traders and the Institute of Automobile Engineers.

39 There is an abundance of bus books for the popular and enthusiast audience. Though many of these volumes do not offer a systematic understanding of the development of the company in question, they do provide evidence which is otherwise unavailable to the academic historian. The authors have often worked in the bus industry, have access to company records and have interviewed bus workers, albeit more often management than shopfloor employees. See, for example, volumes published by Ian Allen, British Bus Publishing, Transport Publishing Company and Venture Publications. Several of these volumes have been reviewed in *The Journal of Transport History* in recent years.

40 Doug Jack worked in the bus and coach industry as a consultant, dealer and bodybuilder for twenty-one years. He now runs and has managed Transport Resources International for eleven years. See, for example, *Beyond Reality. Leyland Bus - the Twilight Years* (Glossop, 1994) and *Volvo Bus. 25 Years of Progress* (Glossop, 1997).

41 See the introduction to T. Barker, *The Transport Contractors of Rye. John Jempson & Son, A Chapter in the History of British Road Haulage* (London, 1982), pp. 9-10. This is one of the few company histories written by an academic. As with buses, there is an active book trade on commercial vehicles for enthusiasts.

42 W. R. Childs, *Trucking and the Public Interest. The Emergence of Federal Regulation, 1914-1940* (Knoxville, Tenn., 1985); D. V. Harper, *Economic Regulation of the Motor Trucking Industry by the States* (Urbana, Ill., 1959); C. Winston, T. M. Corsi, C. M. Grimm and C. A. Evans, *The Economic Effects of Surface Freight Deregulation* (Washington, D.C., 1990).

43 For a specialised monograph see G. L. Turnbull, *Traffic and Transport: an Economic History of Pickfords* (London, 1979). Other scattered information is available on lorries in P. Smith, 'The road haulage industry, 1945-79: from statutory regulation to contested terrain' in C. Wrigley (ed.), *A History of British Industrial Relations, 1939-1979* (Cheltenham, 1996), pp. 212-34; J. M. Laux, 'Trucks in the West in the First World War', *The Journal of Transport History,* 3rd series, vol. VI, no. 2 (1985), pp. 64-70 and a sociological work, P. G. Hollowell, *The Lorry Driver* (London, 1968). Peter Scott is currently working on general road haulage. See 'The growth of road haulage in Britain, 1921-58: a problem of measurement', unpublished MS, 1997.

44 See, for example, M. Walsh, 'The Motor Carrier Act of 1935. The origins and establishment of federal regulation of the inter-state bus industry in the United States', *The Journal of Transport History*, 3rd series, vol. VIII, no. 1 (1987), pp. 66-80; *idem*, 'Coordination, cooperation or competition: the Great Northern Railway and bus transportation in the 1920s', in R. Cameron (ed.), *Cities and Markets. Studies in the Reorganization of Human Space* (Lanham, Md, 1997), pp. 163-89; *idem*, 'In whose interest? Public policy and transportation during depression and war', unpublished MS; S. W. Usselman, 'Trying to keep the customers stratified: government, business and the paths of innovation in American railroading and computing', unpublished MS, pp. 1-12; G. L. Thompson, *The Passenger Train in the Motor Age. California's Rail and Bus Industries, 1910-41* (Columbus, Oh., 1993), pp. 63-90; Childs, *Trucking and the Public Interest*; P. Butterfield, 'Branch lines, wayside stations and road competition', *The Journal of Transport History,* 3rd series, vol. XVI, no. 2 (1995), pp. 179-95 and Bagwell, *The Transport Crisis*, pp. 63-75.

45 For the United States see, Interstate Commerce Commission, 'Motor Bus and Truck Investigation', Docket Number 18300, Testimony and Exhibits, 1926-27; *idem*, 'Co-ordination of Motor Transportation', Docket Number 23400, Testimony and Exhibits, 1930-31; *idem*, 'Investigation of Bus Fares', Docket Number MC-C-550, 1946-49, National

Archives Records Group, BMC-C-550 (Microfilm located at the Surface Transportation Board, formerly Interstate Commerce Commission, Washington D.C.; paper copies located at Washington National Records Center, Suitland, Md). More recently moves to deregulate and privatise public transport have produced another batch of evidence in government hearings and inquiries. See, for example, US Congress, *Intercity Domestic Transportation System for Passengers and Freight*, (95 Congress, 1 Session), Committee Print (1977). In Britain, Parliamentary Papers, Royal Commission and Select Committee minutes, Hansard and Ministry (Department) of Transport reports provide evidence which has not appeared elsewhere.

46 See, for example, D. P. Locklin, *Economics of Transportation* (Chicago, 1st edn, 1935, Homewood, Ill., 7th edn, 1972); C. A. Taff, *Commercial Motor Transportation* (Homewood, Ill., 1st edn, 1951; Centerville, Md, 7th edn, 1986). Some general information is also available in M. G. Lay, *Ways of the World: a History of the World's Roads and of the Vehicles that used Them* (New Brunswick, N.J., 1992).

47 M. H. Rose, *Interstate: Express Highway Politics, 1941-1956* (Lawrence, Ks, 1979); B. E. Seely, *Building the American Highway: Engineers as Policy Makers* (Philadelphia, 1987); H. L. Preston, *Dirt Roads to Dixie: Accessibility and Modernization in the South, 1886-1935* (Knoxville, Tenn., 1991). An earlier and useful survey is C. L. Dearing, *American Highway Policy* (Washington, D.C., 1941). For an interdisciplinary approach which incorporates history, geography and culture see K. Raitz (ed.), *The National Road* and *A Guide to The National Road* (Baltimore, Md, 1996).

48 See for example, P. S. Bagwell, *The Transport Revolution, 1770-1985* (London, 2nd edn, 1988); H. J. Dyos and D. H. Aldcroft, *British Transport. An Economic Survey from the Seventeenth Century to the Twentieth* (Harmondsworth, 1969); Aldcroft, *British Transport since 1914*.

1 Slow progress: forty years of motoring research

T. C. BARKER

The number of motor vehicles of all kinds in the world has grown twelvefold in the last fifty years, from 47 million in 1940 to some 600 million.[1] They are now much larger and more efficient machines, often driven at much higher speeds along specially built motor roads. So the world-wide effect of this growth is even greater than this twelvefold increase suggests. There is now more than one, vastly improved and far more efficient, motor vehicle to every ten people on earth in our motorway age.

We are not just thinking of motor cars. Among the 47 million vehicles in 1940 over 8 million were lorries (trucks) and buses, and a further 3 million motor cycles. By 1990 nearly half the total number of vehicles in the world came into these three non-car categories. Motor transport in its various forms, that is to say, has had an increasing influence on most people in most countries whether they belonged to car-owning families or not. It has been an influence which has been cumulatively far greater, socially, economically and environmentally, in the second half of the century than in the first.

For the last half-century this has clearly been a promising subject for present-minded historians. Yet, despite its growing importance, they have been quite slow to turn their attention to it; and when they did so, they concentrated mainly upon motor cars and motor car *manufacture*, to what is in fact business, rather than transport, history, relatively straightforward to write in terms of the business leaders, and household names on the bonnets of cars, with readily accessible company and family records. The many-sided effects of the growing flood of motor cars as they poured on to the poor and limited roads of the early days posed a much greater challenge to historians; far more difficult to analyse and discuss. And the bus and haulage businesses, the latter often small, one-man concerns, were more often than not overlooked altogether. Moreover, when studying road improvement, the historian was confronted with a task far more difficult than that encountered when writing about railway building, for that involved completely new feats of civil engineering, much described at the time, and, as parts of the railway business itself, well documented.

It is hardly surprising that very few research students in Britain chose motor transport as a thesis subject. Their supervisors were certainly most reluctant to encourage them to venture into such *terra incognita*. This is evident from Dyos's thesis survey of May 1960.[2] Significantly, the notable exception included in that list is I. S. Lloyd's 'Rolls Royce: the Growth of a Firm', submitted for a Cambridge M.Sc. in 1951. This remarkable work was subsequently extended and published in three volumes in 1978, with some revealing comments upon his 'academic mentors at Cambridge' and that university's attitude to the subject by its author, then Ian Lloyd, MP.[3] In the event it was the American Allan Nevins who gained credit for producing the first piece of post-war motor transport history,[4] quickly followed by the English scholars Andrews and Brunner's life of Lord Nuffield.[5] There were two further volumes on Ford.[6] In this way motor car manufacture came to masquerade as motor transport history for many years.

The need to shift from what the American scholar James J. Flink rightly described as the 'narrow, uncritical concentration on the automobile industry . . . toward an emphasis upon automobility as a force influencing American life'[7] first gained wider attention at the end of 1971, when a session at the annual meeting of the American Historical Association was devoted to this broader approach. Flink had just published one book, called *America adopts the Automobile, 1895–1910* (1970), and his next (1975) was to be on *The Car Culture*.[8] The next landmark came in 1980 when the *Michigan Quarterly Review* published a double issue also concerned with the broader aspects of the subject, with contributions from over thirty different authors. It was so well received that it had to be reprinted several times and was subsequently published as a book.[9] It quickly went through several editions.

So far, so good; but these American efforts to take a wider view were still confined mainly to motor cars and were concerned chiefly with the United States. It was at this point that I found myself in the fortunate position of being able to arrange a meeting of specialists from many countries to look at the process of motorisation even more widely, for the International Historical Congress was due to meet in Stuttgart in 1985, precisely the part of the world where the first continuous series of experiments with petrol motors, mechanised cycles and horseless carriages had started almost exactly a century before. It was an opportunity not to be missed. To the Stuttgart congress came a remarkable group of transport historians who had never before all met together. Most notable was John B. Rae, the doyen of American specialists, who had produced 'the first complete, authoritative treatment of the whole span of the automobile industry', as the dust jacket on his pioneer work rather prematurely claimed, and then *The Road and the Car in American Life*.[10] He contributed a masterly paper which, *inter alia*, summarised the American achievement by tables of figures showing the growth of inter-city passenger and freight movements by each transport mode between 1950 and 1983, which brought out the growing importance of motor lorries during those years. Two other American scholars, David R. Goldfield and Blaine A. Brownell, considered the effect of motor cars upon cities in the American south, and Gerald T. Bloomfield, from Canada, looked at its effects between 1906 and 1934 in a frontier region, Saskatchewan. He also provided a most valuable graph showing motor *vehicle* adoption rates during those years in the more advanced countries of the world, which included Australia, New Zealand and Argentina as well as the United States and Canada. Another American transport historian, a specialist in French history who, as we shall see, has very recently made major contributions to our understanding of motor transport developments in Europe, James M. Laux, spoke about the spread of diesel lorries and buses in the United States.

Among European contributors, Otto Nübel, archivist of Daimler-Benz, discussed the beginnings of motor cars in Germany, and in a particularly thought-provoking paper the historian of Renault,[11] Patrick Fridenson, used French statistics to show that in France the motor industry employed only 215,000 workers directly but a further 1·9 million (in all, nearly 10 per cent of the entire French labour force) in a whole spectrum of businesses ranging from motor drivers, garage workers and employees in industries like steel, glass and rubber, supplying material for motor manufacture at one end of it, to insurance salesmen, road builders and car parking attendants at the other. Jaroslav Purš considered the effect of the internal combustion engine in the Czech lands and the occupations of motor vehicle owners there, and compared the number of inhabitants per car in Czechoslovakia between 1920 and 1970 with that in many other European countries. Germany, the pioneer, lagged behind. Fritz Blaich explained why this was still the case between the wars. Dominique Barjot looked at advances in road construction in France, while James Foreman-Peck applied his numerical expertise to statistics of fatal road accidents and government responses to them not only in various European countries but also in the United States. Another English historian, Margaret Walsh, also invaded American historians' territory to discuss the early growth of long-distance bus transport in America. Japan's leading motor transport historian, Koichi Shimokawa, managed to compress into twenty pages a succinct summary of the slow start of motorisation in that country and its phenomenal growth after 1960. In contrast, there were two papers on the role of motor transport in developing areas: Soviet Central Asia (M. A. Akhunova, B. A. Tulepbaev and J. S. Borisov) and Zaire (Epanya Sh. Tshund'olela). All these papers, revised in the light of lively discussion at the congress, were edited and published.[12]

The history of motor transport can now be seen as a subject which stretches far beyond motor car production in a given country, or even just the effects of motor *cars*. Much is to be learned from international comparisons and, *per contra*, international generalisations can be helpful in coming to grips with the effects of motorisation in particular countries or in groups of countries with similar characteristics of economic growth. The complexities of the subject remain as challenging as ever, especially when the range and extent of the sources are taken into account. The present essay is inevitably partial and subjective. It is written in the hope that it will be of some help to potential newcomers to the subject and also that, by its omissions, it will annoy those old stagers — particularly the technical experts — who have specialised in some particular aspects to such an extent that they may be goaded into giving us the benefit of some broader-based efforts. It falls into readily identifiable periods: the years before about 1905, when the petrol engine was developing from its early experimental stage; 1905–30, when the United States raced ahead of the rest of the world in motor car ownership if not to the same extent in the ownership of other forms of motor vehicle; and the years between 1930 and the present, when the rest of the world caught up, much helped after 1960 by events in Japan.

Origins and early development

Railways created more short-distance horse-drawn transport on roads to railway stations and in areas still unserved by trains than they eliminated over medium and longer distances. Most of the traffic in the growing towns was also horse-drawn. F. M. L. Thompson has estimated — and nobody has yet challenged his estimates — that even in Britain, which came to possess a particularly dense railway network, the total number of horses categorised as 'horses not on farms' (i.e. mainly for purposes of public or private travel by road or for haulage) grew from an estimated 487,000 in 1811 to 535,000 in 1851 and then, at a much faster rate, to 1,358,000 in 1891 and 1,766,000 in 1901.[13] There are no comparable estimates for the United States, much less urbanised at that time, but at the US census of 1900 there were said to be 2·9 million horses not working on farms or ranges.[14] Of the farm horses, then estimated at 1·5 million in Britain and 15·5 million in the United States, some would also have been used for local transport purposes. Horses are a costly form of traction, for they eat a great deal — sometimes estimated at the yield of three or four acres of land a year and twice that amount when pulling heavy vehicles — and have to be fed even when they are not working. A rich prize clearly awaited anyone who could find some means of replacing the horse for shorter journeys by road by some sort of mechanised power, much as the steam train had already done for longer ones.

The main contenders were (1) the steam engine, tried and trusted, with improved power-to-weight ratio and Serpollet's flash boiler; (2) the electric motor, relatively straightforward and much favoured in the United States, where, without a coal gas industry, electricity was all the rage; and (3) the internal combustion engine, technically the most complex of the three to develop and to drive, for it involved the co-ordination of both eyes, both hands and both feet. The third eventually won because of its advantageous power-to-weight ratio when the portable energy source as well as the engine itself were both taken into account, but in the early years petrol vehicles cheap enough to enjoy widespread commercial sale were low-powered and could be used to propel only lighter vehicles: open tourers, motorised cycles and delivery vans. For heavier road transport the electric tramcar, which spread from the later 1880s onward, when the petrol motor was still at an early experimental stage, enjoyed growing popularity but suffered from having to follow a fixed track and draw its energy from overhead wires. (The portable source of electrical energy — numbers of heavy lead batteries requiring regular changing or recharging — proved quite unsuitable.) More modern oil or coke-fired steam engines found favour for a time as a means of powering lorries and, in some cases, buses. As more efficient petrol (and later diesel) engines were developed, however, they replaced steam vehicles and, in most cases, electric tramcars.

Just as the steam locomotive had been pioneered in Britain, where stationary steam engines had been developed over previous years, so the first serious attempts to put gas engines on wheels took place in Germany, where stationary gas engine development was most advanced. Gottlieb Daimler, the world's leading expert on the subject, was, however, interested in selling his petrol engine on its own for all purposes, not in building complete motor vehicles. Carl Benz, who did see motor-driven vehicles as his objective, produced a much inferior, slower-speed engine which was hard put to it to move a 600 lb tricycle. Brief biographies of Otto, Daimler, Benz, Diesel and Bosch have been translated into English[15] and provide a valuable background to the German part of the story.

Contrary to widely held present-day views of the relative strengths of German and French industry at the time, it was the French who exploited German inventiveness commercially, particularly the Paris metalworking concern of Panhard & Levassor (P&L), which made Daimler engines under licence from 1887, and Armand Peugeot, the French cycle maker at Valentigney, not far from the Swiss frontier, who was persuaded to fit a French-made Daimler engine to a light quadricycle in 1890. In the following year Levassor turned his attention to designing a heavier vehicle, putting the engine at the front instead of at the rear, under the seat. Emile Roger, who had been French agent for Benz's stationary engines, started to sell his primitive vehicles — called Rogers, because of Franco-German animosity. Contests along France's superior roads — especially the race to Bordeaux and back in 1895 — showed the advantages of the petrol engine over steam or electricity and, aided by much publicity, made France for a few years the centre of world motoring. All this is well described by James Laux in his *In First Gear*, as well as at the beginning of his most recent book, where he indicates the extent of French ascendancy.[16] Progress was very slow at first. In the years before 1898 the Benz company had sold only 1,132 cars altogether, 334 of them in Germany and 509 in France. The French, however, produced 1,500 motor vehicles in that one year, 1898, alone. By 1903 Germany was making 1,450 motor vehicles and France 14,100; by 1906 the figures were 5,218 and 24,400 respectively.[17]

The very small demand for petrol-driven vehicles on the continent of Europe — and in the United States, as we shall see — before the mid-1890s causes us to reconsider whether the so-called Red Flag legislation delayed the development of the new industry in Britain. Laux has noted that P&L's first sales (six) and Peugeot's (four) had come only in 1891. According to this latest count, 'through 1895 Peugeot sold a total of 169 cars and P&L 164, compared with Benz's 271 (135 exported to France) over these years'.[18] (Benz had also started making four-wheelers in 1893.) Even at the end of 1895 — that is to say, after the successful publicity gained by Levassor in the Bordeaux race — there were still only a very few, very primitive petrol-driven vehicles on the continent of Europe compared with the 8,000 steam traction engines already at work on the roads of England and Wales (and others in Scotland).[19] It was to limit the speed and movement of these cumbersome and fiery monsters, terrifying to horses, that legislation had been passed in 1865 and 1878 to warn man and beast of their approach. In any case, this legislation was repealed in 1896. Motors weighing under three tons unladen were allowed to travel on Britain's roads from 14 November that year, subject to a speed limit of 14 m.p.h., which local authorities had the power to reduce if they wished. Enforcement, however, was another matter.

Britain already had one or two budding motor car makers even before the Red Flag legislation was repealed: Herbert Austin and Frederick Lanchester in England and George Johnson in Scotland, for instance, we know about because they went on to found businesses of their own. Opportunities for the resourceful were still immense, for, as the English journal *Engineering* put it in 1896, at the time of the repeal, 'at present the science of designing mechanical road carriages is in a very elementary stage, and much remains to be done before it can be claimed that a motor car has been produced to take its place on the highway as a commercially successful carriage to do general work in competition with horse-drawn vehicles'.[20] Enterprising development was not helped, however, by the general business boom, then particularly strong in the allied pedal cycle industry. On the contrary, the boom encouraged the activities of scheming speculators. Chief among them was H. J. (Harry) Lawson, who had already learned how quick fortunes could be made out of company promotion in transport; he had been involved in some schemes, notably Dunlop Rubber and Humber, in association with the most notorious promoter of all, Ernest Terah Hooley. The Dunlop and Humber companies did lead, however, to end-products. Lawson's motor vehicle promotions, on the other hand, raised very large sums of money but produced very few cars or cycles. His was a deterrent, negative influence at a critical time.

His first move was to acquire, late in 1895, for £35,000, the Daimler Motor Syndicate, owners of the UK Daimler licences. He immediately refloated it for £150,000 as the British Motor Syndicate, with the intention not of producing cars, as the French had done, but of acquiring further UK licences to extend his control over the new industry. These rights he would either sell on to others and/or charge royalties on every vehicle they made or imported. (Among the rights subsequently acquired were those for De Dion and Bollée motor tricyles.) T. R. Nicholson, who has picked his way through all these financial manoeuvres,[21] goes on to explain how the 'sleazy, dynamic Lawson' then launched the Daimler Motor Company in January 1896 with 100,000 £1 shares, all of which were taken up. A disused cotton mill was bought at Foleshill, Coventry, the scene of a fire five years before. In May 1896, with the repeal of the Red Flag legislation in prospect, the suspicious-sounding Great Horseless Carriage Company was floated for £750,000 to acquire part of this factory, and in mid-June the more respectably named New Beeston Cycle Company was set up with £1 million capital to make pedal bicycles as well as 'self-acting bicycles and tricycles'. All this amidst a blaze of optimistic publicity, aided by *The Autocar*, started in November 1895 and soon dependent on Lawson for its advertising, and by his Motor Car Club, formed in January 1896 not only to arrange exhibitions and demonstrations but also to give 'help to inventors in perfecting and disposing of their inventions and rights' and introductions to 'buyers and capitalists' for manufacturers and inventors.[22]

It was Lawson's Motor Car Club which organised the first Brighton run on 14 November 1896, the day the Red Flag legislation was repealed. It was a great advertising stunt to enable him to unload more shares upon the public, the way having been prepared with the declaration of a third interim dividend (110 per cent) on British Motor Syndicate shares (bringing the total for the year to 150 per cent) but payable in Great Horseless Carriage Company stock.[23] A week after the Brighton run Lawson asked the investing public for another £1 million to enable the British Motor Syndicate to be reorganised so that it could acquire yet more licences. No British-built Daimlers were yet forthcoming, however, and those in the know began to expose the insubstantial (if not dishonest) basis of all Lawson's much publicised activities. He preferred to collect royalties on foreign imports, and by July 1897 only twenty vehicles of the Panhard type had been completed by Daimler in Britain: it needed 200 men to turn out three of these a week. By November 1897 only four British-built Bollées had been sold. But by then the value of Lawson's companies had collapsed, investors had lost their savings and Lawson himself had disappeared from the motoring scene. The confidence trick was over. 'Whatever the advertised intentions of Lawson's businesses,' Nicholson has concluded, 'they were not interested in delivering goods . . . public confidence in him had disappeared; nothing would now convince even the most gullible investors that his motor car shares had any value.'[24] The Daimler company eventually survived after reorganisation, but the whole British motor industry had been given a bad name, making it more difficult for honest manufacturers to raise capital. There is still scope for further enquiry into this whole complex financial diversion in an attempt to discover how close motor vehicle technololgy was in the mid-1890s to the point at which British management, and capital, had it been well directed, could have seized the initiative and developed the new industry on a larger scale, using the technical and marketing expertise that the British had already acquired as world leaders in the pedal cycle industry. So far as Lawson was concerned, he eventually came to a sticky end, being sent to prison for six months with hard labour after being found guilty of fraud connected with electric tramways in 1904. When he died in 1925 he left £99 gross, as Richard Storey has told us in the only brief biography of him.[25]

As more imported motor vehicles appeared on the roads of free-trade Britain, other British manufacturers started to emerge, keen to gain a share of the very small but growing home market. Z. E. Lambert (his daughter) and R. J. Wyatt have described Austin's beginnings, and Roy Church has written a much fuller, business history.[26] After the collapse of the pedal cycle boom, firms such as Singer, Riley, BSA and Sunbeam went into motor manufacture in and after 1898 and were followed later by Lea-Francis and Rover. S. B. Saul explored these in a very important, and still too little consulted, article, in 1962.[27] He discovered fifty-nine British firms making motor cars before 1900, twenty-one of which were still in existence in 1914, though 'most of the early British cars were an adaptation of French models (Napier and Daimler in particular) and some were in part French . . . De Dion and Aster engines were widely used.' When the British did produce their own models, they concentrated on the top end of the market, with engines requiring 'high finish, quality materials, painstaking erection and elaborate testing' at high prices.[28] This prevented them from gaining the cost advantages of scale production as the Americans were able to do after 1900. While certainly agreeing with this conclusion, at the Stuttgart meeting I argued that the British were behaving quite rationally. They took account of the nature of the British and British Empire market, which lacked the Americans' social depth of demand. More credit should be given for Britain's logical concentration upon heavy vehicles, on the one hand, and upon cheaper, more affordable, motor bicycles on the other.[29]

The heavy vehicle trials carried out in the Liverpool area in 1898, 1899 and

1901 were backed by the merchants there, who were becoming increasingly concerned at the effects upon their port of the Manchester Ship Canal, opened in 1894, which allowed ocean-going shipping to sail direct to Manchester instead of unloading in Liverpool and despatching their cargoes from there. In order to compete more effectively, the Liverpool men sought better terms from the railways to Manchester but the railways would not oblige. Mechanised road transport would provide the competition to bring the necessary pressure to bear, much as the Liverpool–Manchester railway itself had brought the intransigent waterways to terms eighty years or so before. In the event, the road trials did not produce a new, commercially viable form of mechanical traction for heavy vehicles; but they did give much encouragement to the makers of steam waggons, including Leyland Motors in Lancashire and Foden's in Cheshire. About 1,000 steam waggons were running on Britain's roads by 1903, and some were carrying loads of cotton from Liverpool to Manchester, in competition with the railways, in, or soon after, 1905. From about that time, however, petrol engines had been developed to the point at which some manufacturers, like Leyland Motors, diversified into petrol-driven lorries and buses.

British-made motor bicycles also gained favour: owners of pedal cycles — and younger men generally — who could not afford motor cars were able to buy and run these much cheaper machines. At first many of the engines were bought in, often from abroad, but by the beginning of 1904 the recently launched periodical *The Motor Cycle*, itself a sign of the machines' growing popularity, told readers that Britain no longer imported much, 'except certain parts that are to be obtained cheaper abroad . . . and there are very few now'.[30] Sidecars and forecars were fitted to the more powerful models.

It was not until soon after 1900 that America's experience started to differ much from Britain's. The total number of motor vehicles produced in 1899, according to the *US Census of Manufacturers*, 1900, was about 2,500; but, as Flink, the leading authority, has observed, this figure included steamers and electrics, both of which were then attracting many customers in America, and, according to him, 'were responsible for the most significant part of that output'.[31] Nearly 3,000 of the light steam Locomobile, first manufactured in 1899, had been sold by the middle of 1901 at $600. According to Villalon and Laux,[32] it showed the way for the more reliable and economical petrol-driven curved-dash Oldsmobile. At the Stuttgart meeting I hazarded the guess that, in view of these, and other, steamers — and electrics as well — there may not have been more than 1,500 vehicles of the petrol-driven variety running in the United States in 1900, about the same number as in Britain, though a much higher proportion in use in America were home-produced.[33] Certainly the tiny output of each of the American petrol vehicle manufacturers and their belated appearance suggest a rate of development very similar to that in Britain in the later 1890s.

Henry Ford, superintendent of the Detroit Edison Illuminating Company's engineering department, who had built an experimental petrol-driven quadricycle in his spare time in 1896, left Detroit Edison only in 1899, when the Detroit Automobile Company was formed to market another Ford vehicle. Flink notes that 'it was by no means obvious at the turn of the twentieth century that the four-cycle internal-combustion engine was vastly superior as an automotive power plant over alternatives', but he goes on to quote with approval the June 1900 *American Monthly Review of Reviews'* comment that the petrol car had

> developed more all-round good qualities than any other carriage. In spite of its clumsy and complicated mechanism, it does not get easily out of order. It will climb all ordinary hills; it will run through sand, mud or snow; it makes good speed over long distances — say an average of 15 miles an hour . . . It carries gasoline enough for a 70-mile journey, and nearly any country store can replenish the supply.[34]

The big development of petrol cars started to come very soon after this. The one-cylinder, curved-dash, tiller-steered Oldsmobile sold 425 units in 1901, 2,500 units in 1902, 4,000 in 1903 and 5,000 in 1904, plus a further 6,500 straight-dash models in the latter year. At the beginning of 1905 *The Motor Age* (Chicago) claimed with some justice that Detroit already made 'more motor vehicles than any other city in America, or in the whole world for that matter'. John Rae has explained how the new industry came to cluster there;[35] Oldsmobile, Cadillac, Ford and others were leading the world into a new era.

Although statistical information for the years before 1905 is scattered, and difficult to interpret when located, an increasing amount of literary evidence awaits further historical investigation. From the mid-1890s a specialist motoring press began to supplement the cycling and engineering journals, and the daily papers which had previously dealt from time to time with motoring topics now did so to an increasing extent. *La Locomotion automobile* made its appearance in France in 1894, the *Autocar*, as we have seen, in Britain in 1895, when *The Horseless Age* started publication in New York. Other journals followed to advertise the new products and to appeal to a growing readership, who, as owners, engineers or enthusiasts, were keen to learn anything they could about these new mechanical developments. The motorists themselves were often keen to contribute accounts of their exploits. These often involved breakdowns or ended in the abandonment of their vehicle and returning home by train or (especially on some of the very poor tracks in rural America) having to be ignominiously pulled out of the mud by farm horses. These pioneers were soon publishing books of reminiscences and advice. Alfred C. Harmsworth (later Lord Northcliffe) and others were among the first in *Motors and Motor-driving* (Badminton Library, 1902). Filson Young's *The Happy Motorist* (1906) provides another good example, and Dorothy Levett's *The Woman and the Car: a Chatty*

Little Handbook for all Women who Motor or who want to Motor (1909, reprinted 1970) is a further commendable, if rather idiosyncratic, sample of the genre.

Most people in the early days bought motor vehicles mainly for sport or recreation, though some found them useful for work. Writing to Daimler almost at the very outset, in November 1893, Levassor noted, 'We have sold our cars to different types of people, generally those who use them for pleasure; but we have sold them also to people who use them for business purposes, in particular six doctors, five travelling salesmen and three insurance agents.'[36] These early motorists, coming from backgrounds where clubs were the norm, were quick to form motoring clubs which were soon issuing journals, year books and guides. It was a matter of honour among them to stop and offer help if, as so often happened, they came across a fellow motorist in distress. Wealthier motorists had chauffeurs not so much to drive, for that would have deprived the owner of his pleasure, but to get out and get under when the vehicle broke down.

The spread of motor vehicles after 1904: the United States races ahead

When motor vehicles began to appear in larger numbers the authorities started to register them, for they were particularly lethal. Those who treated motoring as a sport tried to drive their often unreliable vehicles as fast as they could. Brakes failed. Tyres — and even wheels — came off. People were killed or injured. Property was damaged. Huge clouds of dust were raised in dryer weather. Vehicles needed not only to be licensed but also to be prominently numbered at the front and rear so that offenders could be brought to book. Statistics assembled locally were collected nationally and published. They help the historian to clear a way through the growing thicket of literary evidence.

In Britain the Motor Car Act, 1903, which related legality more to reality by raising the maximum speed limit from 12 m.p.h. to 20 m.p.h., laid down that registration should be carried out from the beginning of 1904 by the larger local authorities, the counties and county boroughs. Many of the original handwritten registers have survived and may be consulted in local record offices. They state the names and addresses of owners (thus indicating the status of those who bought motor vehicles), the make and type of vehicle (including whether it was steam or petrol or a motor cycle or not), the purpose for which it was used (private or business) and, in another hand later, when registration was cancelled. These records have been reported upon in a preliminary way for various counties, most recently by Richard Storey, who has produced two articles on the registration records of Warwickshire.[37] These early British registers deserve much more study. Do other countries have their equivalent?

The first national returns for the United Kingdom, distinguishing registration by county and county borough throughout Great Britain and Ireland up to 1 January and 1 April 1904, published as a British Parliamentary Paper,[38] show that by the latter date 15,637 motor cycles and 14,339 'other cars' (i.e. other than bicycles and cycle-type vehicles) had been licensed in Britain, just under 30,000 altogether. Numbers were growing fast. Later returns, collected for the Royal Commission on Motor Cars, showed that by the end of 1904 just over 49,000 motor vehicles of all kinds had been registered and by 30 September 1905 nearly 71,000.[39] These national totals deserve to be checked against the local registers, for there may have been double counting when vehicles changed hands and were re-registered in another local authority area. But in general they seem to be more reliable than the considerably smaller totals (45,000 for March 1906, for instance) reproduced by Mitchell and Deane,[40] which are usually quoted. If this suggestion is correct, Britain by 1905 possessed more motor vehicles than France, for, according to estimates quoted by Barjot, France had only 21,523 cars and 29,954 motor cycles even at the end of 1905.[41]

US official statistics give a total of 78,800 motor vehicles in 1905 (77,400 automobiles and 1,400 trucks).[42] If these figures are to be believed, they suggest that at that date the *ownership* of motor vehicles in Britain and America was still of the same order of magnitude, despite America's far greater area and having twice Britain's population. Comparisons, however, may not have been of like with like, for by 1905 America possessed more petrol-engined cars, not the motor bicycles and lighter cycle-type vehicles which accounted for half the British total. Some statistics from sixteen separately itemised states, supplied by the US authorities for Britain's Royal Commission on Motor Cars in 1906, not only seem to confirm this subsequently published national total for 1905 but also show that ownership was still confined to the eastern part of the country, where most American production had originally been concentrated. Of the 63,373 cars in the sixteen states from which returns were made in 1905, nearly 36,500, more than half the total, were to be found in only two of them: New York (22,490) and New Jersey (14,150). Massachusetts had 9,977. California, on the other hand, then possessed only 3,902 and what was described as 'Illinois (Chicago)' a mere 3,716.[43]

The increase in the number of motor vehicles running on the roads of various countries can be collected from the motoring press and from consular reports, especially those published by the UK and the US. Of particular value is the special US consular report No. 53 of 1913, over 140 pages long, *Foreign Markets for Motor Vehicles*, which gives details of markets throughout the world outside the USA and the way they were organised. From the beginning of the 1920s the data were collected independently by the Automotive Division of the US Department of Commerce and the *American Automobile (Overseas Edition)*, the first list (for 1921) appearing in the department's *Commerce Reports*, 12 February 1923. In the 1930s and during the Second World War the series, often with additional textual matter, was published in the *American Automobile (Overseas Edition)* itself, which also printed from time to time other valuable comparative material such as (in August 1934) the length of highway in various parts of the world, unsurfaced and surfaced. The League of Nations also published national statistics of the four main types of motor vehicle in its *International Statistical Year Book* from 1927 to 1931 (covering the years 1926 to 1930 inclusive) but then ceased publication, presumably because of the depression. The United Nations resumed the series, though specifying only passenger cars and commercial vehicles without any disaggregation, in its *Statistical Year Book* from 1948 onwards, the first in the new series including totals for 1928, 1932 and 1937 as well as for 1946 and 1947.

Government departments and private agencies also made available fuller series of statistics from the First World War onwards. For Great Britain, for instance, the UK Statistical Abstract for 1939 contains details of cars, cycles, commercial goods vehicles, motor hackneys and 'other dutiable vehicles', together with those exempt from taxation, for the four quarters of every year from 1913 to 1937. It also includes comparable details for horse-drawn vehicles which show the extent to which they were eclipsed by the new motors, and the number of fatal and non-fatal accidents caused by vehicles in England and Wales, Scotland and Northern Ireland in 1913 and every year from 1924 to 1937. This reveals a startling increase in the years before 1934, when the upward trend in deaths was arrested by the introduction of driving tests, speed limits and the Safety First campaign.

The Society of Motor Manufacturers & Traders also published many conveniently assembled statistics, such as in 1926 a breakdown relating incomes to the number of people in the United Kingdom who were potential owners of one car (estimated at 660,000) and those who could afford two (87,700). The SMMT also produced in that year details (with a graph) of the consumption of motor spirit in the UK in 1913 and between 1919 and the second quarter of 1926.

America's growing ascendancy before the 1930s is the outstanding feature of any statistical enquiry. Ownership of motor vehicles, other than motor lorries, increased impressively there from 1904, exceeding 100,000 in 1906, 300,000 in 1909 and a million in 1913. Britain then possessed only about 220,000 cars, light vans and runabouts, and France 91,000, 50 per cent more than Germany.[44] While Europe was at war the total in the United States went on growing, reaching 4·7 million in 1917. America's involvement in the war, though costly and crucial to that country, did not affect motor vehicle production or ownership. Nearly a million more cars were running there in 1918 than in the previous year. In 1921, the year for which we have the first tabulated international totals, of 12·3 million cars in the world as a whole, 10·5 million were running on the roads of the United States.[45] Second on the list came Canada, with 473,000. The UK then, according to this source, possessed 353,000 (which must also have included motor buses, for the official British total for cars was 243,000 that year) and France 201,000. Argentina and Australia, each with about 78,000 cars, neared the total for Germany (82,500 in June 1922). The American total kept streaking ahead during the roaring '20s. By the end of 1928, the last full year before the Wall Street crash, the United States still remained at the top of the list, with 24·5 million cars out of a world total of 27 million.

The explanation of this pioneering lead lies at the heart of American writing about motor transport. The United States had the largest potential market in the early years of the present century, not just because of its large population but mainly because a larger part of that population than elsewhere earned higher incomes. 'The same class of people that find it easy to pay $650 for a car in the United States,' wrote an experienced dealer in American cars in Britain in 1911, when the exchange rate was nearly five dollars to the pound sterling, 'find it difficult to lay aside half that sum here.'[46]

Detroit's ascendancy was confirmed when Henry Ford started to produce a lighter, sturdier vehicle, the Model N (1906) for $600 and the logically developed and superior Model T (1908) at $825 for the runabout version and $850 for the tourer. These cars were so sought after that the demand would have been insatiable had Ford not moved to a larger site, introduced a moving line for sub-assembly (1909) and for the car as a whole (1913/14). By 1916 he had sold 577,000 of his tourers at $360 each. After the war, with the even more capital-intensive River Rouge plant, he managed to reach sales of 2 million cars a year in 1923. Meanwhile General Motors, a holding company formed in 1908 to control Buick, Cadillac, Olds and other concerns, having suffered from Ford's competition, staged a dramatic comeback in the 1920s.[47] By then American buyers preferred to 'trade up' for something better than the Model T. Manufacture of the famous 'Tin Lizzie' ended in 1927, just after 15 million had been produced. Ford's delay of about a year in marketing its successor, the Model A, gave Walter Chrysler the chance to launch his own cheap car, the Plymouth, and the Chrysler Corporation to establish itself as the third of America's Big Three.

This success story has been told briefly by John B. Rae and at greater length and more recently by James J. Flink.[48] In the telling an important point made by S. B. Saul is often forgotten. The Europeans looked down on America's substitution of machines for human skills. This, they claimed, might produce cheaper cars but was bound to produce inferior ones. But, as Saul pointed out:

> there was a disastrous inability on the part of America's critics to see the technical as well as the commercial side of the American approach, how accurate workmanship had only been dispensed with where it did not matter. The large, slow-speed engines used by Ford were kept relatively inefficient deliberately so as not to overload any other part of the car; they gave smooth running, used lower quality material, did not have to be machined to a high degree of accuracy and were consequently assembled with a minimum of fitting. It was a new concept of technical perfection.[49]

A number of motor history specialists, Jean-Pierre Bardou, Jean-Jacques Chanaron, Patrick Fridenson and James M. Laux, in 1982 related the American manufacturing experience to other countries,[50] and in that year I used consular reports to look more particularly at ownership and the more general effects of international motorisation in its early years in a contribution to a festschrift in honour of W. W. Rostow.[51] The most recent version of the story, half of which has been devoted to events since the Second World War, is to be found in Laux.[52]

That the state of the roads did not deter intending motorists from buying cars is evident from the growing number of purchasers in the United States, where the roads were among the worst in the world. In 1900, as Professor Rae has pointed out, there were fewer than 200 miles of surfaced road there outside the large cities.[53] Even in the early 1930s 2·3 million miles out of a total of 3 million in that vast continent were still described as 'unimproved earth and non-surfaced'.[54] The most popular early cars were built high off the ground so that they could negotiate the worst tracks. In any case, they were bought at first to replace horses (or public transport) for short journeys where, presumably, drivers knew the state of their local roads well. Such vehicles were particularly useful in rural America, as Reynolds M. Wik has explained.[55] Longer journeys continued to be made by train. Only drivers with a spirit of adventure went on exploratory holidays, usually in the dryer summer months. Among car owners were many with some local influence who, either individually or through their motoring clubs, soon began to bring pressure to bear on the authorities to improve some of the worst stretches. From about 1920 the Americans voted motor spirit duties to finance more extensive road improvements on a federal basis.

On the main roads of western Europe the major routes had been improved long before, in stagecoach days. The main problems were caused by the clouds of dust raised by vehicles, especially those with pneumatic tyres, passing over water-bound macadam surfaces. They were solved by tarring the surface. In Britain the County Surveyor of Northamptonshire, E. P. Hooley, patented a method of mixing iron slag with tar to produce a road surfacing material he christened Tarmac.[56] Taxes were raised on motor vehicles and petrol by the budget of 1909 to enable the Road Board, set up in the following year, to supplement local funds spent on improving the surface of existing roads, widening roads, improving buildings and building new roads. When Sidney and Beatrice Webb came to complete their *Story of the King's Highway* in 1913, however, they could find no evidence of road-building. Only one such stretch of new road had been approved when war came. The real start upon by-passes and other improvements came in the 1920s, presided over by a Ministry of Transport which had succeeded the Road Board, and even these were halted with the onset of the depression in 1930.[57] In France, where the Administration des Ponts et Chaussées had already provided the fine stretches of straight road from which the early motor trials had benefited, tarmacadam was also used. The Colas process of cold-mix asphalt was developed between the wars.[58]

With a few exceptions, notably the early German *Autobahnen*, specially built motor roads came only after the Second World War. There was some turnpiking in the United States but the really big development came under the Interstate Highway Act, 1956. The first full stretch of motorway in Britain was opened three years later. By then Germany was building more *Autobahnen*, France opted for toll roads and most countries were constructing their own specially built motorways.

People movers still relatively neglected by historians

Transport historians' emphasis on private cars has caused insufficient attention to be paid to other means of passenger transport. Rae and Flink, for instance, limit their interest in taxis mainly to attempts to run electric cabs in the 1890s, though Rae does make the significant observation that in the mid-1960s, when he was writing, motor cabs comprised 'half the motor vehicles in downtown Manhattan'.[59] In Britain, petrol-driven motor cabs replaced horse-drawn hackneys quite quickly in the years after 1905. The number of motor cabs in London grew from nineteen in 1905 to 7,260 in 1914. (They came to be called taxis after the installation of taximeters from 1907.) Georgano takes a wider geographical view of this form of motor transport than his book's title suggests.[60] In 1926 there were nearly one-tenth as many cabs as cars in Britain (61,000 and 684,000 respectively)[61] and, although the proportion of cabs fell subsequently as that of private cars rose, the taxi remains significant to this day — especially with the advent of breathalisers. For the United States, Gilbert and Samuel's work on taxicabs deserves more attention than it has received.[62] For France, the spread of Renault taxis in Paris in the years before 1914[63] and the use of this taxi fleet to rush reinforcements to the Marne is one of the staples of motor transport history, but in all the growing towns of the world the taxi, despite its varying fortunes, continued to play a significant role, particularly as the advent of parking meters (in the United States from the mid-1930s and in Britain from the end of the 1950s) made the use of private cars in urban centres increasingly costly and growing urban congestion made it increasingly time-consuming.

The motor bus has gained some attention in Britain, partly because of histories of particular bus businesses, but mainly because of John Hibbs's work, the second edition of which includes an updated bibliography.[64] He also edited a collection of papers read to the Omnibus Society.[65] In the United States the fortunes of local bus operators have been discussed to some extent in terms of what has been called 'the auto–oil–rubber complex' and its contest with electric tramways.[66] Inter-city services in America have been most recently studied by the English historian Margaret Walsh, who acknowledges earlier American writings in end-notes to her contribution to the Stuttgart meeting[67] and in two articles published in this journal.[68]

In powering buses the internal combustion engine for many years made a greater contribution to personal mobility than the private car. That the bus has failed to cater so well for the majority in the longer run is the result of greater car ownership. The heyday of the motor bus occurred at different times in urban and non-urban areas and in different countries. In many cities the electric tramcar carried the main traffic flows until the 1920s, by which time buses, larger and more efficient, had started to replace them, though in some towns they were replaced, for a time at least, by electric trolley buses. In the United States the private car took over, as has been shown by Bottles for Los Angeles.[69] In more lightly trafficked suburbs or outside town, and in developing countries, where tramways and railways were less important — as Epanya Sh. Tshund'olela has demonstrated in the case of Zaire and M. A. Akhunova and others have shown for Soviet Central Asia[70] — bus services were starting to be developed even before the 1920s. A bus passing along a major thoroughfare could pick up and set down anywhere. It was more accessible, and often cheaper, than the train even in districts served by branch-line railways. As traffic grew and frequencies increased it became easier to travel into the nearest town for shopping or even for a night out at the cinema. Brunner remarked that the driver, 'almost always a local man', knew the passengers on country services.[71] This book, which grew out of a master's thesis submitted at Manchester University in 1924, is an important source for all forms of motor transport in Britain in the mid-1920s. It contains valuable observations and judgements on them all. We have nothing like it for other decades.

The school bus was of significance because it made it possible to group schools and provide more specialist teaching. When Ralph Epstein wrote in 1928 he noted that, of 80,000 buses then in use in the United States, 30,000 were school buses.[72] By 1977 there were 250,000 of them in operation there.[73]

The relative importance of the bus in various countries and at various dates can be traced from national and international statistics, although the latter often make the task difficult by listing buses and lorries together. Historians of British road transport, however, are particularly favoured by having at their disposal Munby and Watson, section B of which deals with road passenger transport and section C with London's transport.[74] The decline of shorter-distance stage carriage services, elsewhere as well as in Britain, caused by the spread of private cars (which, in turn, led to a reduction in services which *obliged* many people to buy private cars) has often been offset by a greater number of longer-distance coach journeys along modern motorways and by an increasing amount of contract and private-hire work.

The importance of the motor cycle, also ignored until recently by transport historians, despite a flourishing motor cycle press and innumerable books about the motor cycles themselves, is also best approached by tables of international statistics, which provide separate totals from 1921 onwards, country by country. Motor cycles were never of much importance in the United States, where the level of purchasing power and the cost-reducing effects of mass production allowed buyers to go straight to cars. (At the end of 1922 there were only 210,000 motor cycles there and over 11 million cars.) The Canadian position was similar (9,713 and 473,260 respectively). Elsewhere, however, being much cheaper to buy (and run), motor cycles enabled increasing numbers of people to own their own private motor transport who would not otherwise have been able to afford it. Outside the United States there were 663,000 motor cycles and 1·8 million cars in 1921; 916,000 motor cycles and 2·3 million cars in 1922. In Britain, which had led the world in pedal cycles, the motor cycle industry became equally strong. Motor cycle ownership in the years 1920–24 exceeded that of motor cars (288,000 motor cycles and 187,000 cars in 1920; 496,000 motor cycles and 474,000 cars in 1924). As cheaper cars became available, however, and purchasing power rose, car ownership moved ahead faster than that of motor cycles (the totals in 1930 were 1·56 million and 724,000 respectively and in 1938 1·944 million and 462,000). Many of these motor cycles were of higher power, large enough to carry not only a pillion passenger but also another passenger (and also perhaps a child) in a sidecar. In Germany just before the Second World War the proportion of motor cycles to motor cars resembled that in Britain just after the First, though the totals were, of course, far greater: in 1938 1·583 million motor cycles and 1·306 million cars. Motor scooters became popular in Italy after 1945 and quickly spread from there. Motor cycle registrations, for instance, rose in Britain to 1·8 million at the end of the 1950s but then declined to 1 million in 1970, since when there have been further fluctuations. By then the Japanese had taken the lead, having developed a strong home market for their now internationally famous makes. Motor cycles (two- and three-wheelers) established the modern Japanese motor industry and there were more motor cycles than cars in Japan until 1973. Even a decade later, with 26 million cars on Japan's roads, there were still 16 million two-wheelers.[75] The role of the motor cycle/scooter in the history of motorisation and the explanation of national differences over time still await further study.

Goods transport, even more neglected

'The commercial goods vehicle and the road haulage industry built upon it' are still as overlooked by historians as when G. L. Turnbull remarked upon this glaring gap in 1979.[76] Nobody loves a lorrry, though everybody now depends upon it.

Light vans, built upon car chassis, became popular for local goods deliveries when cars themselves were beginning to spread. In Britain *The Commercial Motor* mentioned (and photographed) them from its inception in 1905. They provided faster shop deliveries, and the shop's name prominently displayed on the side of the vehicle advertised the fact. The technical development of heavier motor vehicles took longer, however, and, as we have seen, steam lorries enjoyed some popularity for a time. The advantage of the petrol engine over the horse was not so obvious for freight as for passengers, especially as the larger fixed capital cost was often offset by much time lost in waiting for, and despatching, loads. Their slow speeds at first limited the distances they could travel. Only in the 1920s, for instance, did it become worthwhile for a chain store like Sainsbury's to employ them to supply shops more than twelve or fifteen miles away from its headquarters. For branches farther away everything had still to be crated, carted to a railway, sent by train, carted away at the other end and then uncrated again until better and faster motor lorries, running on reliable pneumatic tyres, became available. Not until 1937 did Sainsbury's part with their last horses and vans.[77] There were few large general hauliers before then, though the account of one of them, the Pickford business, which amalgamated with others in 1912, is still the best description of the motorisation of a larger concern and the problems involved.[78] I have told what I believe is still the only account, based on records of the business, of the growth of a sizeable road haulage concern which started from a one-man business, as most of them did.[79] In his remarkable work *Road and Rail* Gilbert Walker noted that in 1936 only 135,000 out of 441,000 motor vehicles were above two and a half tons' unladen weight in Britain, which was probably the smallest weight suitable for longer-distance work (over seventy miles) and likely to deprive the railways of most of their traffic — and even some of these heavier vehicles did not compete with the railways, for they were used by breweries and other businesses for local deliveries.[80]

The continued use of horses for freight haulage long after they ceased to be used for passengers explains why we hear so little about unemployment resulting from this important transition. Some horse men certainly switched to motors, but the pace of the transition allowed those no longer needed to service or drive horse-drawn passenger vehicles to switch to horse-drawn carts, vans or waggons and gradually to retire from the transport business rather than to be thrown suddenly out of work. The number of horse-drawn vehicles in Britain, still over 200,000 in 1923, took the rest of the decade to fall to 50,000. By 1937 there were still nearly 12,000 of them, many owned by railway companies. In other, less urbanised countries the transition was even more prolonged. Its extent and variation may be seen from the number of lorries in Europe in 1938 (2·493 million when there were 6·301 million cars) and in Asia (2.3 million and 4.2 million cars). The best introduction to inter-war developments in Britain, including the legislation of 1933, is to be found in the PEP report on commercial vehicles.[81]

The motorway age

The twelvefold growth of motor vehicles during the last half-century, which we remarked upon at the outset, and the new roads which accompanied it, have brought the process of motorisation to a quite different order of magnitude. The number of these motor vehicles, and the congestion, pollution, safety and other problems they create, are largest in the more developed countries and especially in and around their vast conurbations; but even in the developing parts of the world their growing influence, particularly that of commercial goods vehicles and buses, affects the economic and social life of most people.[82] No single technical development — or, more precisely, no series of interconnected technical developments — has had such a profound effect upon mankind in all parts of the globe.

American writers have provided the English-reading world with the best introduction to this vast expansion, particularly John B. Rae and James J. Flink on America and James M. Laux on Europe in the later part of their books.[83] Yet even though Flink moved from car manufacture to car culture and discusses motor buses briefly in a section on the decline of public transit[84] (taking account of David J. St Clair's doctoral thesis, subsequently published),[85] he ignores the very important freight transport aspect of the subject, which must, surely, be taken into account when discussing, for instance, road congestion or atmospheric and noise pollution. Laux does take account of lorries, but motor cycles and scooters get left out and, at the back of it all, he remains very car manufacture-driven. The case against gas-guzzling 'overblown, overpriced monstrosities built by oafs for thieves to sell to mental defectives'[86] is not ignored in the American story, nor are Ralph Nader's *Unsafe at any Speed* (1965) and Emma Rothschild's *Paradise Lost* (1973), but these were not historians' contributions, and historians have still not stood far enough back from their subject to see the arguments for, as well as against, motorisation as a whole. Have they really taken account, for instance, of the extent to which present-day retailing would be possible without the unloved lorry as the means of supply via regional centres to supermarkets from where customers collected their purchases by private car?

That surprisingly little is published on motor transport in Britain is clear from the *Economic History Review's* long annual list of publications on other aspects of transport history. Compared with the American efforts — and in particular with James M. Laux's recent *European Automobile Industry*, with its most useful citations and bibliography — Britain's contributions since the war, even to the history of motor manufacturing, have been slight. Jonathan Wood's aptly named volume *Wheels of Misfortune*, which also includes a good bibliography,[87] is the only serious attempt to write about the British industry after the war, and its first 100 pages, concerned with the industry's rise before 1939, are a welcome addition to Kenneth Richardson's work.[88] David Thoms and Tom Donnelly have written about the motor industry in Coventry, and Steven Morewood about its top management.[89] Both draw upon the catalogues compiled earlier by Joan Lane and Jane Lowe.[90] Maxcy and Silberston adopt an economists' approach to the subject which is in many ways more revealing and certainly more full of insights.[91] Two books have resulted from British television series. That by Harold Perkin, the well known professor of social history, deals with the car since the war in its broader social context,[92] taking account, for instance, of Colin Buchanan's book and report.[93] Julian Pettifer and Nigel Turner's, on the other hand, while also containing much pre-1945 material, is very much more a media creation: a whole chapter is devoted to 'The car and courtship' and there are many illustrations, especially from, and about, films. It is strong on the international side, including the developing world.[94]

A number of British writers have dealt with specific aspects of motorisation and deserve reference. Plowden, for instance, deals with the causes and effects of legislation.[95] The title of Michael Frostick's book on advertising explains itself, as does Eric Tomkin's on the pneumatic tyre.[96] Harold Nockolds explains how a small Midland cycle lamp business became the main supplier of electrical and other components to the British motor industry, and Peter Pugh tells how an oil refining business at Hackney Wick in east London developed a highly refined motor spirit and gave it the trade name Petrol.[97] A useful commentary on road surfacing will be found in J. B. F. Earle's two books.[98] Notions of road pricing, outlined by the Ministry of Transport, were further considered by Gabriel Roth, and most recently in an important report from the Chartered Institute of Transport.[99] For the best introduction to motor transport's most neglected aspect in Britain since the war the report of the Ministry of Transport committee chaired by Sir Arthur Armitage may be consulted, especially the first chapter, which, having given tables of relevant statistics, concludes, 'Lorries now have the major role of carrying goods in our economy, being more important on the measure of either tonnage or ton-mileage than all other modes of transport combined. The lorry has become the essential sinew of the economy.'[100]

Motor haulage, and motor transport generally, receive some attention in Derek Aldcroft's *British Transport since 1914*[101] and towards the end of three other general texts on transport. Of these, Dyos and Aldcroft indicate the need to use Stone and Rowe's work on consumer expenditure and behaviour and Feinstein's on domestic capital formation and national income.[102] Philip Bagwell's is the text which treats motor transport, including motor haulage, most fully and brings it most nearly up to date.[103] It is certainly the starting point for anyone who is looking for an introduction to the subject from the

1880s onwards and for clues, to its changing relationship with other transport modes. When I came to revise Savage[104] I did my best to give more prominence to all aspects of motor transport, but that was nearly twenty years ago, just as the first oil shock was being experienced.

There is now a great opportunity for younger scholars to give this promising subject a great push forward, concentrating not upon motor manufacture but upon the contribution of the millions of lorries, buses and motor cycles, as well as cars. They need to look particularly at the past half-century, when motor traffic has grown at such a pace, one of the most significant aspects of quickening technical change during those years. Its twelvefold growth has, along with the revolution in air travel, greatly contributed to human mobility and, by cutting distribution costs, to improved standards of living. At the same time it has confronted mankind with greater human and environmental hazards. How much has been gain and how much loss?

Notes

1 *The American Automobile (Overseas Edition)* (March 1940); the United States *Year Book for 1988/9* (New York, 1992) gives 537 million, excluding motor cycles and scooters at the end of the 1980s. According to *The Overseas Motor Cycle Industry in a Nutshell* (1982) there were then over 60 million motorised two-wheelers in the world.

2 H. J. Dyos, 'Transport history in university theses', *Journal of Transport History*, 4 (1960), pp. 161–73.

3 Ian S. Lloyd, *Rolls Royce: the Growth of a Firm* (1978). His other two volumes, published then, were *The Years of Endeavour* and *The Merlin at War*.

4 Allan Nevins, *Ford: the Times, the Man, the Company* (New York, 1954).

5 P. W. S. Andrews and Elizabeth Brunner, *The Life of Lord Nuffield* (Oxford, 1955). R. J. Overy produced another biography of the English manufacturer, *William Morris Viscount Nuffield* (1976).

6 Allan Nevins, *Ford: Expansion and Challenge, 1915–32* (New York, 1957), and *Ford: Decline and Rebirth, 1933–62* (New York, 1963).

7 James J. Flink, 'The car culture revisited: some comments on the recent historiography of automotive history', in David L. Lewis and Laurence Goldstein (eds), *The Automobile and American Car Culture* (Ann Arbor, Mich., 1983), p. 405.

8 James J. Flink, *America adopts the Automobile, 1895–1910* (Cambridge, Mass., 1970), and *The Car Culture* (Cambridge, Mass., 1975).

9 Lewis and Goldstein, *The Automobile.*

10 John B. Rae, *American Automobile* (Cambridge, Mass., 1965) and *The Road and the Car in American Life* (Cambridge, Mass., 1971).

11 Patrick Fridenson, *Histoire des Usines Renault, 1898–1939* (Paris, 1972).

12 Theo Barker (ed.), *The Economic and Social Effects of the Spread of Motor Vehicles* (1987).

13 F. M. L. Thompson, 'Nineteenth-century horse sense', *Economic History Review*, second series, 29 (1976), p. 80.

14 US Bureau of the Census, Twelfth Census, 1900, V, tables 37, 39, 41.

15 Eugen Diesel, Gustav Goldbeck and Friedrich Schildenberger, *From Engines to Autos* (Chicago, 1960; originally published in Stuttgart, 1957).

16 James M. Laux, *In First Gear: the French Automobile Industry to 1914* (Liverpool, 1976), and *The European Automobile Industry* (New York, 1993).

17 Laux, *European Automobile*, pp. 3, 8.

18 Laux, *European Automobile*, p. 3.

19 Select Committee on Traction Engines on Roads, *Parliamentary Papers*, 1896 [272], XIV, IV, and evidence of E. B. Chittenden, questions 224, 238, 241.

20 Quoted in *Nature*, 26 November 1896.

21 T. R. Nicholson, *The Birth of the British Motor Car* (1982), III, *1769–1897*.

22 Nicholson, *The Birth*, pp. 386–7.

23 Nicholson, *The Birth*, p. 465.

24 Nicholson, *The Birth*, p. 473.

25 Richard Storey, 'Henry John Lawson', in D. J. Jeremy (ed.), *Dictionary of Business Biography*, 3, *H–L* (1985), pp. 685–7.

26 Z. E. Lambert and R. J. Wyatt, *Lord Austin — the Man* (1979); R. Church, *Herbert Austin: the British Motor Car Industry to 1941* (1979).

27 S. B. Saul, 'The motor industry in Britain to 1914', *Business History*, V (1962), pp. 22–44.

28 Saul, 'Motor industry', p. 42.

29 Theo Barker, 'A German centenary in 1986, a French in 1995 or real beginnings about 1905' in Barker, *Economic and Social Effects*, pp. 39–43.

30 *Motor Cycle*, 12 January 1904. For the history of a well known British motor cycle see J. R. Clew, *The Best Twin: the Story of the Douglas Motor Cycle* (Norwich, 1974).

31 James J. Flink, *The Automobile Age* (Cambridge, Mass., 1988), p. 10.

32 L. J. Andrew Villalon and James M. Laux, 'Steaming through New England with Locomobile', *Journal of Transport History*, second series, V (1979), pp. 65–82.

33 Barker, *Economic and Social Effects*, p. 15, table 1.2.

34 Flink, *Automobile Age*, p. 10.

35 John B. Rae, 'Why Michigan?', in Lewis and Goldstein, *Automobile Age*.

36 Jacques Ickx, *Ainsi naquit l'automobile*, 2 vols (Lausanne, 1961), quoted by Laux, *In First Gear*, p. 18.

37 Richard Storey, 'The beginnings of motor registration in Warwickshire', *Warwickshire History*, V (1983/84), pp. 185–9, and 'Motor vehicle registration in Warwickshire, 1914–18', *ibid*, VIII (1992), pp. 159–62.

38 *P.P.* 1904 [292], LXXIX.

39 *P.P.* 1906 [3081], XLVIII.

40 B. R. Mitchell and P. Deane, *Abstract of British Historical Statistics* (Cambridge, 1962), p. 230.

41 Barker, *Economic and Social Effects*, p. 303.

42 *Historical Statistics of the United States* (Washington, D.C., 1960), p. 462.

43 Royal Commission on Motor Cars, *P.P.*, 1906 [Cd 3080], XLVIII, p. 69.

44 US consular reports, January and July 1914.

45 Official US figure for 1921 in *Historical Statistics*, The total cited for the United States in the first world census related to December 1922, when it was just over 11 million.

46 *US Daily Consular and Trade Reports*, 21 June 1911, p. 1260.

47 For General Motors see Arthur Pound, *The Turning Wheel* (New York, 1934), and Alfred P. Sloan, Jr, *My Years with General Motors* (1963).

48 Rae, *American Automobile*; Flink, *Automobile Age*.

49 Saul, 'Motor industry', pp. 41–2.

50 Jean-Pierre Bardou, Jean-Jacques Chanaron, Patrick Fridenson and James M. Laux, *The Automobile Revolution: the Impact of an Industry* (Chapel Hill, N.C., 1982).

51 'The spread of motor vehicles before 1914', in Charles P. Kindleberger and Guido di Tella (eds), *Economics in the Long View* (1982), II, pp. 149, 167.

52 Laux, *European Automobile*.

53 John B. Rae, 'The motor vehicle and the revolution in road transport: the American experience', in Barker, *Economic and Social Effects*, p. 68.

54 *The American Automobile (Overseas Edition)*, August 1934.

55 Reynolds M. Wik, 'The early automobile and the American farmer', in Lewis and Goldstein, *The Automobile*.

56 W. J. Reader, *Macadam* (1980), p. 206.

57 Alan Day, *Roads* (1963), p. 13.

58 Dominique Barjot, 'Advances in road construction technology in France', in Barker, *Economic and Social Effects*, p. 299.

59 Rae, *American Automobile*, p. 222.

60 G. N. Georgano, *A History of the London Taxicab* (Newton Abbot, 1972).

61 B. R. Mitchell, *British Historical Statistics* (Cambridge, 1988), p. 557.

62 Gorman Gilbert and Robert E. Samuel, *The Taxicab: an Urban Tansport Survivor* (Chapel Hill, N.C., 1982).

63 Fridenson, *Renault*, pp. 55 ff.; Bardou, *Automobile Revolution*, pp. 21–2, 90.

64 John Hibbs, *History of British Bus Services* (Newton Abbot, 1968, 1989).

65 John Hibbs (ed.), *The Omnibus: Readings in the History of Road Passenger Transport* (Newton Abbot, 1971).

66 Glenn Yago, *The Decline of Transit* (Cambridge, 1984).

67 Margaret Walsh, 'The early growth of long-distance bus transport in the United States', in Barker, *Economic and Social Effects*, pp. 81–96.

68 Margaret Walsh, 'The Motor Carrier Act of 1935: the origins and establishment of federal regulation of the interstate bus industry', *Journal of Transport History*, third series, 8 (1987), pp. 66–80; *id.*, '"See this amazing America": the long-distance bus industry's use of advertising in its first quarter-century', *ibid.*, 11 (1990), pp. 61–88.

69 Scott L. Bottles, *Los Angeles and the Automobile* (Los Angeles, 1987).

70 Epanya Sh. Tshund'olela, 'Motor transport in a developing area (i) Zaire, 1903–59', and M. A. Akhunova, B. A. Tulepbaev and J. S. Borisov, 'Motor transport in a developing area (ii) Soviet Central Asia', in Barker, *Economic and Social Effects*, pp. 236–55, 256–63.

71 Christopher J. Brunner, *The Problem of Motor Transport* (1928).

72 Ralph Epstein, *The Automobile Industry* (Chicago, 1928), p. 12.

73 James M. Laux, 'Diesel trucks and buses: their gradual spread in the United States', in Barker, *Economic and Social Effects*, p. 108.

74 D. L. Munby and A. H. Watson, *Inland Transport Statistics: Great Britain, 1900–70* (Oxford, 1978), pp. 219–455, 457–659.

75 Koichi Shimokawa, 'Japan: the late starter who outpaced all her rivals', in Barker, *Economic and Social Effects*, pp. 224–5. Professor Shimokawa, the leading Japanese authority on this subject, has a book in English in the press.

76 Gerard L. Turnbull, *Traffic and Transport: an Economic History of Pickfords* (1979), p. 148.

77 James Boswell (ed.), *J.S. 100: the Story of Sainsbury's* (1969), pp. 48–9.

78 Turnbull, *Traffic and Transport.*

79 Theo Barker, *The Transport Contractors of Rye: John Jempson & Son* (1982).

80 Gilbert Walker, *Road and Rail* (1942), pp. 20–1.

81 *Planning*, 28 February 1949.

82 James M. Laux, 'Diesel trucks and buses', in Barker, *Economic and Social Effects*, pp. 97–113.

83 Rae, *American Automobile*; Flink, *Automobile Age*; Laux, *European Automobile.*

84 Flink, *Automobile Age*, pp. 359–73.

85 David J. St Clair, *Motorisation of American Cities* (New York, 1986).

86 Flink, *Automobile Age*, p. 281, quoting John Keats, *The Insolent Chariots* (Philadelphia, 1958), p. 13.

87 Jonathan Wood, *Wheels of Misfortune: the Rise and Fall of the British Motor Industry* (1988).

88 Kenneth Richardson, *The British Motor Industry, 1896–1939* (1977).

89 David Thoms and Tom Donnelly, *The Motor Industry in Coventry since the 1890s* (1985); Steven Morewood, *Pioneers and Inheritors: Top Management in the Coventry Motor Industry, 1896–1972* (Centre for Business History, Coventry Polytechnic, 1990).

90 Joan Lane, *A Register of Business Records of Coventry and related Areas* (Coventry, 1977); Jane Lowe, *A Guide to Sources in the History of the Cycle and Motor Industries in Coventry, 1880–1939* (Coventry, 1982).

91 G. Maxcy and A. Silberston, *The Motor Industry* (1959).

92 Harold Perkin, *The Age of the Automobile* (1976).

93 Colin Buchanan, *Mixed Blessing: the Motor in Britain* (1958), and *Traffic in Towns* (1963).

94 Julian Pettifer and Nigel Turner, *Automania* (1984).

95 William Plowden, *The Motor Car and Politics, 1896–1970* (1971).

96 Michael Frostick, *Advertising and the Motor Car* (1970); Eric Tomkins, *The History of the Pneumatic Tyre* (1981).

97 Harold Nockolds, *Lucas: the First 100 Years*, 2 vols (Newton Abbot, 1976, 1978); Peter Pugh, *Carless, Capel and Leonard* (1986).

98 J. B. F. Earle, *A Century of Road Materials: a History of the Roadstone Division of Tarmac Ltd* (Oxford, 1971) and *Black Top: a History of the British Flexible Roads Industry* (Oxford, 1974).

99 *Road Pricing: the Economic and Technical Possibilities* (1964); Gabriel Roth, *Paying for Roads: the Economics of Traffic Congestion* (Harmondsworth, 1967); Chartered Institute of Transport, *Paying for Progress: a Report on Congestion and Road Use Charges* (1990).

100 A. Armitage, *Lorries, People and the Environment* (1980), p. 10.

101 Derek H. Aldcroft, *British Transport since 1914: an Economic History* (Newton Abbot, 1975).

102 H. J. Dyos and D. H. Aldcroft, *British Transport: an Economic Survey from the Seventeenth Century to the Twentieth* (Leicester, 1969; Harmondsworth, 1974); J. R. Stone and D. A. Rowe, *The Measurement of Consumers' Expenditure and Behaviour in the United Kingdom, 1920–38*, II (1966); C. H. Feinstein, *Domestic Capital Formation in the United Kingdom, 1920–38* (Cambridge, 1966) and *National Income Expenditure and Output of the United Kingdom, 1855–1965* (Cambridge, 1972).

103 Philip S. Bagwell, *The Transport Revolution, 1770–1985* (1988).

104 C. I. Savage, *An Economic History of Transport* (1957), and T. C. Barker and C. I. Savage, *An Economic History of Transport in Britain* (1974).

2 *Markets and marketing in the British motor industry before 1914, with some French comparisons*

ROY CHURCH

In an important article dealing with the formative years of the British motor industry[1] Professor Saul concluded that its crucial weakness was to be found not in the size of the market but in the industry's approach to it. Quoting from *The Times* in 1912, he emphasised the contrast between the failure of the British industry to produce low horsepower motor cars at low cost for a popular market with the more democratic character of automobile ownership not only in the United States but also in France.[2] The contrast between developments in the British and American markets are well known and readily understood, but comparisons with the French have been neglected, for while it is true that in terms of population size and average *per capita* incomes[3] the British market offered a more favourable potential for wider car ownership than in France, the French manufacturers' lead, stemming from the initial innovation of the automobile, provided a head start which enabled French cars to dominate both French domestic and export markets before 1914.

The disparity between the size of markets and the respective production of the two countries, with Britain lagging behind France, has been remarked upon most recently by Dr J. S. Foreman Peck, who proceeds to argue that had the domestic market been protected, as it was to be from 1915, British car production would have been greater and the weakness in the industry would probably have been remedied.[4] He maintains that 'peculiarly French conditions, permitting cost reductions as scale economies were utilised, [gave] the French vehicles a competitive advantage in Britain'. Such an analysis, however, displays a misunderstanding of the character of the market for motor cars before 1914, which for most of the period was dominated by the pioneering efforts of British manufacturers to make up lost ground in production by learning to copy, to adapt and to improve upon French cars imported by agents and producers attempting to develop a domestic market for motor cars. Laux's discussion of the approach by French manufacturers to markets at home and overseas finds little room for low costs from large-scale production in explaining export success, which even for Renault depended more upon the quality and availability of the product.[5] Furthermore, while it is probable that before 1912 French manufacturers were producing more low-priced cars in volume than were British makers, those who advocated tariff protection for the British industry in 1912 were seeking to anticipate the appearance of American cars on the British market selling at prices with which they could not compete. It was for this reason that in 1912 the *Daily Express* organised a conference on the 'American Invasion of the British Motor Industry'. Cars imported from France were regarded as complementary to, rather than competitive with, cars produced in Britain, and the trade was far from unanimous in supporting the advocates of protection.[6] Further evidence to support our verdict on the counterfactual protection thesis will follow in the more specific context of the 'weakness' of the industry, the character of markets and the role of marketing.

First, we shall argue that Professor Saul's analysis of the weaknesses of the British industry is valid for the period before 1912, but elaboration is required if we are to identify the character and origins of the commercial failure, which he has explained in terms of 'the industry's approach to the market'. In so far as it is possible, it will be important to try to distinguish the role and production orientation of the engineer-entrepreneurs from the contribution of the commercial men, whose motivation and approach to business differed more than merely in style. Second, while accepting the self-evident failure of the British compared with the American industry, we shall question whether in terms of democratisation the British industry's commercial performance was at all inferior to that of the French by 1913, and attempt to explain the reasons why. In order to develop these arguments we shall focus first upon evidence relating to the initial conceptualisation of the market for motor cars in the two countries and to the initiatives which promoted further market development. In relation to this we shall consider the role and contributions of the commercial men in the trade, followed by an attempt to present quantitative evidence, based on estimates for production and sales, to support our comparative analysis of market structures in the two countries.

Conceptualisation of the market for motor cars

In 1912 an American consular report on the French domestic market revealed a general preference for cars of greater than 10 h.p., with accommodation for four passengers in addition to a chauffeur.[7] These were in the medium price range, equivalent to between £300 and £400. Below this category was the *voiturette*, typically the most popular. With seating accommodation for three people, such vehicles developed 8 h.p. from two cylinders and cost at a minimum about £240. This type of car was purchased for use by businessmen and physicians. The third popular category included the coupé 6 and 8 h.p. models, also with two cylinders, and commonly employed as taxi cabs. The price range was about £160 to £240.

The low-to-medium-priced car was also referred to as the most likely growth point in the British market from 1912, especially those below 16 h.p., though as in France the 'doctor's car' at the lower end provided a focal sales point for British manufacturers and agents.[8] An advertisement in *The Motorist* in 1913 revealed an American company's perception of the important constituents of the British market for motor cars on the eve of World War I, when the Willys Overland 'car for the owner-driver' was described as being 'just the car for the owner-driver, whether doctor, traveller, tourist or sportsman. It is ideal, too, for the Lady-driver.'[9]

Any difference in the degree of 'democratisation', if it existed, is not explicable in terms of British manufacturers' 'approach to the market' in the sense in which Professor Saul employed the phrase.[10] For French manufacturers, like their British competitors, also tended to approach the problem of the cheap car from the design side rather than from the marketing standpoint: 'when it came to the low price range, the question the [French] engineer usually tried to answer was, "How can we design a cheap car?", rather than "How can we manufacture a car more cheaply?" '.[11] It is true that for many years the technical lead held by French manufacturers enabled them to dominate world exports, but by 1913 the technical gap had narrowed, and although French cars accounted for the major share of British vehicle imports, by that time 'British' Daimlers and Napiers[12] were exported to France and British car production was rapidly catching up. The justification for minimal French interest in marketing derived only in part from the premier reputation of French automobile technology, but it did owe much to the aggressive marketing role played by Englishmen acting either in conjunction with French or Anglo-French companies,[13] or as independent agents importing French cars into Britain.[14] Indeed, whereas Professor Saul's criticism of British motor *engineers* for their lack of commercial acumen is valid in the main before 1914 (though they were not markedly different in their practices from the French engineers), we need to consider also the record of the commercial men in the motor trade, for theirs was the responsibility for creating and shaping the market for motor cars.

In the pioneering phase of the motor industry the initial problem – or opportunity – presented to British businessmen was to identify and assess the character and permanence of market possibilities for the petrol-driven motor vehicle. The introduction of this momentous invention offered an interesting test not only of British technical receptivity but also of commercial sensitivity, for this was a case where the growth of an industry depended upon the creation of a market in response to an autonomous potential supply. The major British initiative was taken by F. R Simms, the distinguished professional engineer at work in Germany, at whose instigation in 1891 Gottlieb Daimler's high-speed internal combustion engine first appeared in Britain. Four years later, through observation and by report, a handful of relatively wealthy men had become persuaded of the attractions of motor-car ownership and had imported vehicles from France. F. R. Simms, meanwhile, who had acquired the Daimler patents for the UK and the colonies, was persuaded to sell them to Charles Lawson, a speculator who had made a fortune in the bicycle trade and whose ambitious plans to establish a British motor industry were introduced in 1895 when he formed the British Motor Syndicate. The subsidiary companies of Daimler and of the Great Horseless Carriage Companies (later called the Motor Manufacturing Company) were set up to manufacture motor vehicles under licence from the syndicate (they covered the manufacture of Daimler, Panhard Levassor, De Dion & Bouton, Léon Bollée) and Lawson's co-directors and financiers included H. G. Sturmey, a cycle engineer, and a group of wealthy enthusiasts consisting of Harry Hewetson, the Hon. Evelyn Ellis and Sir David Salamons, who together with F. R. Simms in 1895 had formed the Self-propelled Traffic Association with the aim of securing the repeal of the Locomotive Acts and the critical provision limiting speed on the road to 5 m.p.h.[15]

This step was perceived to be a necessary precondition for the commercial exploitation of the motor vehicle, and not surprisingly Lawson played a leading role in the campaign. He imported several cars to form the nucleus of the motor vehicle exhibition held in October 1895 at the country home of Sir David Salamons, followed in May by the International Motor Exhibition, again mounted by Lawson but organised through his 'Society for the Protection, Encouragement and Development of the Motor Industry', and held at the Imperial Institute in London. Lawson's guest list was carefully chosen and reflects his conception, as Britain's premier motor vehicle evangelist, of what constituted his potential market: among those who attended the reception held to open the exhibition were to be found foreign princes, peers of the realm, a field marshal, a general, the Lord Chancellor, the Attorney General, Members of Parliament and scores of well known public figures. Indeed, the Prince of Wales himself requested, and received, a private demonstration.[16]

Complementary to these activities, in 1896 Henry Sturmey launched *The Autocar* to orchestrate pressure on the government to lift the speed limit. The campaign was an instant success, and Lawson's Motor Car Club sponsored a celebratory run to Brighton on 'Emancipation Day' held on 14 November 1896. Out of thirty-three motor vehicles which set out on the journey only ten finished. The publicity it secured wa sufficient to stimulate others to mount further exhibitions, though none could emulate with such success the thoroughness and flamboyance of Lawson. His weakened financial position, however, was a source of embarrassment to those associated with him, for while his activities created interest in the motor car, many people sympathetic to the popularisation of motoring were fearful of the indirect effects of his dubious private commercial aims. Consequently in 1897 F. R. Simms took the initiative and set up the Automobile Club of Great Britain, based on the French model. A handful of former Lawson associates in the Motor Car Club left to join the new organisation, which gained in reputation both from Simms's own professional engineering status (he was consulting engineer to Daimler) and from his aim to 'professionalise' the motor industry: to achieve for motoring the respectability which Lawson's multifarious speculative ventures had always threatened. A series of tours followed in 1898, designed to demonstrate cars to the public. The first Motor Show, held at Richmond by Charles Cordingley, proprietor of the *Motor Car Journal*, for the Automobile Club, was well attended and widely reported in the press, and the National Show, which had hitherto combined the exhibition of motor cars with cycles, was also held in London in 1899.[17] At last it seemed that the public attitude towards the motor car, regarded hitherto as a bit of a joke and sometimes a dangerous one, was beginning to become less hostile, though the real enthusiasts, comprising the founder members of the Automobile Club, were limited still to a narrow social stratum which included doctors, solicitors, professional engineers but very few motor agents and manufacturers.[18]

The real turning point in the image of the motor car was reached in 1900 with the RAC's One Thousand Miles Trial. Two of the principal figures responsible for its conception and organisation were Alfred Harmsworth, the leading proprietor of the *Daily Mail* newspaper, whose recently acquired Mercedes inspired his enthusiasm, and Claude Johnson, full-time secretary of the Automobile Club but later to become managing director of Rolls Royce.[19] The trial was aimed at testing the general design of cars and introducing the motor car to parts of the country remote from the London area and other major cities. It is significant that the taciturn engineer Herbert Austin, who had built the first all-British motor car for the Wolseley Company in 1896, himself drove one of his cars and came second in the event.[20] S. F. Edge, a former racing cyclist, was another entrant of note. Lacking knowledge of engineering, but an enthusiast, anxious to learn about the new motor industry, he had worked on a part-time basis for Lawson in the 1890s, and succeeded in persuading Harvey du Cros, one of Lawson's business associates, to finance Edge's Motor Vehicle Company, formed to sell imported cars. He began in the motor trade by selling his own used car, the first of several such transactions.[21] Dealing in second-hand cars soon led to ambitions to sell new cars in a firm of his own. Edge subsequently contracted with Napier, the long established firm of engineers, then experimenting with the building of motor cars, to supplement the cars imported from France by constructing six cars of the Panhard type, and in order to secure publicity for himself and for his cars he entered a Napier for the 1900 Trial.[22] *The Times* also attached importance to this event, a correspondent explaining the idea which lay behind it, which was 'to prove that the motor car is, even in its present state of development, a serious and trustworthy means of locomotion; not a toy, dangerous and troublesome alike to the public and owner'.[23]

The Trial proved a success, and the prospect of an excessive proliferation of trials, events and especially exhibitions, which were all costly to the motor firms, led to the establishment of the Society of Motor Manufacturers and Traders, which was to assume responsibility for arranging an annual motor show, thereby relieving exhibitors of the financial burdens which a multiplicity of exhibitions would have involved. Affiliated companies agreed to a bond giving the SMMT exclusive monopoly over the show in return for benefits arising out of its organisation.[24] F. R. Simms became the first president, alongside whose signature on the articles of association were those of S. F. Edge, Charles Jarrott and W. M. Letts. The first council included Herbert Austin, Lanchester and Thorneycroft, which suggests that even the engineering pioneers of the British motor industry had now become convinced that the invention had reached a stage when it was important to encourage, promote and protect the motor trade through such an association. Already the occasionally vicious manifestations of prejudice against the motor driver had disappeared, but motorists were still sometimes condemned in the press and in public debate as a reckless and selfish minority, causing danger and pollution which incurred costs for the rest of society.[25]

Another aim of the SMMT was to enhance the image of the motor car and of motor traders by providing reassurance, both to those in the trade and to the public, of the respectability and permanence of the motor industry. This explains why the SMMT soon became involved in establishing the orderly distribution of motor cars. Competitive racing also contributed to enhancing the reputation of the motor car, and international recognition was achieved in 1902 with S. F. Edge's victory in a Napier, winning the Gordon Bennett International Trophy only two years after the first British entry in a Continental race. Thereafter confidence in British motor technology grew as the majority of manufacturers and the public came to accept a particular combination of definitive features in a motor car. In 1903 the speed limit was raised from 12 to 20 m.p.h., marking the acceptance of the motor car as having passed the experimental pioneer phase.[26]

Market development

The origins of the motor industry explain why the marketing practices customary in the engineering trades were adopted in the marketing of motor cars, not the least relevant factor being the engineering origins of the firms which took up motor car production.[27] The motor car possessed characteristics both of the machine tool (as a complex piece of machinery) and of domestic hardware (for example, a bedstead), whose appeal depended upon appearance and style as well as utility; the motor car was also a very expensive luxury consumer durable. A product which combined these features and was sold in a highly competitive trade to the general public clearly offered maximum scope for an intermediary possessing both technical knowledge and powers of persuasion. In the earliest stages of the industry manufacturers sold direct to customers as an arrangement suited to production on a handicraft basis in numerous tiny firms. But as soon as cars could be produced in multiples, each year it became customary to appoint an agent who commonly also represented several other manufacturers and who was often able to demand a relatively high commission. To such intermediaries, who rapidly increased in number after 1900 and who were mostly individual enthusiast entrepreneurs in search of cars to sell, commercial initiatives passed, the early clubs, associations and proliferating journals having established the respectable image of the motor car.

The rise of the early agents, and the evolution of the early distribution arrangements for the sale of cars, owed much to the practices developed in the bicycle trade. By the 1890s cycling was a well organised sport and pastime, national and local associations and clubs arranging races and trials, and the enthusiasm of cyclists was shared by the owners of the numerous repair shops established by mechanics in many towns throughout the country. As the cycle industry grew, manufacturers appointed authorised agents to handle sales, parts, supplies, and to carry out repairs, and when some of the leading companies, such as Humber, Rover, Singer, Swift, Triumph and BSA began to make motor cars, too, a distribution system already existed.[28]

Others took the initiative by approaching car makers whose models they wished to sell, dropping the cycle trade as they gained a foothold in the sale of cars. This was the pattern adopted by a handful of leading independent motor agents who contributed much to the popularisation of imported cars between 1895 and 1910, including S. F. Edge, Charles Friswell, Harvey du Cros, Harry Hewetson, William Letts, Charles Jarrott, George Heath, David Carlaw, C. S. Rolls, G. N. C. Mann, H. W. Egerton and others. In many instances the impetus towards car dealing often came as much from a sporting enthusiasm for cycling or motoring as from economic and rational investment considerations, though active participation in the sport and a sensitivity to the commercial prospects for the sale of the motor cars constituted an advantageous coincidence in the formative years of the trade. Typically the cycle agent was a prominent member of the local cycling community, and the same became true of the early motor agents, who no doubt recognised the opportunities for arranging a similar conjunction of social and sporting activity with commercial penetration.[29]

Frequently the initiative came from independent agents whose business had been established originally on the basis of imported vehicles, not uncommonly in piratical fashion. An important example of this is provided by the origins of Renault in Britain, which began in 1900 when Robert Moffat Ford's Motor Car Company entered two MCC Triumph cars for the RAC One Thousand Mile Trial, one of which won a prize, and both of which were subsequently exhibited as MCC Triumph cars at the Motor Show . Louis Renault took legal action to expose Ford's misrepresentation of Renault cars, the agency for which had been secured by Mors Motors. When the agency passed to the Roadway Autocar Company, under the management of W. L. McBride, success was immediate, for whereas the Mors Motor Company had sold about thirty cars annually, McBride sold 250 in 1902–03 and 450 in 1903–04. The sequel was the formation in 1904 of Renault Frères under McBride's management, his Roadway Autocar Company now merged with Renault Frères Ltd under the joint ownership of McBride and the Renault brothers.[30] In the development of British-made cars, too, the trend among some manufacturers was towards a separation of manufacture from distribution, for engineers seemed to be only too pleased to be relieved of the selling role in order to concentrate their attention upon the sound construction and production of motor cars. For example, Napier contracted to supply Edge with six cars, built on lines very similar to the Panhard but incorporating a Napier engine. Bodies were to be built to customers' specifications by Mulliner's coachbuilding firm at Northampton, the contract stipulating fixed prices but with Edge reserving the power to fix the retail price to the customers.[31]

Charles Friswell, who, like Edge, was formerly an agent for cycles combining other business interests too, established his London enterprise in a similar manner. He had registered a limited company in 1896 and by 1900 was advertising several small cars imported from the Continent. The features advertised by Friswell's Automobile Palace Ltd are indicative of his ambition and style, for having sold three of his cycle depots he invested in a five-storey building, complete with car and passenger lifts, garaging space and showrooms for hundreds of vehicles, with departments for repairs, painting, clothing accessories, machinery and facilities for auctions and safe repository. The premises also contained ladies' dressing rooms, gentlemen's lavatories, hot water plant and an extensive electric charging station. Between 1904 and 1907 sales averaged £172,000 and gross profit amounted to 43 per cent on turnover.[32]

The firm of Mann Egerton, a partnership between an electrical engineer and a motoring enthusiast, in 1898 established an agency in Norwich, the remote yet wealthy capital of East Anglia in the midst of good touring country around the broads (very flat, Norfolk). From here the company sold cars of various makes to doctors, clergymen, leading families in banking and insurance, and other local gentry; potential purchasers could rely on the use of waiting rooms 'replete with every possible convenience, with leather armchairs, newspapers, writing materials and a coal fire', while the ladies' room contained 'every requisite from a long mirror to a pair of curling tongs'.[33]

The increasingly common practice of building cars to order for an agent was presenting difficulties for the manufacturers even before 1905. Herbert Austin recalled how the problem of cash flow in the early days as a major reason why the production of large and relatively expensive cars was preferred to the smaller models, for the high profit margin helped to pay for the faults and failings of the pioneer manufacturers.[34] In 1903 the chairman of Daimler, Sir Edward Jenkinson, reflected upon the difficulty of selling a car in advance of its appearance in the showroom. He found that customers were loath to accept late delivery, which risked the introduction of a new foreign model in the interim, and which might then be preferred. Because potential buyers waited until spring, when they expected to see the newest designs and improvements from which to choose, Sir Edward stressed the need to manufacture and maintain ample stock in order to meet demand, which was seasonal when it came, though this required more working capital.[35]

Indeed, it was the offer of working capital through the payment of deposits on car orders which made the distribution of cars through agents an attractive solution to the problem of liquidity which expansion generated. Even by 1902 Wolseley had agreements with twelve agents in London and other major cities in the regions, Rover had eight, and when Austin commenced production in 1906 he appointed agents in the principal cities and by 1912 had established showrooms in Norwich, Manchester and London.[36] Overseas sales were more often secured through the services of specialist overseas distributors, one of the most important before 1914 being Tozer Kemsley Milbourne Ltd, who acted as London agent for many firms. Through Tozer's activities, manufacturers and agents received cash against delivery to provide credit overseas.[37]

From the manufacturers' standpoint, distributing through a 'free' agent was accompanied by risk and uncertainty for production planning, which is why in 1907 R. W. Maudsley, founder and chairman of the loss-making Standard Motor Company, negotiated an agreement with Charles Friswell. On the latter's initiative Friswell became the sole agent for Standard cars, Standard undertaking to supply a specified number of cars at fixed prices in return for representation at home and overseas and financial backing to underwrite the expansion planned as a result of this arrangement.[38] The agreement between the Hon. C. S. Rolls and the engineer Henry Royce was similar, for while initially Rolls added Royce's car to the Minerva, Panhard Levassor and Orleans cars, for which he acted as agent, Rolls came to trade only in Rolls Royce cars even before Rolls's distributing agency merged with Royce's engineering firm in 1906. This was an indication of the absolute confidence of Rolls in Royce's engineering brilliance and in the enduring appeal which the Rolls Royce would exert in the market place.[39] The attractions of control for the manufacturer were the avoidance of the practice, common among agents and condemned strongly by Herbert Austin, of allowing discounts over and above the normal trade discount to agents touting for commission on sales.[40] The establishment of showrooms and depots outside the place of manufacture was one way of trying to reduce risk by uncertainty due to agents' activities, and Rover, Armstrong Whitworth and Austin were among the first to adopt this policy shortly after 1900. It was a policy open only to the larger and more enterprising companies willing to commit resources and to manufacture for stock rather than to order.

During this pioneering phase of the industry's development the propaganda disseminated both by motoring organisations and by individual firms succeeded in persuading only a tiny elite to purchase motor cars. In 1907 a writer in *The Economist* described the British motor car as a substitute for a carriage and pair, opining that until it could compete with the horse and trap it would not come into general use.[41] Encouraged by some, accepted by most, the limited size and exclusive character of the British market for motor cars, certainly before 1912, meant that purchasers required personal attention, which at the upper end of the luxury market was carried to extreme lengths. For example, a Napier brochure for 1907 invited customers to visit the works and see their cars in every stage of construction. In 1909 the *Autocar* reported that Lord Wemyss, then aged ninety-two, who was buying a landaulet, had personally attended at the works and offered several useful suggestions during the construction of the body.[42] The division of chassis manufacture from the construction of motor bodies, the latter taken on mainly by coachbuilders often working to customers' specifications, made things difficult for car manufacturers who wished to introduce a degree of standardisation in output and to influence demand in the direction of greater homogeneity.

Not only were the motoring pressure groups and organisations addressing themselves to an elite; agents and manufacturers, too, chose to penetrate the ranks of the aristocracy – even royalty – in order to demonstrate the desirability of car ownership and to influence aspiration levels. Thus Lawson had succeeded in evoking the interest of the Prince of Wales in 1896; car ownership, it was implied, was a symbol of recognisable socio-economic status. After taking on the Standard agency, and subsequently becoming chairman and managing director, Friswell had made a similar bid for royal patronage by mounting an extravagant promotional exercise which succeeded in securing the contract for seventy Standard cars to meet transport requirements during the visit of King George V and Queen Mary to India in 1912. But the colossal expense did little to solve Standard's dire financial problems, leading instead to a revolt of his co-directors, who during his absence in India unilaterally terminated the sales agreement with Friswell's and embarked upon a policy of direct sales from the Coventry factory.[43] Daimler, Napier and Rolls Royce were equally anxious to publicise sales to the aristocracy, domestic, foreign or colonial. Napier published lists of satisfied customers, consisting mainly of dukes, viceroys, earls, lords, marquesses, etc. The advertising copy of these and many other firms was clearly aimed at the chauffeur-driven owner, or those with the wealth and/or pretensions to become one. Only during the years immediately preceding World War II did the concept of the motor car as a utility vehicle, as distinct from a means of sport or recreation, begin to advance in Britain, though doctors (who under the Finance Act of 1909 became entitled to pay only half the duty when licensing a car for professional activities) had figured among buyers from the beginning; one suggestion puts cars purchased for business purposes at less than one-third before 1914.[44]

Certainly by 1905 most British manufacturers who had taken up the Continental challenge of competitive motor racing had decided that they could no longer afford to continue, besides which the technological lessons could still be learned more cheaply from trials employing standard production vehicles. Exposure to the public was achieved through participation in the numerous reliability trials and international competitions for production models. But even Herbert Austin, outwardly sceptical of pushful sales methods, in 1908 built a 100 h.p. sports car and attracted considerable publicity when the car was purchased by Jack Johnson, the British boxing champion.[45] Furthermore, publicity could be achieved by imaginative planning and ingenious execution – as had been done in the past. S. F. Edge and Napier cars led the way, both on the racetrack and in stunt activity, whether it was by driving up Porlock Hill, with a one-in-four gradient, as a wager in 1900, or driving a Napier non-stop for twenty-four hours and 1,581 miles round the newly opened Brooklands track at an average speed of 66 m.p.h., a record which he established in 1907 and which lasted for eighteen years. Edge also exploited the feats of others. In the following year an obliging American owner of a 24 h.p. Napier car, Charles J. Glidden, began a series of marathon tours throughout Europe, including the Alps, even the Arctic Circle, and, with railway wheels fitted in place of tyres, along the track of the Canadian Pacific from east Canada to Vancouver, through to Australia and New Zealand, on tyres and back to London, then to the Far East. Not until 1909, having covered nearly 50,000 miles in thirty-nine countries, did the motoring exploits of Charles J. Glidden disappear from the Napier catalogue and publicity. By this time, however, Edge's success in pushing Napier to the forefront of car manufacture led Napier himself to become over-confident and choose greater independence in the firm's commercial as well as technical affairs. A successful public flotation provided him with the financial support to do this, and in 1912 Edge and Napier eventually parted, the latter taking over Edge's Motor Vehicle Company, while the 'pugnacious', 'mercurial' and 'egocentric' Edge became temporarily neutralised for seven years, by agreement, in retirement as a pig farmer in Sussex.[46]

Leading agents like Friswell and Edge certainly attracted publicity for their own activities and for the cars they sold, and both were responsible for defining the particular segment of the market in which the cars should be sold, for they set retail prices; indeed, when Friswell became chairman of Standard he was also responsible for blocking the plans proposed by Maudsley, founder of the company, to build cars which would appeal to a less exalted market than that cherished by Friswell.[47] Napier eventually took over Edge's agency of Napier cars after a dispute over pricing, Napier accusing Edge of pricing his cars so high in order to secure excessive profits, which had the effect of limiting Napier's sales.[48] In fact Edge and Friswell, among the most flamboyant persuaders in the motor trade, became increasingly exceptional in their behaviour. The formation by agents and retailers in 1910 of the Motor Traders' Association, a branch of the SMMT, showed that by this time the major concern in the trade was not excessive pricing but price cutting, and it was to prevent this by taking such steps as were legal that the Association was formed. It was not the first time that price maintenance by manufacturers and agents had been mooted, but hitherto manufacturers had not succeeded in forcing such a policy upon dealers. In 1911 the MTA issued a 'stop list' of companies and individuals with whom its members were instructed not to deal, the Association underwriting legal fees if necessary. Before 1914, with membership growing, the MTA had introduced a degree of orderly trading and a standard 15 per cent agents' discount, though the 'stop list' also grew.[49]

After more than ten years of rapid technical development in motor car design and construction, the prospect of retaining second-time purchasers as well as attracting first-time buyers became a consideration. For this reason Daimler in 1908, Austin in 1911 and Ford in 1913 introduced monthly magazines, each seen, as the *Austin Advocate* expressed it, as a 'weapon in the advertising armoury'. Described by the editor as 'an interesting, instructive and humorous' publication, the *Advocate* was designed to advise Austin owners of the best way of using Austin motor cars, to establish brand loyalty and to foster good internal relations. Rover did not produce a magazine, but the company did issue *What They Think of Us*, consisting of a bound reprint collection of testimonials from various sources, and a tract entitled 'Experiences of an 8 h.p. Rover'. Rover cars were under three months' guarantee in 1909, extended to six months in 1910, a practice introduced by Rolls Royce in 1907, when the company guaranteed the cost of replacement not only of defective parts but of parts which became obsolete through technical improvement, an expensive way of achieving good publicity.[50]

Marketing methods in France were similar to those to be found in Britain before 1914. French manufacturers sold cars through regional distributors who dealt with local agents. Automobile journalism and substantial advertising were employed to raise the level of interest in motoring and motor cars, and considerable publicity was attracted by exhibitions, stunts, competitive trials and racing. In the earliest days the standard purchase agreement required a deposit of one-third of the price to accompany the customer's order, but following Charles Rolls's initiative in 1903 a number of French dealers began to allow customers to purchase cars by instalments. The establishment of branches to assist with distribution and to provide after-sales service under guarantee is another practice which became well established during the first decade of the twentieth century.[51]

In these various ways the marketing of motor cars in Britain before 1914 did not differ much from those adopted by French manufacturers and dealers, and they reinforced the fairly rapid growth of the British market which followed the 1900 Reliability Trial. Not only were methods of sales and promotion similar; so too, with notable exceptions, were the kind of motor cars on offer to the two markets, in design, power and price. Professor Laux has concluded that the major area of weakness in the French automobile industry before 1914 was in marketing, where after an initial vision of the potential for the motor car French businessmen revealed themselves to be 'somewhat myopic'.[52] Much the same could be said of British businessmen in the years before 1912, but the notable exceptions were of sufficient importance to succeed in beginning that lengthy transformation of the luxury market into a market for popular cars.

Democratisation and the motor trade: a comparative review

Not surprisingly, and with ample justification, in 1912 the *Motor Trader* referred to the lack of attention shown by British manufacturers and traders towards the creation of a market for inexpensive motor cars.[53] There was one exception, a British motor agent named Percival Perry who by 1912 was beginning to overcome the earlier reputation of low-priced American cars in Europe as 'cheap and nasty'. Perry is interesting in the history of marketing because of his resounding success, and because his experience raises the question of the importance of national characteristics of markets. With a grammar school education, a passion and facility for writing poetry, no knowledge of engineering and possessing meagre financial resources, Perry had become interested in motor cars and secured employment with H. J. Lawson during the peak of his speculative career in the 1890s.[54] He became involved in the formation of the Central Motor Car Company in 1904, selling Ford cars, becoming managing director in 1906, but the relative failure of the Models A and C in Britain led shortly to its liquidation. Undeterred, and encouraged by the prospect of the new Model N, in 1907 a new agency – Perry Thornton and Schreiber – came into being, taking over the right to sell Ford cars from the Central Motor Car Company. Perry left the new firm after a dispute with the other two parties and, after selling low-cost Reo cars, from the American, R. E. Olds, for a couple of years, he reopened links with Henry Ford, who in 1909 appointed him manager in charge of the English Ford enterprise, registered as the Ford Motor Company (England) Ltd in 1911. Assembling cars costing between £125 and £135, far lower than the prices of cars remotely comparable in the British market, by 1914 Ford in England easily outsold all other British companies and in 1913 accounted for nearly 30 per cent of total production.

Perry's initial publicity campaign to introduce the Model T was familiar in approach but spectacular in results. As the Royal Automobile Club's reliability trials had died out, Perry decided that Ford should conduct its own, driving a Ford across the rugged South Downs countryside for two days. In 1911 he arranged for the Scottish Ford dealer to drive a Model T up Ben Nevis, Britain's highest mountain at 4,600 ft. The public impact was enormous. Sales increased rapidly, even though the concessions made by Henry Ford to the design of cars assembled in Manchester for the British market were minimal, consisting of little more than the substitution of right-hand for left-hand drive, though some dealers made special bodies for the standard Ford chassis. Contrary to Ford practice in the United States, Perry adopted the customary British pattern which allowed dealers (nearly 1,000 of them) to sell cars other than Fords. Agreements allowed 15 per cent discount on cars purchased in return for an undertaking not to sell below a recommended price, which Ford, outside the MTA, enforced in the courts.[55]

British manufacturers misinterpreted the conception of a market for low-priced cars, which Perry had been so successful in identifying and exploited so effectively thanks to Ford's low-cost production, for the attempt to bridge the gap between the motorcycle and sidecar and tricar and the cheapest four-wheeled motor car then available resulted in the cyclecar. This was a crude hybrid, typically combining unreliability, underpowering and discomfort, whose only feature in common with the Ford was low initial cost. Alldays & Onions, Humber, Swift and Wolseley were among the few larger or established British motor car manufacturers to venture into this segment of the market, while Jowett, Morgan, AC and GWK were other firms which built cyclecars and yet survived as car manufacturers, albeit on a small scale, after World War I.[56] Renault, formerly Renault Frères, the Anglo-French agency operating in Britain since 1905, directed by local management under the chairmanship of Fernand Renault, also achieved success in the low-to-medium-priced segment, more than 20 per cent of the 663 Renault cars sold in Britain in 1913 consisting of two-cylinder cars of 8 or 9 h.p., priced below £200.[57]

Only a handful of motor manufacturers read the market reasonably accurately in response to Perry and his Model T Ford and by 1913 offered low horsepower two- to four-seater models for less than £250, which both the *Times* correspondent and the author of an American consular report identified as the upper limit below which was to be found a potentially large and expanding section of the population aspiring to car ownership. These included Singer, Standard and Hillman, each of which was more or less dominated by engineers, Standard having rid itself of its commercial albatross, Charles Friswell. Moreover, even in those cases where there was a perception of a demand for relatively low-priced, low horsepower cars, the scale of production necessary in order to compete with Ford was seen to be far beyond the resources available to them, and the successful sale of medium-priced cars on higher unit profit margins offered insufficient incentive to take the plunge.[58] Such had been Herbert Austin's view in 1912, and in 1913, while Rover's directors acknowledge the potential demand for 'a small runabout car to sell at about £100', they also agreed that as trade in their existing models was satisfactory and the sale of motorcycles buoyant, no further action should be taken at that time.[59] Similar discussions occurred between the directors of Standard in 1910, but financial difficulties hampered development in the direction of a single model of 'small size and ample power' produced on economical lines.[60] An article in *The Times* in 1912 commented on the avoidance of this branch of the industry even by the big firms as explicable 'possibly on financial grounds'.[61]

The lowest-cost British car in this range in 1913 was the Morris Oxford, with a basic price of £175, compared with the Ford at £125–£135. And it was William Morris, like Perry lacking engineering expertise and formerly in his own business of selling, rather than building, motor cars, who achieved the breakthrough for British manufacturers. Both in the design of the Morris Oxford and in the adoption of assembly methods of production on a sizeable scale, certainly unprecedented in the history of British producers before Ford, Morris provided the commercial initiative which after World War I was to push the British industry into the stage of volume production, with all the implications this carried for mass marketing methods and distribution. It is significant, then, that prior to 1914 it was left to the two commercial men, Perry and Morris, to set the pace in further 'democratising' the British market for motor cars.

While the complete transition to mass demand was to be a protracted process both in France and in Great Britain, there is evidence to suggest that, contrary to an impression conveyed by the literature, Britain was probably not behind France in the development of a market for low-cost motor cars in 1913. It is also possible to reinforce this conclusion by attempting to quantify the extent to which by 1913 the relatively low-priced motor car had affected market structures in the two countries. By 1910 estimated registration figures suggest that the rate of car ownership *per capita* was similar in the two countries but rising faster in the UK, where by 1913 the estimate of 250,000 motor vehicles registered may be compared with roughly 125,000 in France.[62] Production in the two countries has been estimated at 34,000 in the UK and 45,000 in France, the difference being explained by substantial French exports to the principal car-owning countries, and especially to the UK.[63] It is possible that a higher *per capita* car ownership in the UK might have reflected nothing more than the difference in *per capita* incomes in the two countries, and that in the sense of Professor Saul's quotation from *The Times* the British market for motor cars was more exclusive, less 'democratic' than the French. In order to be able to test that hypothesis, however, we require an examination of market structure in the two countries, for the *Times* correspondent claimed that cheaper cars were more prevalent in France than in the UK. If this were found to be true, it would add weight to Professor Saul's criticism of the relative lack of development of this segment of the market in Britain and, by implication, would suggest that French businessmen had countered the disadvantages of their own small domestic market, not only by successful exporting but also by tapping a demand in the domestic market by offering smaller and cheaper models, perhaps supported by more vigorous marketing methods.

Comparisons of market structure are difficult to make without much more detailed information than is available, and it is necessary to rely on little more than informed guesses at the proportion of the French and British markets secured by cars costing less than about £200, the figure which the *Economist* correspondent quoted as the upper price limit for what he described as 'moderate priced cars',[64] and may be regarded as the approximate price separating the medium-quality market from the first-time buyers who formed the basis for a potential popular demand. Professor Laux has suggested that a very rough estimate of 6,000 cars in this category were produced in France in 1913 and 1914, which is approximately 15 per cent of the total.[65] For the United Kingdom a comparable tentative estimate (table 1) would lie between 4,000 and 5,000 low-priced cars, excluding Ford; but between 10,000 and 11,000 with Ford included.[66] Including Ford, the comparable percentage figure for low-priced cars in relation to UK production may have been greater than 30 per cent and even excluding Ford would have been perhaps 12 per cent.

A more useful indicator of the comparative degree of 'democratisation' of the markets for motor cars in the two countries would be the proportion that purchases of relatively low-priced cars represented of total car sales in each country, a com-

Table 1 *Estimates of cars priced below £200 produced in Britain in 1913*

Ford	6,139	Hillman	50 (Hillman, Swift, Star, Belsize)	Humber	2,000
Morris	300	Swift		Wolseley	750
Singer	675	Star		GWK	200 (GWK, AC, All other cyclecar producers)
Standard	200	Belsize		AC	
				All other cyclecar producers	
		Total	10,314		

Note. It cannot be emphasised sufficiently that most of the figures shown in tables 1 and 2 are estimates and guesses, some of which are based on qualitative evidence only, though in every case relying upon contemporary sources. The Ford figures are reliable and are taken from *Ford Times*, June 1914, and P. L. D. Perry, 'The Ford in England', M. Wilkins and F. E. Hill, *American Business Abroad*, p. 51; those for Morris and Humber are from S. B. Saul, p. 25, and those for Renault have been calculated from the Renault Car Register for 1913. The figures for Singer, Standard and Wolseley are guesses based on the known production figures for these companies and rely on judgement of the proportion of their total production likely to have been accounted for by their smaller 'popular' models. Figures for 'all British producers' in table 2 assume no exports of smaller models, the justification being that the average price of British car exports was almost twice as high as the average price of imported cars, and that alternative figures are not available. All remaining 'estimates' are pure guesswork, but count for a relatively small proportion of the totals. There is not even quasi-quantitative information on the production of cyclecars, except for some of those companies listed here (Humberette and, even less reliably, Wolseley Stellite), but it seems likely that the figures produced here are considerable under-estimates. For a list of motor cars and cyclecars in the categories covered by these tables see W. C. Bersey and W. V. Foucard, *A List of Motor Cars, 1908–1914* (London, 1914), and in much greater detail Fletcher's *Motor Car Index, 1913–24* (Norwich, 1925).

parison which is even more fraught with difficulties, as there is information only on the *value* of aggregate French exports before 1914. However, as France was a negligible importer of automobiles, it may be argued that if Ford imports into France are added to the estimates of French production of low-priced cars, the result will provide a crude upper limit of popular car purchases when the sum of relatively low-priced cars produced is expressed as a proportion of car registrations. The figure for 1913 (6,676 as a proportion of 125,000) is slightly above 5 per cent. The UK also poses a difficult problem because of the very large imports of motor vehicles; however, most of the low-priced units will have been Fords, though in value terms French imports to the UK were larger than from the US.[67] It seems unlikely that the pattern of exports to the UK from Renault, one of the two largest French manufacturers, through Renault Frères, was unusual or, at least, was exceeded by other French companies; in 1913 about a fifth of Renault cars imported in the UK cost less, when sold, than £200.[68] We have assumed that Renault's sales of such cars in the UK in 1913 were equalled by the aggregate sales of comparable models by all other European exporters.

The output of British cars in this category, including Fords (imported but assembled at Trafford Park) may have accounted for nearly 5 per cent of registrations (table 2). These rough estimates suggest that, adopting the £200 criterion, by 1913 the British market was no less democratised than was the market in France. 'Democratisation', however, was relative and in Britain did not extend further than the professional and business sections of the community. A point of contrast between the two markets was that whereas such limited social dispersion of car ownership as existed in France was due to the domestic supply of relatively low-priced vehicles, a considerable number of which were exported to Britain to swell the burgeoning market for taxi cabs,[69] in Britain it was Ford (propelled by Perry) that led the incipient movement towards mass motorisation.

Table 2 *Estimates of cars priced below £200 sold in Britain in 1913*

Ford	7,310
Other British producers	4,175
Renault	158
Other imported models	158
Tota	11,801

See note to table 1.

Undoubtedly the successful penetration of the free-trading British market by Ford was an advantage to Percival Perry in his campaign to widen the market for cheaper cars, though Professor Laux has dismissed the retardative effect of the French tariff of 8–12 per cent, maintaining that 'French pride in the home-manufactured product' served as a much more potent contraceptive against Ford's automotive thrust.[70] It may be so, though it seems worthwhile to recall that the French jibe of 'hardware' aimed at American cars had its counterpart in the 'cheap and nasty' reputation which accompanied the arrival in Britain of the low-priced American cars. Furthermore, in 1912 a US consular report noted declining resistance to low-priced cars, concluding that, while the French market would continue to be difficult, prospects for the growth of small car sales were better.[71] Perry's success in presenting Ford in the UK surely throws into doubt the notion of national characteristics of markets impervious to commercial erosion.

In other respects there are distinct similarities between the approach of manufacturers to the market, both in the type of models offered and in the methods of marketing. In each country the evolution of the market for the lighter-weight, low-powered, low-cost cars was slow in comparison with the US. Renault had been successful with the 8–9 h.p. two-cylinder taxi before 1909, though less so with a two-cylinder 10 h.p. car; Austin's 10 h.p. car introduced in 1911 also proved less successful than the larger, more expensive cars. After 1909 an Anglo-French company, Darracq, operating in both countries, began to founder on a policy emphasising cars in the lower half of the price range. Not surprisingly, both Renault and Austin concentrated on larger models in supplying the private passenger car market after 1911. It was left to other manufacturers in both countries to develop the compact lower-priced models, first by experimenting with cyclecars and then from 1912 with small cars proper: the Zèbre four-cylinder model,[72] the Peugeot Bébé, and with other small cars from Clément Bayard, Gregoire and Sizaire & Naudin. In Britain Singer, Standard, Hillman and, in 1913, Morris led the way. Both in Britain and France *manufacturers* can be criticised for a relative lack of interest in aggressive marketing methods before 1912, but in Britain the importing agents, praised for their dynamism by Professor Laux, were instrumental in developing a market considerably more extensive than in France, although French production was larger. Perhaps it is significant that both Renault and Austin, who rejected low-priced car production in the immediate pre-war period, were very profitable companies at this time, while Peugeot and Unic (Zèbre cars) whose profitability was much lower, successfully pioneered the production and sale of economy cars in France.[73]

Among the British firms tempted to experiment at this end of the market, both Humber and Wolseley experienced financial difficulties, which the Humberette and Stellite cyclecars may have been developed to alleviate.[74] Both at Standard and at Singer the introduction of light cars in 1912 followed capital reconstruction, and in the case of Standard was the sequel to a financial crisis and boardroom changes,[75] though the new models were designed to expand sales and the scale of production rather than to compensate for unprofitable trading. Rover's directors, on the other hand, rejected further expansion, content with current motorcycle and car sales in the medium price range. While it might be possible to explain why particular firms in Britain and France were tempted to produce smaller lower priced motor cars after 1911, it would not be sensible to try to explain the differential growth in economy car sales in terms of differential profitability between the two industries, for in both countries there was a wide dispersion throughout the pre-war period.

It is possible that the campaign launched in British newspaper circles round about 1912 to encourage 'economical motoring', and the production of a type of car to appeal to a family of modest means played a part in the emergence of the cyclecar and small car proper,[76] but the evolution of low-priced models occurred simultaneously in both countries. Reports of the popularity of low-priced cars in the United States raised expectations of a similar trend in European countries, and, even disregarding the alleged national pride of the French in home manufactured products, the impact of Ford cars imported to France was likely to be less than in

Britain, where cars were assembled on British soil by British workers and promoted by the extraordinarily commercially sensitive Percival Perry. By 1913 more than 6,000 Model T cars had been sold in Britain, compared with fewer than 700 in France. Perry, it seems, broke through the prejudice against the image established by the early American cars, an achievement which is a testament to the importance of marketing in the history of the motor industry before 1914.

While the lack of tariff protection cannot be considered to have contributed to it, Saul's strictures on the commercial weakness of the British industry are well founded. Commercial men, though, must share the blame with engineers for the tardy realisation that the future of the industry depended upon the development of a sizeable market for low-priced cars. In this the British industry was no worse than the French, and for similar reasons; moreover by 1913 Perry and a handful of others had demonstrated a commitment to achieve democratisation of the market for motor cars in Britain.

Notes

1 S. B. Saul, 'The motor industry in Britain to 1914', *Business History*, V (1962), pp. 42–3.

2 *The Times*, 20 August 1912.

3 A. Milward and S. B. Saul, *The Development of Continental Europe, 1850–1914* (1977), p. 515.

4 J. S. Foreman-Peck, 'Tariff protection and economies of scale: the British motor industry before 1939', *Oxford Economic Papers*, N.S., vol. 31 (1979), pp. 241, 257.

5 J. M. Laux, *In First Gear: the French Automobile Industry to 1914* (Liverpool, 1976), pp. 202–3.

6 *The Motor Trader*, 25 September 1912.

7 US Bureau of Domestic and Foreign Commerce, *Special Consular Report* No. 53 (Washington, 1912), 'Foreign markets for motor vehicles', pp. 59–66.

8 A series of biographical articles by 'owner drivers' on their early experiences included several doctors as owners. Dr A. Elmslie Craffe presented evidence to show just how economical it was to substitute car for horse and carriage for the conduct of his duties. (*The Motorist*, 23 August 1913.) The Star Motor Company's four-cylinder 10 h.p. car called the 'Doctoris Victoria', offered at £265 in 1912, and BSA's 'Doctor's Coupé', introduced in the same year at £350, are clues to the price range perceived by manufacturers as appropriate for the income of physicians. (*Motor Car Journal*, 20 January 1912.)

9 The two-cylinder 'Overland' was priced, complete, at £275, including starting handle. *The Motorist*, 20 September 1913.

10 Saul, 'The motor industry', p. 43.

11 Laux, *In First Gear*, pp. 202–3.

12 *Motor Export Trader*, 9 March 1913.

13 Laux, *In First Gear*, Chapter 8, p. 203.

14 See below, pp. 7–8.

15 L. T. C. Rolt, *The Horseless Carriage* (1950), pp. 40–2, 70–2; St John Nixon, *The Story of the S.M.M.T.* (1952), pp. 17–23.

16 Rolt, *The Horseless Carriage*, pp. 70–2.

17 *Ibid.*

18 K. Richardson, *The British Motor Industry* (1977), pp. 20–1.

19 H. G. Castle, *Britain's Motor Industry* (1951), pp. 56–8.

20 St John Nixon, *Wolseley* (1949), pp. 11, 51–8.

21 *The Motorist*, June 1913.

22 S. F. Edge, *My Motoring Reminiscences* (1934); C. Wilson and W. Reader, *Men and Machines* (1958), p. 71.

23 Wilson and Reader, *Men and Machines*, p. 72.

24 Nixon, *The Story of the S.M.M.T.*, pp. 25–31.

25 W. Plowden, *The Motor Car and Politics* (1971), pp. 36–9.

26 Rolt, *The Horseless Carriage*, p. 77.

27 For the origins of distribution see G. C. Allen, *Industrial Development of Birmingham and the Black Country, 1860–1927* (1966), pp. 344–51.

28 Richardson, *The British Motor Industry*, pp. 211–12.

29 *Ibid.*, pp. 211–19.

30 'The Story of Renault in the United Kingdom', *Auto-world*, 1979.

31 Wilson and Reader, *Men and Machines*, pp. 71–8.

32 Pollitt Papers, 398/3; *Automotor Journal*, 31 August 1907.

33 Richardson, *The British Motor Industry*, p. 217.

34 'Sir Herbert Austin, KBE: his life story', *Autocar*, 23 August 1929.

35 *Automotor Journal*, 5 December 1903.

36 J. K. Starley, one of Rover's managers in 1909, explained to the directors that a shortage of finance the previous winter had prevented the ordering of materials for building a new model, which is why the 1909 car programme was late. Rover Company Ltd, Directors' Minutes, 20 April 1909; Nixon, *Wolseley* (1949), p. 50; Roy Church, *Herbert Austin: the British Motor Car Industry to 1941* (1979), p. 25.

37 Castle, *Britain's Motor Industry*, p. 56–8.

38 Standard Motor Company, Minute Book, 18 January, 8 February 1907.

39 Ian Lloyd, *Rolls Royce: the Growth of a Firm* (1978), p. 11.

40 Church, *Herbert Austin*.

41 Quoted by Plowden, *The Motor Car*, p. 39.

42 Wilson and Reader, *Men and Machines*, p. 87.

43 J. R. Davy, *The Standard Car, 1903–1963* (1967), pp. 17–18; Standard Motor Company, Board Minutes, 15 February 1912.

44 D. G. Rhys, *The British Motor Industry* (1972), p. 9.

45 Church, *Herbert Austin*, p. 27.

46 Wilson and Reader, *Men and Machines*, pp. 99–100.

47 Church, *Herbert Austin*, pp. 187–8.

48 Wilson and Reader, *Men and Machines*, p. 97.

49 K. C. Johnson-Davies, *The Practice of Price Maintenance* (1955), pp. 1–4.

50 G. Oliver, *The Rover* (1971), p. 29; Church, *Herbert Austin*, p. 25.

51 Laux, *In First Gear*, pp. 70–2, 201–3.

52 *Ibid.*, p. 201.

53 *The Times*, 20 August 1912.

54 M. Wilkins, *American Business Abroad: Ford on Six Continents* (1966), pp. 23–5.

55 Richardson, *The British Motor Industry*, p. 220.

56 C. F. Caunter, *The Light Car: a Technical History* (1970), pp. 43, 52–3.

57 These included some vehicles for sale overseas, mainly through Tozer Kemsley to imperial markets. Renault Ltd, Minute Books, 1905–1910; Renault Frères Minute Book, 1910–13; Renault Car Register, 1911–13.

58 Church, *Herbert Austin*, pp. 39–41.

59 Rover Company Ltd, Directors' Minutes, 24 February 1913.

60 Standard Motor Company, Directors' Minutes, 5, 19, 26 April 1910.

61 *The Times*, 20 August 1912.

62 Laux, *In First Gear*, p. 196.

63 *Ibid.*, p. 209.

64 *The Economist*, 22 November 1913.

65 Laux, *In First Gear*, p. 202. This figure includes one, two and four-cylinder cyclecars and motor cars.

66 This is made up as follows: Ford, 6,139; Morris, 1,300; Renault imports, 147; and remaining guesstimates: Humberette, 2,000; Stellite, 1,000; Singer, 1,000; Standard, 500; Star, 200; Belsize, 250; Hillman, 20. As there were many tiny producers of cyclecars, the total figure of cheap cars, adopting the definition used by Professor Laux, may have exceeded our figure of approx. 12,500, though as the suggested figures for the main small car producers are so tentative no additions have be.. made to take account of them.

67 Laux, *In First Gear*, p. 209, table 12.

68 Renault Company Register, 1911–13.

69 G. N. Georgano, *A History of the London Taxi Cab* (1972), pp. 95–101.

70 Laux, *In First Gear*, pp. 101–2.

71 US Bureau of Domestic and Foreign Commerce, *Special Consular Report No. 53* (Washington, D.C., 1912), 'Foreign markets for motor vehicles', pp. 59–66.

72 Laux, *In First Gear*, p. 160.

73 See Laux, *In First Gear*, appendix, table 14.

74 *Motor Trader*, 11 December 1912.

75 Standard Motor Company, Directors' Minute Book, 14 January, 16 August, 19 October 1910; 5 January, 15 February, 19 November, 31 December 1912; 30 January, 18 October 1913; Pollitt Papers, Coventry volume.

76 *Automotive Industries*, 19 February 1920.

3 *The outstanding potential market: the British motor industry and Europe, 1945–75*

TIMOTHY R. WHISLER

This study analyses the failure of the British motor industry to achieve a significant market share in western Europe from 1945 until 1975. Although company executives, government officials and industry observers regarded Europe as a lucrative market, the British were unable to capture more than 5 per cent of annual sales in Europe, with the exception of the immediate post-war years. The time frame of this investigation allows a comparison of the activities and strategies of the firms during the horizontal merger movement, which culminated in 1968 with the creation of British Leyland Motor Corporation (BLMC), and its nationalisation, which occurred in 1974 when the government rescued BLMC from bankruptcy. It also permits an examination of the ramifications of the British decision to join the European Free Trade Association (EFTA) rather than the European Economic Community (EEC) and the reversal of this policy in 1973.[1]

Chandler argues that, historically, a 'three prong investment' in management, production and distribution was essential for firms to exploit the economies of scale and scope.[2] Various studies of the post-World War II British motor industry, however, have demonstrated that the indigenous companies generally refrained from investing in the recruitment, training and specialisation of managers, resulting in a lower skill level of personnel and the slower development of corporate structure and strategy compared to rivals.[3] The limited capabilities of management also produced a resistance to new manufacturing techniques. Investment in production facilities occurred more frequently, but capital expenditure tended to be made in amounts insufficient to modernise and integrate plant and machinery. Competitors, however, instituted capital-intensive automated production methods and reaped the cost benefits of achieving minimum efficient scale. Finally, the British failed to invest in the facilities and personnel to co-ordinate production and distribution functions. British export campaigns were hindered by poor marketing, high prices for and chronic shortages of cars and spare parts, and low quality of dealers and distributors. In contrast, European and Japanese exporters committed large sums of capital to create national sales subsidiaries which controlled the activity, inventory and general standard of their distribution structures.

The failure of the British firms to make the 'three prong investment', particularly in distribution, was the underlying cause of the relatively low sales of British cars in Europe. As Chandler suggests, the interdependence of product characteristics, production methods and scale, marketing skill, and distribution structure is crucial to sales success: it is difficult to construct and maintain a viable product channel without offering products that meet demand, and products in demand will not be sold in volume without establishing an effective distribution structure. The British often failed to acknowledge this relationship, and when firms did recognise the association they were unable or unwilling to enact the measures to ensure sales success in Europe.

British distribution structures and immediate post-war Europe

Distribution structure performance depends largely upon the degree of co-operation between members. Usually a leader emerges within the product channel which persuades or forces, through net pricing, discounting product supply, administration and/or satisfying member needs, the structure to act as a unit. Generally a short product channel confers greater control on the leader and reduces the number of transactions, thus lowering distribution costs. A leaderless or poorly guided channel, however, allows members to pursue their own interests, to the detriment of the whole. As a result, the transfer of information and products becomes costly and inconsistent.[4]

By its nature, the franchise distribution structure, traditionally used in the motor industry, placed the manufacturer in the leadership role. American motor firms were quick to use their power to reduce costs and control dealer inventory by reducing the number of tiers in their domestic product channel. By the end of the Second World War direct delivery of cars and spare parts from the factory to the dealer was general practice. Corporate regional offices co-ordinated the process as well as directed marketing campaigns. The British motor firms, however, preferred a multi-tier product channel in the domestic market. Distributors, which often held retail rights, and main dealers purchased cars from the factory and sold them on a commission basis to franchised dealers. In some cases, 'area dealers' passed cars on to small, non-franchised dealers. The structure allowed the firms to reduce their inventory and sales costs, but the length of the channel diluted their control.

In view of the British domestic distribution structure, it is not surprising that the early post-war export product channels were based upon loosely affiliated agents who assumed the costs of financing shipments and inventories of cars and spares. In effect the British domestic product channel — with an additional tier — was recreated in overseas markets. The product channel was lengthened even further when export sales divisions, which purchased cars from line divisions for shipment abroad, were created in England. Profit-taking at each transaction increased export retail prices. Perhaps more important, the long product channel led to frequent clashes of interest among structure members. The disadvantages inherent in the British export distribution structure were clearly evident in the European market during the 1940s and 1950s.

In 1945 the British motor industry appeared to be in a strong competitive position for the short and long term. Most firms emerged from the war with undamaged plant and machinery, new 'shadow factory' capacity as well as war-time mass-production experience and profits. A world shortage of US dollars, combined with Detroit's inability to fulfil domestic orders and the dislocation of European manufacturers, seemed to offer, as the *Manchester Guardian* claimed, 'a golden opportunity to secure a large and permanent export trade'.[5] The industry's prospects convinced the Treasury that, in the face of a national foreign currency shortage, motor exports could be used to earn the funds needed to pay for imported materials and food. In April 1945 the President of the Board of Trade, Hugh Dalton, informed the sector that 50 per cent of its output was to be exported. Two years later the 'Export or Die' campaign increased the requirement to 75 per cent. The Labour government exercised no formal control over model production or export destination, but encouraged, through exhortation and public announcements, sales in hard-currency markets, particularly the US and dollar areas.[6]

The manufacturers were unenthusiastic. In 1947 the Nuffield board commented that while previously exports had been considered 'an expensive but unavoidable nuisance . . . now our very existence is dependent upon it'.[7] Nuffield and other British car makers preferred to concentrate their sales efforts in the domestic market, but sales were restricted by government quotas. Moreover the producers had relatively little pre-war exporting experience. In 1938 Britain was the third largest car exporting nation, but the British shipped 44,000 units, compared with German exports of 60,000 cars and American shipments of 162,000 units.[8] Nearly 85 per cent of British exports were shipped to the dominions/empire. Eire was Britain's largest European market. Sales in Ireland were more than double the combined value of sales in Belgium, Denmark, the Netherlands, Portugal, Sweden and Switzerland.[9]

The Political and Economic Planning Group (PEP) consultants noted in 1950 that the motor firms had to launch an export drive without established distribution structures in most overseas markets. Prior to the war British cars were imported by foreign agents who appointed and then supplied distributors and dealers. The product channel was designed for low-volume sales and minimal manufacturer control and investment. PEP warned that, in the new environment, high-quality sales and service facilities and adequate spare parts and car inventories would be crucial to export sales success. In view of the cost and complexity involved in constructing foreign distribution structures, and the firms' limited resources, PEP suggested, in vain, that the manufacturers join in creating (and sharing the costs of) common export product channels, which would handle all British models.[10]

Throughout the post-war period the British firms regarded Germany as the key to the European market. In the late 1940s the British faced contradictory market conditions in West Germany. On the one hand the dislocation caused by the war, tariff rates of 14 per cent and foreign exchange restrictions hindered sales to civilians. On the other hand, the British Commercial Representative argued that sales to government and military personnel could create a solid base for large-volume sales as the German economy recovered in the longer term. The British entered the market cautiously. Austin established a national agent and several main dealers near US and British military bases. Nuffield appointed two autonomous distributors. Incredibly, Standard-Triumph relied upon its London distributor to supply three small dealers. The High Commission reported that nearly all sales were to military and diplomatic officials and that higher sales, including to Germans, were possible if distributors and dealers kept an inventory of cars and spares. Instead new car deliveries often took eight weeks and one American serviceman waited six months for a replacement engine for his MG Midget sports car. Even the most routine spares were not kept in stock.[11]

When most of the vehicles in the British and Swedish diplomatic motor pools were idled by delays in the delivery of spares, the British Commercial Representative, stressing the need for 'adequate sales and service' to increase British car sales, negotiated an arrangement with American Eucom Exchange Service (AEES).[12] The US military merchandiser agreed to import direct, retail and stock a designated minimum level of spares and cars. In addition, the British High Commission offered $25,000 to finance parts stocks in Germany. But Ford and Austin accepted only $5,000 each, while Nuffield drew upon just $1,000. Standard-Triumph declined to participate, insisting that all parts come direct from England.[13]

A mystified High Commission and Ministry of Supply demanded that the firms explain their actions. The manufacturers replied that the AEES scheme would decimate existing product channels; moreover, German foreign exchange regulations prevented large parts stocks. Citing these circumstances and low annual sales, the companies claimed they 'would prefer not to do the business at all'.[14] The industry response was curious. The British had a virtual monopoly in the market, and sales to servicemen and diplomats earned hard currency. In catering primarily to these customers, the AEES scheme appeared advantageous. The obvious drawback of relying upon the AEES was the uncertain duration of the American military occupation of Germany. Yet the firms were doing little to ensure the long-term viability of their existing product channels. The indifferent response to the High Commission financing offer revealed that the companies had delegated responsibility for inventories to the agents.

In addition, the European market, as the manufacturers had implied, was a low priority. The government emphasised earning hard currency in the North American market, and the industry preferred to sell in the Commonwealth, particularly Australia, which had been Britain's largest export market in the pre-war era. In the immediate post-war years the manufacturers believed that the small indigenous industry would be incapable of supplying the expanding Australian market. Both the industry and the government were committed to short-term objectives. Successs in the European market, however, required long-term vision. The opportunity to establish a viable distribution structure and marque loyalty was largely ignored during the late 1940s.

Changing market conditions: the rise of Volkswagen

Several developments in the early 1950s affected the British position in Europe. With the outbreak of the Korean War in 1950 and the consequent shortage of alloy and non-alloy metals, the Ministry of Supply allocated materials largely on the basis of exports to hard-currency markets, especially North America. Two years later, as the rationing programme was ending, Australia imposed currency exchange restrictions and high tariffs on imported cars, which effectively closed Britain's largest overseas market. As a consequence the Board of Trade urged the sector to 'spread its efforts even more widely', suggesting that European markets could be exploited if the distribution structures were upgraded. Industry representatives replied that higher sales were necessary to establish effective distribution structures.[15] Apparently no one recognised that both views were essentially correct. The key to sales success was to upgrade distribution structures and increase turnover to stabilise and sustain product channel members.

Equally important, European competition emerged in the form of the German-built Volkswagen. Although Britain had the largest intra-European market share in 1950, with 40 per cent, Germany, led by Volkswagen, held 36 per cent of the market. More worrisome, the British were losing sales in an expanding market. The warning signals had reached London as early as 1947. The Mechanical Engineering Industries Branch (MEI) of the Control Commission for Germany, which supervised the re-start of production at Volkswagen's Wolfsburg complex, stated that the design of the model was 'a good five years ahead of anything being produced in England today'.[16] A Nuffield distributor visiting the Continent and British diplomats confirmed the German car's superior design, characteristics and quality compared with British models. The Volkswagen featured such innovative characteristics as torsion bar suspension, synchromesh transmission and high reliability.

The Volkswagen also had a lower price than the British competition. MEI, High Commission, and Ministry of Supply reports during the early 1950s suggest that the Volkswagen price advantage stemmed from the utilisation of highly mechanised plant organised in line with flow production techniques capable of achieving high annual output, thus reaping economies of scale. It was estimated that the daily installed capacity of the Volkswagen model was 1,000 units. Managers and engineers tightly supervised capacity utilisation rates and labour input, raising productivity by a factor of seven between 1946 and 1952 as Wolfsburg came on stream. In comparison British firms generally maintained their pre-war production methods, characterised by weak managerial control, low capital–labour ratios, low levels of machine integration, and piecework payment systems. Each company also offered a number of different models comprised of unique components, which reduced individual model output and the opportunity of achieving minimum efficient scale.[17] For example, the Morris Minor had a daily installed capacity of about 460 units in 1950, and material shortages and poor production organisation kept utilisation rates low. As a result Nuffield managers complained of overmanning and high product prices in the European and North American markets.[18]

Volkswagen's advantages in product characteristics and price were reflected in the market. In 1953 British diplomats noted that the German car threatened to 'completely oust the British light car' from the Swiss market. The Board of Trade acknowledged the role of price and characteristics in the German sales success, but argued that the impressive standard of Volkswagen sales and service facilities was also a critical factor. As early as 1947, two years before the firm's export drive began in earnest, the British Commercial Representative in Frankfurt reported that Volkswagen was giving 'special attention' to organising service facilities, including company-owned repair shops and spare parts depots, throughout Europe. The firm, not an agent, created its distribution structure. Members were chosen upon the basis of financial and marketing attributes and geographical location. This strategy ensured a high-quality structure for the company while providing each member with a potentially lucrative sales volume. This structure also allowed Volkswagen to exert far greater control over its product channel compared with the British. National sales subsidiaries were established to co-ordinate sales strategy, provide factory technicians to assist dealer repairs and monitor member adherence to designated car and parts inventories.[19]

Requests for a Volkswagen franchise by prospective wholesalers in Belgium and Holland during 1949 vividly demonstrate how the interrelationship of product, manufacturer and distribution is fundamental to a successful sales effort. Strong franchise demand, based upon product characteristics, price and manufacturer support, allows the producer to choose among the best distributors and dealers. In this relationship the firm has, if it possesses the managerial and marketing skills, the control to enforce its standards upon the structure members. In turn, channel members, willing to submit to the leader to secure product supply, earn profits while providing the level of sales required to ensure efficient factory operations. The interests of the product channel members and producer are integrated in the pursuit of higher sales and profits. Neither the relationship between nor the benefits to product channel members existed in the British distribution structure.

With the closing of the Australian market for built-up exports, the British shifted their sales target to North America and Europe. Austin, which had merged in 1952 with Nuffield to form the British Motor Corporation (BMC), informed the Ministry of Supply that it intended to 'capture a large share of the European market' with its new Austin Seven model. The Ministry agreed with the firm's optimism that the small car would sell well.[20] But Austin enacted few measures to improve its European product channel. In contrast, Standard-Triumph reorganised its distribution structure by appointing agents in Austria, Belgium, Denmark, Germany, Holland, Ireland, Italy, Switzerland and France, but the firm's model range remained unattractive. British diplomats in Europe considered the Standard Eight markedly inferior to the Volkswagen, and the larger Vanguard was priced higher than German and French rivals.[21] In effect, Austin upgraded its model range and Standard-Triumph improved its product channel, but neither firm attempted to do both simultaneously. Thus sales prospects remained essentially unchanged.

The British outside the EEC

Table 1 demonstrates that annual sales of British cars in western Europe increased slowly during the latter half of the 1950s. By 1958 the British were selling the fewest units of the four major European car-producing countries. The British failure was pronounced in the EEC, where annual sales actually declined slightly from the 1956 peak in a market that was growing at an average annual rate of 16 per cent. The British performance cannot be attributed solely to the EEC tariff. Marketing efforts had returned once again to Australia, where local assembly had been established, and the United States, where Detroit had ignored the small car segment. Equally important, as *Motor Business* revealed, the problems that had previously plagued the British sales effort in Europe remained unresolved. The British offered a limited model range, and the design, price, characteristics and quality of the cars continued to be inferior to those of Continental rivals. The journal also argued that the standard of sales and service provided by the British distribution structures was poor. Frustrated European product channel members complained that the British devoted little attention and investment to advertising and marketing. Sales leaflets were not even translated into native languages.[22]

Table 1. *British, German, French and Italian new car exports to Europe, 1946–75*

	Britain		*Germany*		*France*		*Italy*	
Year	*EEC*	*EFTA*	*EEC*	*EFTA*	*EEC*	*EFTA*	*EEC*	*EFTA*
1946	7,757	n.a.	n.a.	n.a.	n.a.	n.a.	n.a.	n.a.
1947	18,245	n.a.	n.a.	n.a.	n.a.	n.a.	n.a.	n.a.
1948	21,440	n.a.	n.a.	n.a.	n.a.	n.a.	n.a.	n.a.
1949	22,676	n.a.	n.a.	n.a.	n.a.	n.a.	n.a.	n.a.
1950	29,311	n.a.	n.a.	n.a.	n.a.	n.a.	n.a.	n.a.
1951	25,026	n.a.	n.a.	n.a.	n.a.	n.a.	n.a.	n.a.
1952	27,371	n.a.	n.a.	n.a.	n.a.	n.a.	n.a.	n.a.
1953	28,531	n.a.	n.a.	n.a.	n.a.	n.a.	n.a.	n.a.
1954	34,552	n.a.	n.a.	n.a.	n.a.	n.a.	n.a.	n.a.
1955	35,708	38,463	81,020	146,904	33,400	27,370	20,015	24,696
1956	36,196	39,760	91,375	157,111	40,338	28,993	29,739	25,045
1957	34,764	44,849	81,107	177,872	40,482	39,796	45,680	22,832
1958	25,473	41,030	98,009	212,451	55,120	41,284	80,090	19,910
1959	34,718	47,737	104,471	213,507	121,985	69,351	102,317	29,298
1960	50,974	44,137	141,102	279,412	134,455	100,281	93,971	28,964
1961	62,860	52,000	187,326	282,128	128,627	71,001	128,508	32,115
1962	105,825	93,573	244,029	309,116	255,413	78,086	172,130	41,727
1963	142,192	107,950	382,339	335,844	287,554	76,134	141,834	39,605
1964	115,870	128,168	368,001	402,697	211,100	86,142	148,964	59,619
1965	116,128	135,037	352,007	411,929	247,676	87,374	171,724	52,847
1966	87,711	114,404	397,040	352,858	233,662	94,847	214,552	69,903
1967	87,304	113,874	377,544	283,466	252,137	106,867	223,722	76,334
1968	114,610	133,600	524,445	301,392	303,292	105,899	308,859	92,005
1969	152,189	152,189	605,134	351,845	410,932	137,182	318,200	93,203
1970	142,881	151,046	700,874	336,651	584,433	195,489	335,908	115,502
1971	165,417	139,776	739,764	388,867	614,481	235,998	334,473	122,749
1972	159,673	98,774	738,959	449,478	653,310	289,729	327,770	139,689
1973	231,791	55,164	958,358	324,134	870,734	130,408	394,186	82,633
1974	158,653	45,546	691,388	284,286	708,794	143,906	317,323	82,630
1975	120,475	36,395	722,615	268,600	772,025	122,306	356,215	74,118

Source. Society of Motor Manufacturers and Traders, *Yearbooks.*

A study conducted by the Standard-Triumph Export Sales Department during 1956 provides greater insight into the British position in Europe.[23] The report stressed that the German market remained the key to European sales success. It had the lowest tariff rate (17 per cent), the highest import sales (almost 7 per cent of total sales) and the largest new car sales of the countries entering the EEC. Despite long waiting lists for German cars during 1955–56, the British captured only about 1 per cent of total sales, and military personnel still accounted for an overwhelming majority of the British sales. BMC held nearly half of British sales. Standard-Triumph's share of British import sales was just 12 per cent.

The report suggested that Germans preferred the design, characteristics and price of domestic models. Therefore Standard-Triumph would have to capture sales from other imports. The Triumph TR3 sports car was introduced to attract military sales from BMC's MGA, while the Standard Super Ten small car was aimed at the Morris Minor, Renault Dauphine and Fiat 600. The study argued that the firm should not compete on the basis of price, but adhere to what Maxcy and Silbertson termed 'model–price strategy'.[24] Routinely practised in the British market, model–price competition was characterised by higher-priced manufacturers attempting to lure buyers from the acknowledged price leader within a market segment by offering more characteristics in their models. For example, the report proposed that the Super Ten (DM 5,990) would gain sales from the Renault (DM 5,490) and Fiat (DM 4,280) if the Standard had automatic transmission, a heater, windscreen washer and interior lights. In short, the study revealed the essence of model–price strategy when it claimed the key to sales was 'to offer . . . more than the competition at the right price'. Model–price strategy was an acknowledgement that Standard-Triumph, and the British in general, could not compete directly on the basis of price or design.

At a price of DM 5,990 (compared with the Volkswagen price of DM 3,790), the report acknowledged that the ex-works unit profit of the Super Ten would be low, owing to Standard-Triumph's high manufacturing costs. Consequently the report suggested an increase in the ex-works price to improve unit profits. This recommendation illustrated once again the firm's ignorance of the distribution structure relationship. The manufacturer clearly put its interests above those of the product channel components. A price increase forced members either to raise prices and risk lower sales or to maintain prices and accept lower profits. Given the low demand for the Super Ten, the revenue of the structure members declined, regardless of which price strategy they chose. Lower revenue, in turn, reduced members' ability to finance car and parts inventory and service facilities. The company's manufacturing inefficiency and selfish policies provided little incentive to product channel member loyalty.

During the early 1960s Britain again turned its sales efforts towards Europe, as Table 1 reflects. The switch was motivated by the reduction in North American sales as Detroit launched its compact models and by the first British application for membership of the EEC. BMC, which had shipped nearly half its exports to North America (110,144 units) in 1959, announced in its 1960 annual report that the firm intended to investigate its market prospects in the Common Market and European Free Trade Association. But the company noted that it was waiting for the government to 'define our position in Europe as between the Common Market and Free Trade Association'.[25] The manufacturers, unsure of the country's trading membership status, appeared to regard Europe as the market of last resort.

Standard-Triumph, which was purchased by the Lancashire-based lorry manufacturer Leyland after facing bankruptcy in 1960, faced a similar European dilemma. As the French veto kept the British outside the EEC, and Leyland managers struggled to return the car maker to profitability, the firm's Marketing and Research Department compiled a series of reports concerning the European market. The first study,[26] conducted in 1961, predicted that the largest growth rate in total sales and imports during the remainder of the decade was 'likely' to be in EEC rather than EFTA markets. However, the report claimed that increasing external and decreasing internal EEC tariffs would prevent the British from gaining higher sales. Moreover the British did not, in many cases, have a price advantage in EFTA markets, owing to higher internal duties and lower external tariffs compared with the EEC. Although the Leyland-Triumph study concentrated upon the effect of tariffs, it ignored a vital factor in higher British prices: the growing gap in productivity rates between British and European motor firms.[27] Greater efficiency and higher output, resulting in lower ex-works prices, allowed the Europeans, particularly the Germans, to export assembled cars to EFTA markets. The British were increasingly forced to circumvent the EEC tariff by shipping knocked-down (KD) kits to associated or subsidiary assemblers in Belgium and Italy.

Nonetheless the 1961 Leyland-Triumph report[28] argued that the key to achieving Leyland-Triumph's long-term sales objectives was greater sales in Europe. In 1960 the company held 1 per cent of the EEC import market and 3·5 per cent of the EFTA import market. The design and characteristics of the new Herald model were considered superior to those of the Super Ten, though it was stressed that price would be a major factor in increasing sales. More important, the company was beginning to realise the importance of a viable distribution structure in improving sales. The report stressed that, regardless of price, Herald sales would remain low until a 'sound nationwide' dealer organisation was established. A survey of distribution structures revealed that Sweden and Denmark were 'at best dormant', Norway was 'non-existent', the Netherlands and Italy were 'inadequate' and France and Germany were focused 'mainly to US service personnel'. Nearly all distributors were financially unsound and acted like British main dealers, conducting more retail than wholesale activities.

Acknowledging that the previous pricing policy had been ineffective in creating and maintaining viable product channels, the report proposed several options. The wholly-owned sales subsidiaries of Volkswagen, Renault and Fiat impressed the researchers. The structure seemed to offer the advantages of cost savings in administration and inventories as well as enhanced control over channel member performance. The major disadvantage, according to the study, was the large initial staff and inventory costs. The report also noted that individual attempts by BMC and Rootes to institute this structure in Scandinavia had met with disaster. No analysis was made of the Nordic failures, though it appeared to be an ominous sign that the British lacked the marketing and managerial skill and the financial commitment to construct and maintain a sophisticated distribution structure. Citing the large investment requirements, the report rejected this option.

The study preferred alliances with non-competitive European manufacturers. It was argued that Leyland-Triumph's model range, consisting of the Herald saloon, TR3 sports car and Triumph 2000 executive model, would complement the products of NSU in Germany, Citroen or Peugeot in France, Lancia in Italy and Volvo in Scandinavia. These associations would provide the British firm with comprehensive regional distribution structures at virtually no cost. They also offered the potential for local assembly without investment requirements. The obvious disadvantages of loss of control over inventories, model offering, pricing, marketing strategy and dealer performance were never addressed. Nor did the study determine why foreign firms should find it in their interest to handle Triumph products.

In the end, Leyland-Triumph was forced to return to using price incentives and model offerings to build its European product channels. The model range was moved away from the mass market by improving product features in existing cars and launching new models, such as the Spitfire sports car and Vitesse saloon, while unit production costs were decreased by reducing installed capacity and achieving higher utilisation rates. These moves allowed Leyland managers, experienced in exporting commercial vehicles, to institute a more flexible ex-works pricing policy, compared with Standard, which had set only US and 'rest of world' prices. Leyland-Triumph's regional pricing scheme was less comprehensive than Volkswagen's individual market pricing. Nonetheless the new models and pricing system seemed to be a factor in the firm's turnround: between 1961 and 1963 Leyland-Triumph's exports to the United States increased from 19,137 to 30,898 units, and shipments to Europe rose from 7,673 to 17,979 units. In 1963 the firm exported about 49 (1961: 32) per cent of total output and declared a net profit for the first time since 1959.

In April 1964, however, the Leyland-Triumph board suggested that the firm 'had fallen in the habit of depending upon the US market'.[29] One month later the Export and Sales Division released another report outlining the company's export prospects.[30] Since the firm's model range consisted of sports cars and up-market saloons, the study argued that sales efforts should be concentrated in the US and Europe. In view of rising personal disposable income levels and car sales, Europe was considered to be 'the outstanding potential market'. The case for concentrating upon Europe was based upon the premise that a 'tiny increase' in the company's market share would translate into a substantial increase in unit sales. This logic would tantalise British export managers over the next two decades.

In addition the Leyland-Triumph report argued that Britain would eventually join the EEC. Interestingly, the study stated that, if the country remained outside the EEC tariff walls, then the prospects for all British industry would be 'very dubious'.[31] The optimism concerning entry into the EEC is surprising in view of the first Wilson government's indifference towards the Community and Labour's preference for closer ties with the Commonwealth.[32]

Just as in the 1961 report, the 1964 study argued that action had to be taken to improve Leyland-Triumph's European distribution structure. The company was slowly learning from its mistakes and incrementally adopting many of the measures implemented by Volkswagen two decades earlier. To improve the control and performance of the product channels, the report suggested that the firm's export staff should be expanded from seven to nine members. The two additional representatives, who would double the number dealing with European affairs, were to be based in Europe. They were to supervise structure members, developing 'trust and confidence' in the company. The report acknowledged that the previous policy of occasional visits from factory officials, who lacked decision-making authority, had not bound the channel members to the firm's goals.

The study also admitted that past pricing strategies had been detrimental to the product channel. Although current sales of the Herald returned little or no profit to the company, owing to high manufacturing costs, the report argued that the ex-works price should be lowered on the grounds that structure members would not only earn higher profits but would have more capital to invest in service facilities and parts and car inventories. The Herald, therefore, was to be sacrificed to maintain the product channel, enabling the firm to earn profits on the sale of low-volume but high unit profit sports and executive cars.[33]

The 1964 export and sales analysis provides many clues to the company's poor performance in Europe. The new pricing strategy appeared to address the basic problem of providing product channel members with a steady source of income. But, as Table 2 indicates, the Herald was still higher-priced than most of its rivals, rendering member sales volume (and income) uncertain. An attempt to compensate for high production costs by increasing spare parts prices sustained the complaint of high parts prices, which did little to promote car sales. The appointment of field staff might have reduced the referral of administrative and technical matters to England, yet two 'men on the spot' could not perform the same range of operations as a sales subsidiary. The ineffectiveness of Leyland-Triumph's European strategies during the 1960s was illustrated by the board's comment in 1968 that 'the steady volume of exports to North America' ensured the profitability of overseas sales.[34]

Table 2. *Prices of mass-market models in selected European markets, 1964*

Model	*Austria (Sch.)*	*France (fr.)*	*Germany (DM)*
Volkswagen 1200	33,800	6,950	4,200
Renault Dauphine	n.a.	5,900	4,750
Fiat 1300	n.a.	9,590	6,890
Mini	31,200	6,995	5,780
Austin 1100	38,500	10,450	n.a.
Triumph Herald 1200	38,600	9,900	7,610

Source. University of Warwick, Modern Record Centre, MSS 226/ST/2/3/3.

Given Leyland-Triumph's difficulties in increasing sales in the European market, Table 3 suggests that BMC, which quadrupled its European sales between 1960 and 1967, was a major factor in the higher British sales on the Continent during the early 1960s. The increase in BMC sales coincided with the introduction of the Mini and 1100 models and a reorganisation of the corporation's product channel. Unlike most previous British offerings, these new cars featured unique designs and characteristics suited equally to European and British driving conditions. Indeed, the Mini accounted for nearly 70 per cent of BMC's Continental sales during this period.[35]

Table 3. *BMC export sales as percentage of total*

Market	*1955–56*	*1965–66*
EEC	5·7	20·1
EFTA	8·6	16·4
North America	12·2	13·4
Australasia	31·4	20·4
Other	42·1	29·7

Source. Motor Business, 49, January 1967, p. 7.

In 1961, the year Britain first applied for EEC membership, and two years after the launch of the Mini, BMC undertook a reorganisation of its European distribution structures. Over the next six years BMC created a corporate administrative facility in Lausanne to supervise the activities of newly formed sales subsidiaries in Switzerland, Sweden and France. Local assemblers in Belgium and Italy were given national distribution responsibilities. Yet little was done to upgrade the important West German product channel, and, not coincidentally, BMC market share in that country remained very low. *Motor Business* noted some improvement in the performance of the firm's European distribution structure, yet still complained of chronic car and parts shortages as well as poor after-sales service.[36]

BMC's mixed results in Europe can be traced to the firm's manufacturing performance, product range and, despite the improvements, unstable product channels. Sophisticated engineering and complex production methods, as well as low productivity caused by frequent industrial disputes, mechanical downtime and inefficient labour utilisation, made the Mini costly to manufacture. High production costs and competitive retail pricing against other European models led to low unit profits for both the firm and its product channel members, especially when industrial action led to shortages of cars and parts. Table 2 indicates that the prices of BMC models were high not only in the EEC but also in EFTA markets. In spite of the British tariff advantage, the Mini was priced just 8 per cent below the larger Volkswagen 1200 in Austria. Low sales of BMC's other models and the firm's policy of maintaining separate Austin and Morris product channels also resulted in reduced member sales volume (and revenue) and increased administrative, delivery and inventory costs.[37]

Table 1 indicates that annual sales of British cars in the EEC and EFTA did increase during the early 1960s, but French, German and Italian car makers also achieved higher annual sales, compared with 1959 levels. Britain, for example, held only about 2 per cent of the EEC market in 1965. Moreover British sales declined steadily from 1963 until 1968, while the yearly sales of the country's European rivals increased continuously in the latter half of the decade. British annual sales and market share also varied considerably according to individual national markets. The British continued to have low sales in France and West Germany, the markets with the largest new and imported car sales. In addition, the value of British exports to the EEC generally remained below that of shipments to North America. For example, in 1967 Britain earned £44·2 million on sales of 70,766 units in the United States, compared with £42·4 million on sales of 87,304 units in the EEC.[38] The difference in value can be attributed to increased deliveries of KD kits — reaching nearly 40 per cent of the firm's total exports in 1967 — and the high number of small-car sales in Europe, whereas sales in America consisted primarily of built-up sports and executive models.

British Leyland and entry into the EEC

British Leyland Motor Corporation (BLMC), formed by the merger in 1968 of British Motor Holdings (Jaguar had joined BMC as a virtually autonomous division in 1967) and Leyland-Triumph (Rover had been purchased in 1967), brought together the indigenous motor firms one year after Britain's second application to the EEC had been rejected. Essentially controlled by Leyland-Triumph management, the firm announced its intention of increasing Britain's European market share. However, in combining the companies, BLMC brought together the chronic problems of shortages of cars and parts supplies, high product prices, unattractive models, poor product quality and inadequate product channels which had plagued previous British attempts to increase sales in Europe.

BLMC management placed its hopes on a new product range. The Marina (1971) and Allegro (1973) mid-sized mass-market models were to increase the firm's market share and strengthen the distribution channels, while Jaguar, the Triumph TR7 sports car (1975) and the Rover 3500 executive saloon (1976) were to provide the company with large unit profits. Contrary to expectations, the impact of these models was negligible. In 1975 BLMC exported about 125,000 units to Europe — only 500 more cars than BMC had shipped a decade earlier — and the Mini still accounted for nearly two-thirds of sales.[39] Low sales of the Marina and Allegro stemmed from inferior design, styling and characteristics as well as poor quality and reliability.[40] Prices of BLMC products were generally higher than those of European and an increasing number of Japanese competitors, owing to industrial action, equipment downtime and management's inability to supervise newly installed capital-intensive manufacturing methods.

In response to continuing poor foreign sales and distribution structure performance, the corporation in 1970 created British Leyland International (BLI). This division supervised foreign marketing and manufacturing subsidiaries as well as export sales, inventories and service. Prior to the formation of BLI, the firm maintained the haphazard product channels it had inherited, with some controlled by manufacturing divisions and others by sales subsidiaries or BLMC corporate staff. BLI attempted to rationalise this chaotic structure and establish its leadership position by buying out distributors and investing in others. However, limited finances and the large number of European wholesalers reduced the effectiveness of the scheme. In addition the historically poor performance of the channel members and company sales divisions meant that even the best jointly owned distributors were apt to be inferior to their rivals. BLI also failed clearly to define the role of British Leyland Europe, the former sales subsidiary, perpetuating some overlap of distribution functions.[41] Thus BLI's efforts did not significantly improve the length, cost, control or performance of the European product channel.

The structural problems of the channel were aggravated by the deficiencies of BLI itself. The reorganisation was mishandled, leading the Triumph board to note, as late as 1972, that its European channels were being closed before the creation of new ones. The Specialist Car Division (Jaguar, Rover, Triumph) advisory board routinely complained that BLI withheld information concerning warranty claims and service problems. BLI was also accused of creating delivery delays and setting unfavourable prices. A corporate liaison committee, formed to facilitate communication and co-ordination between BLI and the manufacturing divisions, failed to improve the situation. In 1973 the line divisions reassumed responsibility for technical and service matters, leaving BLI to oversee the performance of the distribution structures and foreign marketing. Two years later, however, the advisory board blamed low European sales on BLI, which had only one sales representative on the Continent. A frustrated advisory board planned to establish its own marketing staff across the Channel.[42]

During August 1973, eight months after Britain entered the EEC, the advisory board agreed that BLMC's 'future must lie in Europe'. The board's discussion[43] centred upon the role of prices in increasing sales on the Continent. There was no mention of BLI or the distribution structure. The board acknowledged that, while current prices were generally higher than those of the competition, the unit profitability of certain models varied considerably. In some European markets unit profits were 'much higher' than in the domestic market. Rather than setting prices to maximise unit profits and sales according to individual export markets, the advisory board suggested that BLI should use prices to produce 'a profit equal to all countries for each model'. This policy appeared to result from BLMC's continuing manufacturing difficulties and declining financial position. Amid product supply shortages, the board did not want cars diverted from the domestic market, which had a cultivated customer base and continuity of cash flow. Selected European markets might have offered high unit profits, but they also had lower sales volume, higher financing obligations and a more restricted cash flow. Clearly the corporation's growing problems meant that it could not offer the supply of products and investment necessary to support, much less upgrade, its European market share. Within one year the cash-flow crisis forced the firm to turn to the state for financial assistance.

In December 1974 the Labour government of Harold Wilson justified the nationalisation of BLMC on the grounds that the corporation was one of the country's leading exporters and its domestic sales provided import substitutes. The Ryder committee,[44] which had been appointed by the Cabinet to compile a rescue strategy, argued that the company's low productivity rates could be increased by a massive capital replacement programme funded jointly by the state and the corporation. Ryder also proposed that BLMC's low capacity utilisation rates could be raised significantly through higher sales in western Europe. Ryder essentially repeated the earlier arguments that a small increase in European market share (from 3 per cent in 1975 to 4 per cent in 1985) would result in a large increase in sales (from about 200,000 units in 1975 to 390,000 units in 1985).

The change in ownership and Ryder's plan, however, did not result in a change of strategy or performance. Although Ryder's report acknowledged that Britain had a reputation in overseas markets for delayed car deliveries, spare parts shortages and inadequate after-sales service, his argument for state funding centred upon modernising the firm's plant and machinery. There was a case for Ryder's capital replacement proposal, but, as the Trade and Industry Sub-committee noted, it was illogical to expect substantially higher sales in western Europe without a concurrent investment and reorganisation programme in distribution and marketing.[45] A holistic approach was needed: more attractive products would lead to higher output and lower manufacturing costs and lure high-quality product channel members capable of obtaining large sales volume. Not surprisingly, one year before the Ryder plan was abandoned, a 1976 Department of Industry White Paper noted that British Leyland had failed to achieve its goal of increasing its western European market share.[46]

Conclusion

Over the three decades examined in this article, the British motor companies failed to achieve a large market share in western Europe, for several reasons. The government's export drives of the late 1940s and early 1950s, and its decision to join EFTA rather than the EEC in the mid-1950s, directed, on the surface at least, sales efforts away from the largest European markets. During this period the manufacturers reinforced this trend by preferring Commonwealth and North American markets. In the 1960s and early 1970s high EEC tariffs and Britain's unsuccessful attempts to enter the Community created much uncertainty among the firms' sales staffs. After Britain had entered the EEC, BLMC sales actually declined as the firm's deteriorating financial position prevented it from reaping the advantages of membership. Despite the bold intention of expanding export sales, British Leyland was forced to defend its domestic market share from aggressive European and Japanese rivals.

The fundamental factor, however, was the failure of the British firms to grasp that the interrelationship of product, production and distribution was the key to export sales success. The British consistently emphasised production rather than distribution. Consequently management devoted most of its limited investment to plant and machinery. It was clear, however, that British companies were high-cost producers, owing to their less mechanised production methods, more disruptive labour relations and lower output of individual models as compared with rivals. Models tended to be designed for the domestic market and the levels of product characteristics and quality were inferior to competitors'. Therefore the British firms had great difficulty acquiring distribution structure members of a high standard. Equally important, the companies generally delegated the leadership role of the product channel in order to conserve funds, which resulted in channel member independence, small structure size and low standard of sales and service facilities. Inadequate sales staff, overlapping divisional export responsibilities, shortages of cars and spare parts as well as limited marketing and financial assistance to distribution structure members demonstrated the incompetence and ignorance of distribution that characterised the British firms. The British occasionally had the product, but, in contrast to Volkswagen and several other rivals, never developed the type of distribution structure necessary to achieve a significant market share in western Europe.

Notes

1 Henceforth 'Europe' refers to western Europe and 'EEC' refers to 'The Six' (Belgium, France, West Germany, Italy, the Netherlands and Luxembourg) from 1957 to 1972 and after 1973 to 'The Nine' (adding Britain, Denmark and Eire).

2 A. D. Chandler, Jr, *Scale and Scope: the Dynamics of Industrial Capitalism* (Cambridge, Mass., 1990), pp. 234, 286, 391.

3 See, for example, K. Bhaskar, *The Future of the UK Motor Industry* (1979); D. F. Channon, *The Strategy and Structure of British Enterprises* (Boston, Mass., 1973); P. J. S. Dunnett, *The Decline of the British Motor Industry: the Effects of Government Policy, 1945–79* (1980); W. Lewchuk, *American Technology and the British Motor Vehicle Industry* (Cambridge, 1987); D. G. Rhys, *The Motor Industry: an Economic Survey* (1972); T. R. Whisler, 'Niche Products in the British Motor Industry: a History of MG and Triumph Sports Cars, 1945–81', Ph.D. thesis, London School of Economics, 1992; K. Williams, J. Williams and D. Thomas, *Why are the British bad at Manufacturing?* (1983); *The Motor Industry*, British Parliamentary Papers, 1974–75, XXV.

4 R. A. Robicheaux and A. J. El-Ansary, 'A general model for understanding channel member behavior', *Journal of Retailing*, LII (1976–77), pp. 14–15.

5 *Manchester Guardian*, 18 July 1944.

6 PRO, BT 96/211, T 229/346.

7 British Motor Industry Heritage Trust (BMIHT) Morris Motors Collection.

8 Political and Economic Planning Group, *Motor Vehicles* (1950), p. 156.

9 Society of Motor Manufacturers and Traders, *Yearbooks*.

10 Political and Economic Planning Group, *Motor Vehicles* (1950), p. 104.

11 PRO, SUPP 14/399.

12 The AEES was a retail network primarily for US servicemen, although its customers often included nationals and servicemen of the other occupying powers. Similar structures were established in the Middle East and Asia.

13 PRO, SUPP 14/399.

14 *Ibid.*

15 *Ibid.*

16 PRO, SUPP 14/397, SUPP 14/399.

17 Lewchuk, *American Technology*, p. 366. See also W. Lewchuk, 'The motor vehicle industry', in B. Elbaum and W. Lazonick (eds.), *The Decline of the British Economy* (Oxford, 1986), pp. 140–1, 148–51.

18 BMIHT Morris Motors Collection.

19 PRO, SUPP 14/397, SUPP 14/399.

20 *Ibid.*

21 PRO, SUPP 14/332.

22 *Motor Business*, March 1957, pp. 31–2; June 1957, p. 37.

23 University of Warwick Modern Record Centre (MRC), MSS 226/ST/3/C/197.

24 G. Maxcy and A. Silberston, *The Motor Industry* (1959), pp. 115–16.

25 British Motor Corporation, *Annual Report, 1960*, pp. 16–17.

26 MRC, MSS 226/ST/3/C/272.

27 D. T. Jones and S. J. Prais, 'Plant size and productivity in the motor industry: some international comparisons', *Oxford Bulletin of Economics and Statistics*, XL (1978), pp. 131–52.

28 MRC, MSS 226/ST/3/C/272.

29 MRC, MSS 226/ST/1/1/14.

30 MRC, MSS 226/ST/2/3/3.

31 *Ibid.*

32 M. Steward, *The Jekyll and Hyde Years: Politics and Economic Policy since 1964* (1977), p. 77.

33 MRC, MSS 226/ST/2/3/3.

34 MRC, MSS 226/ST/1/1/15.

35 G. Turner, *The Leyland Papers* (1971), p. 206.

36 *Motor Business*, January 1967, p. 4.

37 *Ibid.*, pp. 4–7; Turner, *Leyland Papers*, pp. 194–6.

38 Society of Motor Manufacturers and Traders, *Yearbook, 1968*.

39 Bhaskar, *The UK Motor Industry*, p. 134.

40 MRC, MSS 226/ST/1/11/1.

41 *Motor Business*, April 1972, pp. 5, 36; MRC, MSS 226/ST/1/7/1.

42 MRC, MSS 226/ST/1/7/1, MSS 226/ST/1/1/15, MSS 226/ST/1/11/1.

43 MRC, MSS 226/ST/1/11/1.

44 *British Leyland: The Next Decade*, P.P., 1974–75, XIV, paras. 16, 24, 3.

45 *The Motor Industry*, P.P., 1974–75, XXV, para. 170.

46 *The British Motor Vehicle Industry*, Cmd 63771, 1976.

4 *Concentration in the inter-war motor industry**

D. G. RHYS

THIS paper analyses the increasing level of concentration which took place in the British car industry during the inter-war period. In addition to that phenomenon, in an industry which in 1918 had contained dozens of producers, mass production methods were introduced. This combination of factors resulted in severe price competition in the 1920s. The beginning of the final stage of development of the car industry took place in the 1930s when, after economies of scale began to assert themselves in the form of a shake-out of smaller companies, the industry became a mature oligopoly of a few companies with much less price competition, especially at the wholesale level. Price competition was still very real, however, and took the form of a firm having to be able to produce, at a profit, cars comparable in price and quality with those of its competitors in each class of vehicle. After 1945 the industrial structure laid down in the 1930s was consolidated, with an added emphasis on exports and capital inves..ent in overseas markets. However, this paper suggests that the pre-war shake-out did not go far enough and that concentration actually decreased in the 1930s.

Concentration has often been linked with a conscious attempt to increase monopolistic powers. For instance, concentration in the U.S.A. during the last 20 years of the nineteenth century can be seen as an attempt to establish monopoly conditions in various industries, while from 1904 the remaining second-rank firms grew by merger in order to combat the power of the market leaders, thereby creating an oligopolistic situation.[1] In Britain the first attempt to eliminate competition was by the establishment of trade associations. The collapse of these led to attempts to monopolize industries by merger. As the remaining independent firms increased in competitiveness, an

*I would like to express my sincerest thanks to Mr Derek Braddon, Research Fellow, Department of Economics, University College, Cardiff, for extracting and collating some of the data used in this paper.

attempt was made to revive trade associations, dominated by the large older companies, as a means of reducing competition, in preference to straightforward mergers. However, the British motor industry from 1900 to 1939 took no significant part in this movement towards mergers. Not one pre-1945 motor industry merger was large enough to be deemed 'important'.[2] It is true that the Rootes Group was the product of a series of mergers, but as all the firms involved were very small the emergence of monopoly power was not a factor. Indeed, Rootes only grew to a position of eminence long after the mergers that had produced the combine, and as a result of the group's own efforts; in effect Rootes' position improved through unitary growth. So did that of Standard, Austin, Ford and Vauxhall, and so in effect did Morris's, for Wolseley was an insignificant producer when purchased, as was Riley in 1938; the creation of the Nuffield Group was a tidying-up of William Morris's own interests. Increased overall concentration in the 1930s, which created an oligopolistic situation, was a product not of mergers but of unitary growth.[3] Indeed, such was the competition in the 1930s that effective concentration was reduced. It was only in the post-war period, with the mergers instigated by AEC and by Leyland in the 1940s and 1950s, and then the AEC–Leyland, the Leyland–Triumph and Jaguar–Daimler–Guy mergers, that concentration by merger became a significant factor in increasing market power. The Austin–Morris, then the BMC–Jaguar–Pressed Steel, and finally the BMH–Leyland mergers were attempts at preserving an existing position, i.e. they were essentially defensive and not offensive mergers. For all its lifetime, therefore,[4] the British motor industry has been highly competitive, with no restrictive trade associations (except on the retail side) or mergers designed to restrict competition. Concentration arose out of vigorous competition, especially in the period 1918–39.

When we consider Europe as a whole, we find that changes in structure and technology in the European motor industry were reflected in a relative increase in efficiency when compared with the U.S.A.[5] This helped the Europeans to increase their share of world trade in vehicles. The emergence of the European small car in the 1920s, especially in Britain, produced a vehicle with a wide appeal, not only in European markets having high vehicle and motor-fuel duties, but overseas as well.[6] Discrimination against the import of American cars by import duty, currency restrictions and the incidence of taxation all helped the relative growth of the European industry. Furthermore, the small car tapped a larger, lower-income, market, and American involvement in production in Europe (often undertaken to overcome trade discrimination) spread mass-production, which helped to reduce unit costs, and this in turn caused greater concentration of output.

However, before 1914 the British car industry's development was lethargic, the car being regarded as a largely hand-made luxury item, for which there was relatively little price competition. Only a few firms saw the real potential for the spread of motoring and even by 1913 only Ford making 6,000 cars, Humber making 2,500, and Wolseley making 3,000 were significant producers.[7] These producers accounted for about 40 per cent of car production in 1913, the other 60 per cent being produced by some 170 firms. The entry of Ford and its immediate rise to leadership meant a sudden increase, in 1911, in the proportion of output accounted for by the largest firm. However, by 1913 this had been reduced. Indeed, over 20 firms could at least *entertain* thoughts of market leadership despite Ford's pre-eminence.

In 1911, Ford began assembling its 1908 Model T at Trafford Park, Manchester, from parts imported from the U.S.A. By the time production of Ford vehicles was transferred to the new Dagenham plant in 1931 this purely assembly facility in Manchester had become a mainly manufacturing one.[8] By 1914, through a combination of price and quality quite unequalled[9] by any other British-based producer, Ford was quite clearly the market leader, and by 1918 it was making 12,000 vehicles (car and commercial vehicle Model T chassis) a year. However, British producers, such as Morris and Austin with cars and AEC and Leyland with commercial vehicles, made great strides during the First World War in production planning and engineering on the one hand and product development on the other. Morris had introduced mass production flow line techniques, based on Taylorism,[10] to produce war materials, while carrying on with a programme of product development to create a motor-car geared to this type of low-unit-cost manufacture and assembly. Consequently, as early as 1923 Morris made more cars than Ford and by 1925 its output of 55,582 far exceeded Ford's total annual vehicle production in Britain of 33,371. Austin had also introduced new production methods[11] and Longbridge was a more highly-integrated plant than Morris's Cowley plant and was, if anything, rather more sophisticated.

As to products, however, Austin pursued the wrong policy; the company was still committed to a more exclusive approach to motoring and relied mainly on a relatively expensive 20 h.p. model. The post-war boom seemed to justify this but when the slump came in 1921–2 the company was ill-prepared.

In order to counter Morris's market penetration and to produce a car suited to the conditions created by the adverse general economic situation and the increased horse-power tax of 1921, Austin introduced the '7'. The car was made by efficient production methods, and since it was small and straightforward only low variable unit costs were added to the relatively low fixed unit costs. However, the slump of 1921–2 hit Austin harder than Morris: the '7' was just newly introduced at a price of £225 (which fell by stages to £130 in 1929), exactly the same as the two-seater 11·9 h.p. Morris Cowley of late 1922. This reduced price for the Morris was clearly aimed at blunting the competition provided by the two-seater Austin 7. Herbert Austin's organization was committed to producing big cars which the market in general no longer wanted. Morris's cheaper Oxford and Cowley, helped by two price cuts in both 1921 and 1922, allowed the company to weather the storm. Austin's plight was such that Herbert Austin sought a merger with Morris and Wolseley, a Vickers subsidiary for which Austin had once worked. Morris, valuing his freedom of action and utilizing his position of strength, refused to join and bought Wolseley as a personal venture in 1927. Then Austin entered into negotiations with the General Motors Corporation in 1925 with a view to selling out, but the Americans estimated that Austin's asking price was too high and his management too weak, the company being very much a one man band. However, with the recovery in the car market and the success of the '7', Austin's finances improved from the near-bankruptcy of 1921, although by 1929 only Morris and Singer were in a really strong and profitable situation. Nevertheless, by 1929 Austin held 25·7 per cent of total production to Morris's 35 per cent and Singer's 15 per cent. Ford's share of car production in Britain was a mere 3·9 per cent.

THE SITUATION IN THE 1920S

During the 1920s the Ford company suffered a relative decline, for although in absolute numbers output continued to grow slowly, British firms such as Austin, Morris, Singer and Clyno grew faster. The 33⅓ per cent McKenna duty imposed in 1915 in order to conserve shipping space was retained after the war as a protective device.[12] This significantly increased the price of imported parts, so until the local manufacturing content was increased this put the Model T at a price disadvantage. However, without lower unit-cost production in Britain the McKenna duty would not have protected the home market from severe American competition if the pre-war price ratios, corrected by American wartime inflation, were to be taken as a guide.[13] There were two processes at work; one was improved British efficiency and reduced British real production costs, and the other was the increased price in Britain of cars like the Model T. Moreover, the Model T at 22·4 h.p. cost more to run, e.g. in petrol consumption, especially between 1917 and 1921 when petrol was about 4*s.* to 4*s.* 5*d.* per gallon (20p to 22p – 100p to 110p in 1975 prices). Only in 1926 when it fell to around 1*s.* 7*d.* per gallon (8p, or 40p in 1975 prices) did petrol become cheap, and even so, real incomes were much lower than in 1974. The Model T also suffered from carrying a higher exise duty than, say, the 11·9 h.p. Morris Cowley.[14] Despite this, Ford vehicle production reached 46,362 in 1920, a total not surpassed until 1933, but between 1921 and 1931 it typically varied within the range 21 to 31 thousand. However, an increasing proportion of these were commercial vehicles,[15] since the Model T chassis was suitable for either car, truck or bus use. Of the 275,000 Model Ts assembled, and later manufactured, in Britain, 100,000 were commercial vehicles and 175,000 were cars. The Model T was replaced in 1928 by the Ford Models A and AF and between 1928 and 1931 15,000 car and 35,000 commercial vehicle chassis were made. However, the Models A and AF, like the Model T before them, were, at 24 and 15 h.p. respectively, large cars and relatively expensive both to buy and to run.[16] Consequently these Ford models were more successful as commercial vehicles where only the other American firm, Bedford, and the one significant British competitor in the light commercial vehicle market, Morris Commercial, were major competitors to Ford.

Until 1927, Morris's greatest rival, apart from Austin, was Clyno. This firm had entered the market in 1922; by 1925 output was up to 300 cars a week which put the firm in third place. However, after a strenuous attempt to compete with Morris the company fell back and ceased operating in 1929 after a life of just seven years. Clyno attempted to, but could not, compete in both price and quality with Morris. An attempt to match Morris's price *and* quality at Clyno's much lower output levels, gave only marginal profits[17] which soon turned into a financial loss. By 1927 the attempt to compete only in price meant the production of a shoddy vehicle of wood and unpainted fabric costing £160, which even at that price proved difficult to sell. So either way, by trying to compete head-on with Morris, the company lost ground and was forced to leave the market. Its head, Herbert Smith, insisted on sole control and refused accounting and financial advice. The company's demise, like Austin's earlier problems, was a consequence of that approach to management which even after the Second World War was to plague the British-owned sector of the car industry – the autocratic style with a purely engineering outlook.

Although in 1929 Morris's greatest rivals were Austin and Singer, by 1939 the share of output of the last-named had fallen from its 1929 level of 15 per cent to a mere 2·6 per cent. In the late-1920s Singer's concentration of output on the successful £160 Junior which sold well between 1927 and 1929, and the Ten, introduced in 1921 at £250, enabled the firm to prosper. However, in the period 1930 to 1933 came a multiplicity of models and model changes. This was expensive in terms of production and development costs, and the company 'lost its way', unable to tap or to anticipate the market's true wants.[18]

As a result of low unit costs, Morris could charge low prices and make profits.[19] Indeed "economical production, careful buying, expanded sales leading to further reductions in price"[20] by Morris and Austin allowed the main car makers to grow. Throughout the 1920s both firms were able profitably to cut prices almost annually,[21] and by so doing Morris was able to fulfil his objective of making the roads of Britain the preserve not of the foreign but of the English car. The severe price competition which this meant for the 96 car firms existing in 1922, proved too much to combat and by 1931, despite the entry of new firms, the number of producers had fallen to less than 40 independent firms. The histograms on pages 256 and 257 below show the number of car and commercial vehicle makers in the industry up to 1940. In the inter-war period,[22] after the rash of new entrants in the boom of 1919–21, the decline in the number of firms was most marked. The slight increase in the number of firms in the early 1930s is misleading: almost all the new entrants were insignificant, only S.S.-Jaguar and Jensen being of any subsequent note, and most had left the industry by the end of the decade with just half-a-dozen surviving into the post-war period.[23] It was the 1920s which saw a tremendous shake-out in the number of individual manufacturers, and by 1930 only two firms could realistically entertain ideas of market leadership compared with ten times that number in 1913.

THE 1930S: FROM ONE-FIRM LEADERSHIP TO SIX-FIRM COMPETITION

From table 1 we can see that although Morris and Austin made up an effective duopoly in 1929, the 1930s saw two trends which affected the structure of the car industry. First, the market share held by firms other than the 'Big Six' continued to fall.[24] Second, competition between the top six markedly increased, so that by 1939 the duopoly of ten years earlier had been replaced by a greater degree of equality between the six firms, so in a very real sense concentration *fell.*

TABLE I

Percentage of Car Output held by Car Producers (1929–39)

Year	Vauxhall	Standard	Rootes	Ford	Morris	Austin	'Others'	Absolute figures Morris ('000)	Absolute figures Ford ('000)	Absolute figures Ind. total ('000)
1929	0·75	3·3	3·0	3·8	34·8	25·3	29·05	63·5	—	182·3
1930	5·1	4·4	4·8	6·09	34·4	32·2	13·01	58·4	—	169·6
1931	4·5	7·5	4·8	2·4	27·4	24·2	29·20	43·5	—	158·9
1932	4·48	10·16	6·4	6·0	29·4	23·5	20·06	50·3	11·9	171·2
1933	4·97	6·23	6·37	13·2	19·9	20·16	29·17	44·0	36·4	220·7
1934	6·96	6·88	6·96	12·4	23·7	23·28	19·82	58·2	34·5	256·8
1935	8·01	7·02	7·47	15·66	29·7	21·87	10·27	96·5	48·5	325·1
1936	5·8	8·9	8·6	20·4	27·3	21·3	7·7	—	74·9	367·2
1937	7·4	8·9	8·7	20·5	25·3	20·9	8·3	—	77·8	379·3
1938	10·4	9·9	10·2	17·5	23·6	20·4	8·0	—	59·9	341·0
1939	9·4	11·5	9·8	13·2	24·2	21·9	10·0	—	48·0	305·0

Sources: Information supplied by the Ford Motor Co.; A. Silberston and G. Maxcy, *The Motor Industry*, 107, provides a table showing the relative position of the 'Big Six', but this can now be modified to produce the above by using the Ford data.

N.B. The comparison is on an 'output' and not a 'share of the home market' basis; output is the determinant of firm size, and moreover, exports were relatively unimportant although the car industry was better than most in this respect.

In 1929 the firms which were to become the 'Big Six' of the late 1930s and the post-1945 period were far from being alone in the mass market sector (although many firms attempted to compete in this sector by utilizing non-mass-production methods, a policy doomed to failure unless the small firm could differentiate its product,[25]) and Singer, with 15 per cent of the market, was larger than four of those firms. Apart from the firms listed in table 1, another nine producers operated in the 'bargain basement' of the car market, i.e. they mainly sold cars which were priced below £250. By 1939 all but two of these had either disappeared entirely or had moved 'up the market' into the more exclusive and higher-priced sectors to avoid direct competition with the Big Six. Table 2 shows the position in 1939 compared with that of 1929.

Rover, by concentrating on market sectors which were not directly competitive with those served by the Big Six, survived as an independent firm until 1967, when it was taken over by the Leyland Motors Corporation still as a thriving concern. Triumph, even by moving up the market, was unable to survive beyond 1939, while

TABLE 2

Firms competing in the Mass Market: 1929 compared with 1939

	1929	1939	'Disappeared'*	'Up-market'	Year
Big Six	Vauxhall	Vauxhall			
	Standard	Standard			
	Rootes	Rootes			
	Ford	Ford			
	Morris	Morris			
	Austin	Austin			
'Medium'					
	Singer	Singer			
	Jowett	Jowett			
	Rover			Rover	(1934)
	Triumph†		Triumph (1939)	Triumph	(1932)
'Insignificant'					
	Trojan		Trojan		(1935)
	G.W.K.		G.W.K.		(1931)
	Swift		Swift		(1931)
	A.J.S.		A.J.S.		(1931)
	Crossley		Crossley		(1937)

*'Disappeared' is here taken to mean leaving the car market entirely or being taken-over in some way by another car maker.

†Triumph went into liquidation in 1939. The assets and goodwill were purchased by the Standard Motor Co. in 1945.

Trojan and Crossley survived to produce commercial vehicles in the post-war period, the former becoming an associate company of Brooke Bond tea and the latter being absorbed by AEC in 1948. AJS subsequently concentrated on motor cycle production.

Duopoly within the Big Six came closest in 1930 when Morris and Austin accounted for 66·6 per cent of total production, but by 1933 this had fallen to 40·1 per cent. Subsequently the 'duopolists' recovered some ground in the period 1934 to 1939. A number of factors accounted for this state of flux during the 1930s.

REASONS FOR THE EMERGENCE OF MULTI-FIRM COMPETITION

First and foremost was the appearance of Ford's new integrated production facility at Dagenham, potentially the most efficient production plant outside the U.S.A. This potential was realized by the first Ford car which was purpose-built for the European market (though American-designed) and which appeared in late 1932 – the Model Y Ford 8 h.p. Armed with its new efficient production facilities, Ford had a number of marketing options open to it in 1932. The Ford 8 could have been built to standards of design and quality similar to those of its most immediate British competitors, and with the improved manufacturing and assembly facilities open to it Ford could then have undercut its rivals by between 15 and 20 per cent.[26] However, this might have produced cut-throat competition which would have harmed Ford's market penetration and thereby made the capital-intensive Dagenham plant a liability instead of an asset.[27] Instead, most of the cost advantage conferred by the Dagenham facility was used to manufacture a product of superior quality. Although Ford cars were, until the early 1950s, always the cheapest in each class in which they competed (8 h.p., 10 h.p., etc.), severe price competition or undercutting was not exercized.[28] In 1932–3 the Ford 8 was slightly more expensive than the Austin 7 (which was really an 8 h.p. motor-car) but cheaper than the 1928 Morris Minor, but its quality and level of appointment were superior. In concentration of output the chief feature of the 1930s was the advance of the Ford Motor Company of England, first with the 8 h.p. model of 1932–3 and then consolidated with the 10 h.p. car of 1935, which significantly eroded Morris's market leadership and Austin's market penetration.

Second, as the economic blizzard of 1929–32 increased in intensity, car-buyers were less able to afford to purchase or run a big or even a medium-sized 12 h.p. car, prices of which were over £200 free of tax, or £1,800 pre-tax in 1975 terms, but they still required something larger than the Austin 7 or Morris Minor, the latter introduced in 1928 to compete with the former. Consequently, both Austin and Morris began to make a 10 h.p. car of between 1100 and 1200 c.c. to give customers a choice of a car bigger than a baby car but smaller than the 12 h.p. Morris Cowley or Austin Heavy-Twelve. The Austin 10, which was Austin's best-selling car for much of the 1930s, appeared in 1932 at £148 and was more successful than Morris's riposte of a year later which sold at £165. However, neither the Austin nor Morris 10 h.p. cars were specifically designed as such, being in essence a quickly designed and produced amalgam of existing models and components. In contrast, the 10 h.p. Hillman Minx and Standard Big Nine, both of 1931, were the first cars designed specifically as 10 h.p. models. These were the quintessence of middle-class motoring in Britain, being true compromises between the old 11·9 h.p. cars and the 8 h.p. babies. The Hillman's extremely competitive price of £159 was made possible by the concentration of most of the firm's output on one specific model, and by common consent it offered new standards of smooth motoring in its class.[29] Standard offered slightly better appointments at prices only just above the Austin/Morris level, again by concentrating expertise and production on a narrow range of models.[30] Therefore, as Austin and Morris vigorously promoted the sales of their 10 h.p. models in what was rapidly becoming the largest sector of the market (see table 3), much of the benefit of this sales promotion was conferred as an 'externality' to Hillman and Standard. Because they had the right product at the right time in what was becoming the most important market sector, Hillman and Standard substantially increased their share of the market.[31] In addition, Standard made very competitive small cars in the 8–9 h.p. class. In 1935 appeared the new Ford 10 h.p. which utilized the same formula of low price and high quality which had proved so successful with the 8 h.p. car. At £135, it was £13 cheaper than its nearest competitor, not an insignificant difference when it is remembered that in 1975 terms the variation was some £117. Together with the £100 Ford 8 of 1935 it increased Ford's share of British output to 20·4 per cent in 1936, very close to that achieved by Morris and Austin.

Morris's position had improved in 1935 with the introduction of the Morris 8, at £120: this proved to be the motor industry's most successful pre-war car.[32] However, between 1930 and 1935 Morris's model range was ill equipped to meet the new economic conditions or to combat the new models from Hillman, Standard, Ford or Austin.[33] The Austin 7 introduced at £225 reached its peak annual output as late as 1935, despite the cut in the h.p. tax from £1 to 15*s*. (75p) per h.p. in that year. Sales

TABLE 3

Shares of the Market, by h.p. Class
('000s)

	1930	1931	1932	1933
8 h.p.	49	36	34	44
9 h.p.	1	6	18	13
10 h.p.	11	14	24	49
12 h.p.	24	17	23	29
14 h.p.	17	12	15	12
15 h.p.	22	12	21	20
16 h.p.	17	14		

Source: Society of Motor Manufacturers and Traders.

of small cars continued to grow, as the increase in demand for all cars in 1935 was sufficient to offset any substitution effects caused by the reduced horse power tax. In that year over 27,800 Austin 7s were made, a total exceeded only by the 8 h.p. cars from Ford and Morris. Nevertheless Austin's market share fell as Morris's increased when the latter introduced a car which the market demonstrated that it had been waiting for: the Morris 8.

A further reason for the change in the relative position of the Big Six in the 1930s was the management problem experienced by both Austin and Morris in the early 1930s.[34] Both firms needed new top management, as well as new manufacturing and assembly facilities utilizing the most efficient techniques.[35] These points, as well as the need to develop new successful models, were attended to between 1933 and 1935. Another factor was the new aggressiveness of the American-controlled firms. Ford, after 1931, and Vauxhall in that year, after the appearance of its first contender in the mass market, albeit right at the top, both emerged as major forces after British firms had made the running in the 1920s. Yet it is worthy of note that relatively small differences in price were not necessarily sufficient to make a particular model into a market leader, since there was evident goodwill and customer loyalty towards Morris and

Austin. The Morris at £20 more than the Ford 8 or the Hillman Minx at £18 more than the Ford 10, still sold in greater numbers than the cheaper car. Customer loyalty and other forms of product differentiation did something to offset the pure price effect. Nevertheless, the price difference had to be relatively small, for over a period of time the protection which product differentiation gave tended to lessen. During the 1930s the long-term trend of Ford's market penetration was upwards, whilst that of Austin and Morris was in the opposite direction.

THE DEGREE OF CONCENTRATION; AN UNDERESTIMATE

It must be emphasized that the degree of concentration shown in table 1 and in the histograms tends to underestimate the situation. Many of the 'makes' which survived in the 1930s as seemingly separate entities were either members of a larger grouping of car makers or came under some common controlling shareholder: for example, until 1935 Wolseley and M.G. were separate private companies controlled by William Morris; both were quite separate from Morris Motors. Therefore, by 1940 the number of independent firms totalled 27 and not 38 as implied.[36] For instance, outside the mass market sector, Daimler, B.S.A., and Lanchester were all part of the Birmingham Small Arms combine, while Rolls Royce bought Bentley in 1931. Within the mass market sector the Rootes Group consisted of two commercial vehicle and four car firms (see table 4), and William Morris's Nuffield Group controlled four of the 1939 surviving car firms.

In table 1 the Rootes total includes the combined outputs of Hillman, Humber and Sunbeam: as the last-named was such a small-scale producer in the 1930s its inclusion

TABLE 4

The Main Constituents of the Rootes Group

Hillman *1927**	
Humber	
1926† *1928*	
Commer	Rootes Group (Sunbeam Trolleybus Sold in 1946)
Karrier *1934*	
Sunbeam	
1920 *1935*	
Talbot	
1919	
Daracq (sold in 1935)	
Tilling Stevens-Vulcan *1953*	
Singer *1955*	

*Italic figures indicate when firms were bought by Rootes.
†Arabic figures indicate dates of pre-Rootes mergers.

after 1935 does not seriously harm the continuity of the series. The Morris figures, however, omit those for M.G., Wolseley, and Riley, and this is rather more serious in terms of underestimating the degree of output concentration.[37] Although at the time of the Morris take-over in 1927 the Ward End factory of Wolseley made only 2,000 cars a year, by 1937 the total was in excess of 10,000 or some 3 per cent of total industry output. On the other hand between 1935 and 1940 inclusive, M.G. made only 11,000 cars, while Riley only began making cars under Nuffield's control in April 1939.[38] However, by the end of the 1930s the inclusion of Wolseley would clearly have materially affected Nuffield's market share.

THE CAR INDUSTRY OUTSIDE THE MASS MARKET

Most of the firms which survived into the 1930s were outside the mass-producing mass-market sector, catering for the more affluent members of society and selling cars in the £250–£800 price bracket.[39] In 1929, apart from the more expensive products of the mass producers, 20 independent producers competed in the 'sports' and 'quality' saloon car sector (see table 5). In addition to these, there were those firms catering for the tiny market containing the 'richest in the land' such as Rolls-Royce, Invicta, or Railton, and those firms catering for the sports car enthusiast such as Morgan, Aston Martin, or H.R.G. However, total sales in these sub-sectors of the market were minute, although competition was severe and the mortality rate of firms was high.

In the rather larger but highly competitive market for cars priced between £250 and £800 the position of Wolseley was particularly interesting. The cars produced by this firm had the same relationship with Morris's Cowley products as those from Pontiac, Buick and Oldsmobile with Chevrolet in the U.S.A. During the 1930s all but the smallest Morris models had their Wolseley equivalent, and before 1936 there was very little rationalization between them. After 1936 the price premium to be paid for a Wolseley over its Morris equivalent was about £75.

Humber's relationship with Hillman was rather different. The smallest and cheapest Humber was typically more expensive than the largest Hillman: therefore Morris's 'parallel marketing' approach did not operate. However, the Talbot Ten of 1936 did follow the Morris-type policy.

In the sports car sector S.S. Jaguar caused a shake-out similar to that produced by Morris in the mass market a decade earlier. Their skilful purchase of proprietary-made parts produced in large quantities, including major components such as engines and axles, made it difficult for small firms like Triumph and Riley (whose cars had a larger bought-in content) to compete successfully in both price and quality without financial embarrassment. Indeed, only William Morris's M.G. and Singer provided S.S. with real competition in sports cars, and even then the competition was not head-on.

Table 5 illustrates that few of the 1929 producers were able to survive as independent entities until 1939. The emergence of market leaders such as Rover and Wolseley who based their competitiveness on sound keenly-priced products in what was a limited market made it difficult for other, often poorly managed, concerns to continue.[40] By

TABLE 5

Firms producing Cars in the £250–£800 Retail Price Sector 1929–39

1929	1939	Disappeared	Merged	Year
Rover	Rover			
Wolseley	Wolseley			
Armstrong-Siddeley	A.S.			
{Daimler-B.S.A.	{D.-B.S.A.			
{Lanchester	{Lanchester			
Humber	Humber			
Sunbeam-Talbot-Daracq			Sunbeam T.-D.	1935
Triumph		Triumph		1939
S.S. Jaguar	S.S. Jaguar			
Riley			Riley	1938
Lea Francis	Lea Francis			
Standard Avon		S. Avon		1937
Crossley		Crossley		1937
British Salmson		British Salmson		1938
Arrol Aster		A. Aster		1931
Rhode		Rhode		1931
Whitlock		Whitlock		1932
Hampton		Hampton		1933
Star		Star		1932
Barclay		Barclay		1937
Jewel		Jewel		1938
Partridge Wilson & Co.		P. Wilson & Co.		1934
Cleco		Cleco		1939

1939 only four firms outside the control of the Big Six were still operating in the £250 to £800 market. Although customers in this sector were prepared to pay something extra for their cars, the relationship of price to quality was such that once the market norm was established car firms failing to meet the norm could not survive by turning to cost-plus pricing in total disregard of the demand curve.

THE IMPORTANCE OF THE 1930S IN MOTOR INDUSTRY DEVELOPMENT

The significance of the 1930s in the development of the motor industry was considerable. This was the period when the industry matured; in the home market short-run price changes, i.e. the relative price reduction of a current model, became very rare. Even the Ford 8's price reduction in 1935, from £120 to £100, was accompanied by a reduction in variable costs, the lower priced car being a 'stripped-down', more austere, version of the £120 Model Y. The position of the 'other' car firms, which had declined considerably in the 1920s, continued to deteriorate in the 1930s until by 1939 a position familiar to students of the post-1945 car industry emerged: the mass market was in the control of a few oligopolistic competitors,[41] the 'executive' car market provided room for a few medium-sized firms, while a number of producers survived at both market extremes, i.e. from Reliant three-wheelers on one side to Rolls-Royce on the other. However, although the motor industry in 1974 was dominated by those names found in table 1, only Vauxhall and Ford remained under the same ownership, and even Ford's status had changed when the 49 per cent British equity participation was bought by Detroit in 1961.[42] Rootes had become Chrysler's British subsidiary, while Standard was saved from oblivion by Leyland Motors in 1961. The latter was later amalgamated with Austin, Morris, Jaguar, Rover and Alvis, among others, to form the British Leyland Motor Corporation. Indeed, the failure of British motor management to progress beyond the stage of the enthusiastic pioneering engineer, running a one-man band, to the commercial management of a large complex mass-producing organization engaged in large-firm competition, had meant the demise of four of the firms listed in table 1, and the emergence of a completely new name on the motor car scene. The main actor in the British-owned car-making sector since 1968 has been the descendant of the small-scale Lancashire-based truck and bus manufacturer, Leyland Motors. This firm had something that was unusual for a British motor firm: a strong sales and service side to back up its expertise in production engineering. Leyland Motors, with the formation of British Leyland, became in 1968 the *de facto* controller of the British-owned motor industry.

In broad summary a number of points can be made. The period 1918–30 saw the relative, but not the absolute, decline of Ford and the rise of Morris, Austin and Singer. Motor-car enthusiasts sometimes regard the period 1925–30 as the most interesting in the history of motoring. By 1925 even the relatively inexpensive car had been developed into a reliable conveyance, while there was still a large number of manufacturers making a variety of products. However, the economist can discern in the 1920s moves that were to bring this state of affairs to an end, and were to make the period 1920–30 highly interesting from the point of view of the economics of the industry. Large-scale production methods were adopted and spread during this period. One important feature was the emergence of the all-steel body utilizing the Budd pressed steel principle. This increased the optimum size of the output level by stimulating the development of specific-use, expensive, high-output, high-speed tools and machinery. In 1927 William Morris and Budd joined forces to establish the Pressed Steel company in Cowley, the output of which spelt the end for the wooden framed metal or fabric body in the mass market. The expense incurred in tooling-up for an all-steel body meant that in the 1930s the annual or rapid body change was no longer economic. Machinery had to be ammortized over long high-speed production runs if the potential benefits of the technique were to be realized in low unit production costs. The period 1930–9 meant the end of many car-makers, especially in the mass market but also in other sectors as well. At the same time, within the mass market the near-duopoly of 1929–30 was replaced by six-firm competition. Of the firms outside the Big Six, Singer declined as Ford rose, although there is little evidence to suggest a direct causal connection. Nevertheless, Singer remained quite prosperous and by 1939 it was, together with Jowett, the only 'other' producer remaining in the mass market.[43] Both survived into the 1950s when Jowett's demise stemmed from the development of a new car, the 'Javelin', which proved unexpectedly expensive to make and which had teething troubles. This meant that customers were being asked to pay a premium price for a product which was initially inferior to comparable cheaper cars made by the Big Six. By the time the car's problems had been eradicated, the company's liquidity had been exhausted and the supply of bodies was below requirements.[44] The company ceased trading in 1954, and just one year later Singer's independence ended.

THE FINAL SHAKE-OUT POSTPONED: REASONS AND CONSEQUENCES

This article has emphasized the major shake-out of firms in the motor industry but it is possible to contend that in the light of events after 1945 this process did not go far enough. The survival of six major firms was a function of the relative decline of Austin and Morris, all of which left the industry in poor shape to face the future when the post-war seller's market disappeared. Too many firms earning marginal profits meant lack of product development and investment in capital equipment, and failure to spend sufficient resources on sales and service facilities. In short, the shake-out of the 1920s left too many firms in the industry, because the 1930s manifestly failed to complete the process of concentration. Indeed the 1930s saw a resurgence of, albeit big-firm, competition both in the numbers involved and in its intensity of long-run price competition. The smaller firms within the Big Six experienced higher unit costs, and faced with a combination of price and quality established by the market they had to accept lower unit profits. At the same time, to protect themselves from the continued advance of the other smaller producers, Morris and Austin had to make their own prices as competitive as possible and thereby earn a barely sufficient rate of profit. Given Ford's very efficient production facilities Austin and Morris had to watch their own prices very carefully. It is instructive to compare, briefly, the situation in Britain with that in the U.S.A. and on the Continent.

In the U.S.A. the position is summarized in tables 6 and 7 below which show a greater concentration by the three leaders in 1929 than in Britain, and which grew further in the 1930s.

Similarly, on the Continent the concentration of output into the hands of the three or four largest firms of 1929 continued during the 1930s. In France, by 1938 Citroen,[45] Renault, and Peugeot held 75 per cent of output, compared with 68 per cent in 1928. In Germany in 1938 Opel (40 per cent), Ford (10 per cent), Auto Union (25 per cent), and Daimler Benz (10 per cent) held 85 per cent of the market, another 17 firms competing for the rest. In Italy, Fiat typically held between 80 and 90 per cent of the market in the 1930s. Only in Britain did the dominant firms of 1929–30 decline in relative power. It is also noteworthy that in 1975 all three Continental countries had more indigenous producers than Britain. The question, therefore, arises whether the

TABLE 6

Absolute Output Figures ('000)

Year	GMC	Chrysler	Ford	Total of 3 leaders of 1937	Total of 7 leaders of 1937	Industry total
1911	36	—	40	76	107	210
1923	755	—	1,917	2,672	2,931	4,034
1929	1,800	422	1,718	3,939	4,508	5,359
1933	779	438	393	1,616	1,720	1,920
1937	1,908	1,114	1,055	4,076	4,454	4,809

Source: Motor Vehicles: PEP, 1949, 111.

TABLE 7

Percentage of Output, 1936–41

Year	GMC	Chrysler	Ford	Hudson	Nash	Packard	Studebaker	Others
1936	42·9	23·6	22·6	3·3	1·5	2·2	2·4	1·5
1937	40·9	24·2	22·6	2·7	2·2	2·8	2·1	2·5
1938	43·9	23·8	22·3	2·5	1·6	2·5	2·3	1·1
1939	45·0	22·7	21·8	2·8	2·3	2·6	3·7	1·2
1940	45·9	25·1	19·0	2·3	1·7	2·1	3·1	0·8
1941	48·3	23·3	18·3	2·1	2·1	1·8	3·2	0.9

Source: *Ward's Automobile Yearbook* (1951).

relative lack of concentration in Britain in the 1930s was a significant factor in the severe post-war shake-out in the British industry, and also in its decline *vis à vis* those on the Continent.[46]

In trying to resolve this question it might be truer to say that it was not so much the survival of too many large firms that was in itself the problem, but rather the failure of too many car-firm managements to identify their correct objectives, which often reflected fundamental managerial shortcomings. This may have been the key to the problem. Indeed, it may be contended that it was only with the creation of British Leyland, and the infusion of both Leyland and Ford talent, that the British-owned part of the car industry came within sight of completing the transition from the era of entrepreneurial-enthusiast to the rule of the professional manager.[47] This process had been largely completed in the U.S.A. by the mid-1920s. The infusion of Ford men was an attempt by BLMC to adopt the American priority of financial and planning control over production. The entire organization was led by the sales-orientated Donald Stokes.

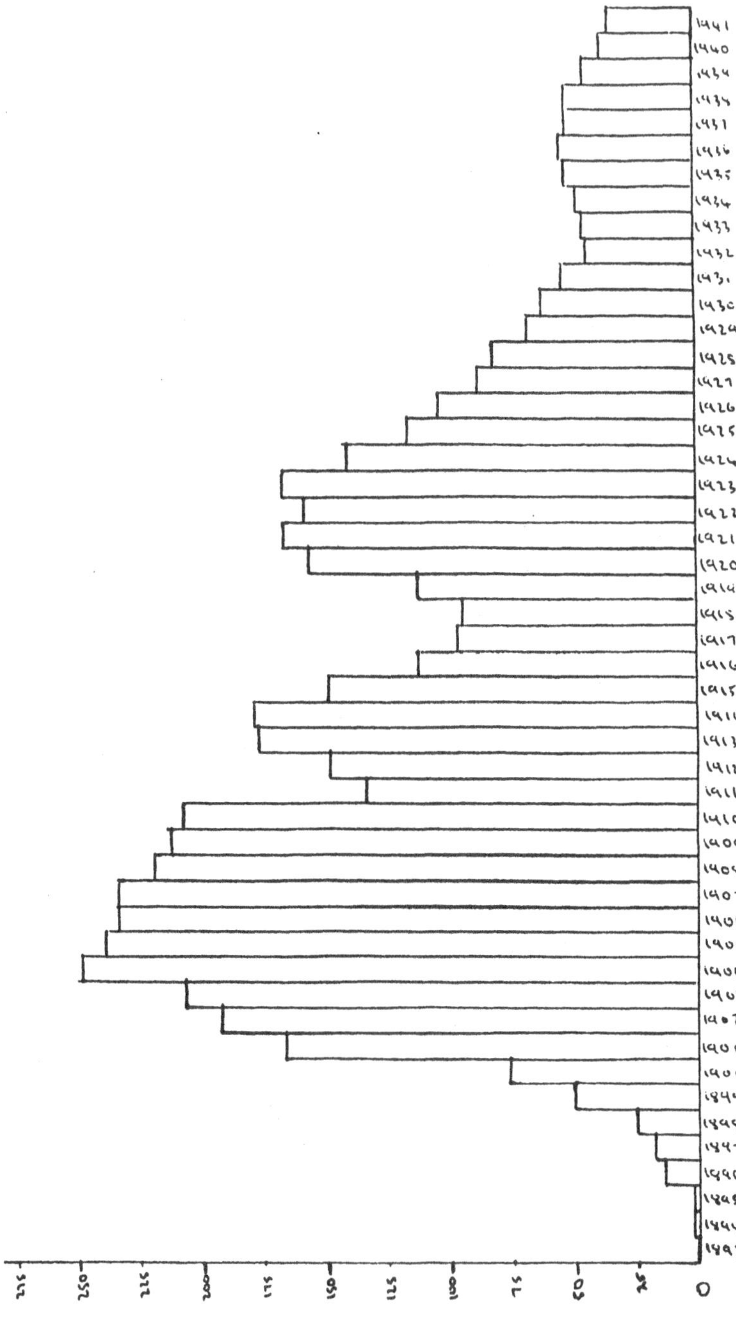

Diagram 1. Automobile manufacturers (U.K.), 1893–1941 (scale 1 cm: 20 makes).

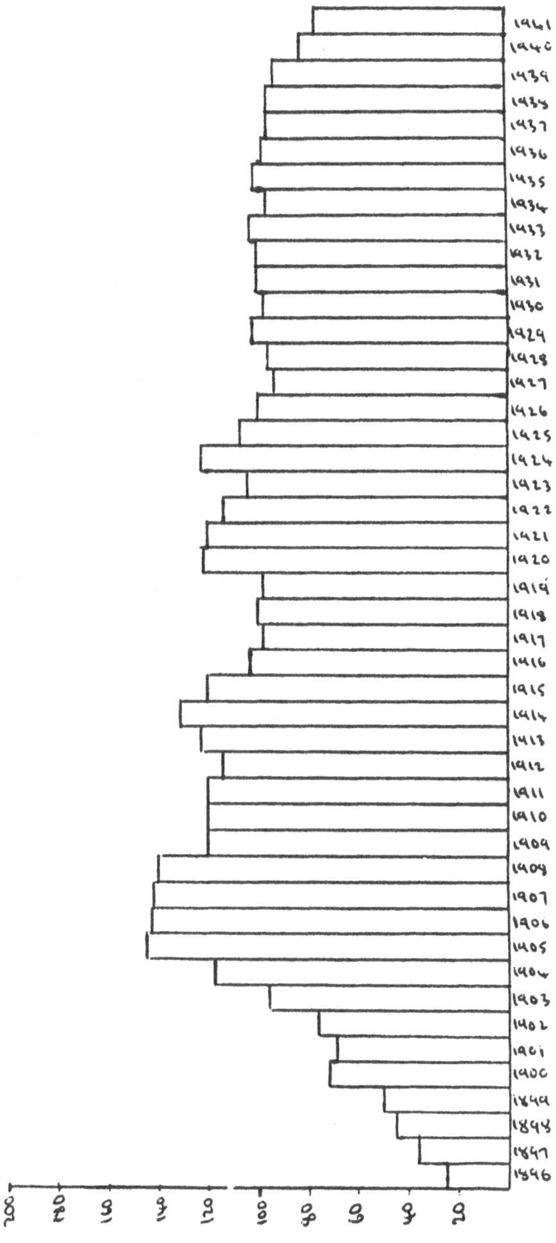

Diagram 2. Commercial vehicle producers (U.K.), 1896–1941 (scale 1 cm: 20 makes).

THE PRESENT-DAY SITUATION AND THE 1930S

The shortcomings of Morris and Austin in the 1930s postponed the final shake-out which was really necessary;[48] smaller firms such as Standard and Rootes were able to survive, and the entry of Vauxhall and Ford into the mass market was made easier than it need have been.[49] The survival of six mass-producers plus some medium-sized firms meant that after the post-war seller's market disappeared in the early 1950s[50] the history of the car industry became one of crisis and disaster, liquidity starvation and stagnation. Even financially successful firms such as Jaguar and Rover only earned small absolute profits and had a low growth performance when compared with Continental firms like Daimler-Benz, Volvo or BMW, which served similar markets. Certainly a shake-out had occurred in the 1920s but shortcomings, mainly of management, had allowed the clock to be put back. In effect, the substitution of six-firm competition for two-firm market leadership meant that the process of shake-out had to begin again in the post-war period; too many firms had survived for all of them to be able to grow to an efficient size within a limited market. As the firms involved were now larger in all respects, the post-war shake-out was more painful and longer drawn-out than that of the 1920s and 30s, and its culmination was the State's rescue of BLMC from bankruptcy in 1975.

The market shares gained by all six firms meant that the two leaders found it difficult to reach output levels which would allow them to reap more significant economies of scale. Consequently smaller firms and larger ones alike found conditions difficult in a highly competitive market. Therefore the postponed shake-out of the 1930s led to the violent financial problems of the 1950s and 1960s, which were encountered first by the smaller firms Standard, Rootes and even Vauxhall, and then by BMC. The latter found it increasingly difficult to earn a sufficient surplus to finance expansion and product development. The curtailment of 'shake-out' in the 1930s had led directly to the problem of survival that confronted BLMC in 1974, and resulted in the State take-over of 1975.

In the post-war period the influence of the Americans was greater than in the 1930s and now Austin and Morris were themselves at risk. The creation of BMC was only a respite and the opportunity fully to rationalize and integrate operations was missed. Although a financial merger had taken place, in practice all that had happened was the cartelization of the two firms with Austin and Morris remaining autonomous beneath the umbrella of the BMC holding company. In the event it was Leyland Motors which rationalized the British-owned car industry.

APPENDIX

To post-war eyes one of the interesting features of the inter-war period was the substantial price reduction of the 1920s and the price stability of the 1930s. For instance the Hillman Minx was introduced at £159 in 1932 and remained at that until 1937 when the price of the basic saloon was increased by £4. In addition the introduction of new or improved models in any sector of price, quality, size or performance was not seized upon as an opportunity to increase prices. For instance, the Hillman Minx

Car Prices

	S.M.M.T.* British car price index	S.M.M.T. 'Corrected' index†
1924	100‡	100‡
1930	68	75·4
1935	50	58·8
1936	49	56·0
1937	51	56·6
1938	49	54·3

*S.M.M.T., *The Motor Industry in Great Britain* (1939).

†As the inter-war period saw a fall in the general price index between 1920 and 1934, the S.M.M.T. index above overstates the fall in the 'real' or 'relative' price of cars. The 'corrected' index makes allowances for the fall in the general price level to extract an index of car prices measured in constant £s (1924). This shows that the fall in car prices was mainly due to (a) improved productive efficiency, and (b) the manufacture of smaller cars with a lower direct cost, and not to the fall in the general price index.

‡The post-war boom of 1919–20 ended in October 1920 and turned into a slump in 1921, but many firms stuck to price levels appropriate to strong demand and 'abnormal' profits. Morris reduced prices in February 1921, some firms followed in April but most were to wait until late 1921 and early 1922 by which time Morris had cut prices for a second time in October. In 1922 Morris again cut prices twice. So whereas in January 1921 the 2-seater Morris Cowley was priced at £465 by the end of October 1922, after four price cuts, it was £225. The latter price was the same as that charged for the newly introduced Austin 7 two-seater; clearly the new price was not unconnected with this new competition and the Morris was 'more car for the money'. By such measures Morris increased its share of output from 5 per cent in 1920 to 28 per cent in 1923. In short the base year of the index was a year in which prices were substantially lower than they had been three years before. However, the price reduction between 1922 and 1924 consisted of the elimination of abnormal profits plus increased efficiency; after 1924 increased efficiency and the appearance of smaller cars were the main factors.

received a completely new body shell in 1936 but the price for the basic saloon remained unchanged,[1] while the De Luxe model's price was reduced. Improved economies in production and severe competition meant that model–price competition took the form of considerable price stability in the 1930s. In the highly competitive climate no firm could afford to take the introduction of a new or improved model as an 'excuse' to increase prices, as so often happened after 1945. In short, model–price competition in the 1930s took on its severest form, i.e. firms had to be able to make a profit by introducing new models at prices identical to superseded models if they wished to conform to the class norm. Clearly if a firm was already a price leader with a substantial price advantage over its rivals, e.g. the 1936 Ford 8 at £100 compared with £112 for the less advanced Austin 7, both being 8 h.p. cars for fiscal purposes, then the opportunity might be taken to increase price and profits. Therefore the new Ford 8 of 1937 was priced at £115,[2] an increase over the previous price but still in line with the class norm and indeed cheaper than the best-selling Morris 8 introduced in late 1934. It must be stressed that the real costs of car production, and also the real relative prices of cars, fell substantially in the inter-war period. The fall in the general price index, i.e. the general deflation, only explained a small part of the fall in car prices; the main cause was lower real unit production costs derived from economies of scale and technological progress. This can be seen from the table on page 259.

A final point here concerns the variety of models and unit production costs. Owing to an attempt by some manufacturers to cater for every whim of their middle-class customers a proliferation of models ensued. In order to compete in terms of market coverage and to give their dealers a chance to compete with the opposition, other firms followed suit. Not only was a wide variety of models placed on what was a limited market but they were often quickly replaced. Therefore production runs were both short and small-scale, especially in the period 1928–34. Even when firms like Morris and Austin made some models in large numbers over many years, the limited production of a wide variety of other types played havoc with unit costs of all sorts,[3] i.e. 'learning economies' as well as technical and other economies were being lost. Ford, however, remained wedded to what was in effect a three-model policy while the Hillman part of the Rootes group made a very limited product range.[4] Morris and Austin, while reaping significant economies specific to the whole enterprise, tended to squander the opportunity to earn greater economies at the plant level by making many cars in small numbers. Therefore the advantages they gained from their larger total scale of operations were not as great as they could have been.

NOTES

1. G. J. Stigler, 'Monopoly and Oligopoly by Merger', *American Economic Review, Papers and Proceedings*, XL no. 2 (1950). He suggests that the early shift in emphasis away from monopoly lies with the early development of anti-trust policy in the U.S.A., 1904 being a key date. In Britain, without such a policy, mergers for monopoly continued into the 1920s.

2. M. A. Utton, 'Some Features of the Early Merger Movements in British Manufacturing Industry', *Business History* XIV no. 1 (Jan. 1972), 51–60.

3. This would not have been entirely so if the merger Austin had proposed in 1924 with Morris and with Vickers' Wolseley subsidiary had occurred.

4. The early attempts at monopoly, e.g. by Lawson's 'British Motor Syndicate', were short-lived failures.

5. Between 1909 and 1923 the index of man-hours per unit of car output in the U.S.A. fell from 1,160 to 158. After reaching 100 in 1929 progress halted. See S. Fabricant, *Employment in Manufacturing 1899–1939* (New York, 1942). However, in Britain and Europe productivity increased and prices fell in the 1930s as can be seen from the S.M.M.T. price index cited in the Appendix.

6. However, most British exports were sports cars and luxury cars, products where Britain had a 'comparative advantage'.

7. See S. B. Saul, 'The Motor Industry in Britain to 1914', *Business History*, v (1962), 25; G. Maxcy and A. Silberston, *The Motor Industry* (1959), 12. The British industry suffered both on the supply side, because its bespoke methods produced high unit costs and prices, and on the demand side. Compared with the American or French consumer, cars may have been further down the British consumer's preference scale because of higher population density, a better railway network, and a smaller proportion of the population living in rural areas. Furthermore, *per capita* incomes, compared with the U.S.A., were much lower. As an aside it is worth remembering that most of the early car makers saw themselves as competing with the horse and not with the train.

8. See *My Life and Work* by Henry Ford, in collaboration with Samuel Crowther (1922), 76.

9. The 22·4 h.p. Ford T was priced at between £135 to £200 depending on the degree of appointment. The British-made 15·8 h.p. Star cost £265, and the smaller 8·9 h.p. Morris Oxford cost £175.

10. Before 1914 only Ford and Sunbeam had fully embraced these methods, although Wolseley went part of the way towards doing so.

11. As did AEC, which had even introduced a moving assembly line during the First World War, something Morris did not do until 1933.

12. In 1914 7,000 cars were imported from the U.S.A., while in 1915 imports were running at 4,000 units a month. Only in 1972 when the 'Kennedy Round' had reduced tariffs to 11 per cent could it be said that the 'infant motor industry' had matured.

13. The possible over-valuation of sterling did not help either.

14. From 1910 to 1920 the annual excise licence duty on a 12 h.p. car was £3 3*s*. 0*d*. (£3·15) while on a 22·3 h.p. car it was £6 6*s*. 0*d*. (£6·30). From 1921 to 1934 tax was at a rate of £1 per unit h.p. and this severely penalized large-engined cars such as the Model T and American imports. (Horse Power was the fiscal h.p. derived from a Royal Automobile Club formula.)

15. The McKenna duty on commercial vehicles was not introduced until 1926, by which time the Model T was being manufactured out of mainly British-made parts. This duty helped the Morris Commercial, introduced in 1924, to break into a market dominated by Ford and GMC 1-ton trucks. See D. G. Rhys, *The Motor Industry, an economic survey* (1972), 341–57.

16. Petrol duty in the period 1928 to 1931 increased from zero to 3½p. This may have had something to do with the switch in demand from 12 h.p. to 10 h.p. cars in the early 1930s. However, the effect of the economic situation on gross income and on *per capita* income was the key factor.

17. In 1927 profits were £24,000 for Clyno but £1 million for Morris Motors Ltd.

18. M. Sedgwick, *Cars of the 1930s* (1970), 290–1. Singer's decline was well under way *before* the Ford 8 appeared in large numbers in 1932, so it is hard to 'blame' Ford for Singer's position.

19. Morris reduced prices *twice* a year in 1921 and 1922. The company's policy was the same as that pursued by Henry Ford before 1910 in the U.S.A., reducing prices to tap a wider market, not waiting until increased demand made it profitable to introduce new techniques which cut costs and then prices. The textbooks state that lower prices follow from economies of scale which *follow* increased demand.

Ford and Morris reduced prices to make large-scale production possible by tapping a larger market, i.e. the reverse of what the textbooks say.

20. P. W. S. Andrews and E. Brunner, *The Life of Lord Nuffield* (1955), 112.

21. See, for instance, R. J. Wyatt, *The Austin Seven* (1972).

22. For a general discussion of the relative growth rates of the U.S. and European motor industries, the importance of the motor industry in the national economy, and comparisons of productivity, see D. S. Landes, *The Unbound Prometheus* (1969), 440–51. In Britain in 1922 there were 96 car factories, in France in 1921 there were 150, and Germany had 200 in 1925. Concentration was very rapid in France where by 1928 three firms had 68 per cent of sales. In Britain by 1929 there were 41 factories and in 1939 there were 32; the number of firms was, of course, smaller. Ingvar Svennilson, *Growth and Stagnation* (1954), 144–52.

23. These new entrants exemplify that "hope springs eternal". The improved market of the post-1932 period meant that many would-be entrepreneurs thought they could make money either at the centre or, at least, on the margins of the car market. The same was still true in 1975, for of the 14 small firms existing in the car industry in 1968 only four had survived unchanged, i.e. still in existence under the same ownership, by 1975. The lack of working capital and a hand-to-mouth existence, plus changes in the economic climate and the vagaries of supplies, put such firms on the margins of the industry and of the market.

24. Although until 1934 the 'others' still did quite well, the decline in Austin and Morris fortunes between 1930 and 1933 helped them as well as the other Big Six makers. After 1933 they had to contend, for the first time, with a situation where Austin and Morris as well as the other large firms were all operating efficiently together.

25. In the European motor industry of 1974 only Saab, outside the big league, produced cars similar in size and appointment to the mass-produced, mass-market vehicles, mainly by stressing the durability of the product. DAF's small and relatively expensive car was highly differentiated by its unique transmission system. All the other medium-sized firms concentrated on specialized market niches away from direct competition with the mass producers.

26. Estimate suggested by a former Ford executive.

27. That is, capital-intensive production leads to low unit-cost production at planned output levels but at output levels lower than this the high absolute capital expenditure tends to increase unit costs markedly and to eliminate profits.

28. The Ford 8 four-seater was introduced at marginally under £120, being some £2 more expensive than the four-seater Austin 7 and some £3 cheaper than the four-seater Morris Minor. In 1935 the Ford 8 at £100 was around £20 cheaper than its rivals, the Austin 7 and the new Morris 8. In 1939 Ford proclaimed that the Eight was £13 cheaper than other 'eights', the Ten £18 less than other 'tens' and the V8 30 h.p. the lowest-priced luxury car on the market. Ford was not afraid to compete on price.

29. Sedgwick, *op. cit.*, 284–5.

30. The growth of all-steel body construction after 1928 and unitary bodywork after 1937 meant that more complicated and more expensive tools and dies were needed. The expense of tooling-up to make the all-steel bodies, especially those with more complicated rounded bodywork, meant that long production runs, if not large annual runs, were needed. This meant that annual body changes were no longer economic. See 'Development of the Passenger Car, Parts 1 and 3', *Autocar* (30 March 1974).

31. The inability of Morris to capitalize quickly on the demand for 'tens' meant that by the time their contender was ready Austin and Rootes were already well established. The growth in the car market after 1931 helped the smaller four to consolidate their position, but Morris did not recover until 1934.

32. Between 1935 and 1938 250,000 Morris 8s were made compared with 225,000 Ford 8s between 1932 and 1939. Between 1922 and 1939 over 270,000 Austin 7s were made, but obviously the Morris 8 was the most successful model, taken on an annual basis.

33. Morris's desperation between 1932 and 1934 was illustrated by the plethora of new models which were introduced and the shortness of production runs, which often failed to cover the overheads incurred in making the models involved (Andrews and Brunner, *op. cit.*). Part of the reason for this was fashion: the specialist makers changed models yearly, and the mass producers felt constrained to imitate them between 1928 and 1934. However, this may have been a rationalization for the effects of producing a poor product range: after all, once a successful model appeared it remained in production unaltered for some five years. Moreover roles were reversed; in 1920–21 Austin had been caught with big cars when the boom burst, whereas in 1929 Austin's 7 was well established in contrast with Morris's newly-introduced Minor. Morris's main seller had been the 12 h.p. models in the range.

34. G. Turner, *The Leyland Papers* (1971), Chapter 6.

35. As late as 1973 visiting production engineers were surprised to see some of British Leyland's main facilities using belt-driven lathes, etc., instead of numerically controlled equipment. Clearly the problem of efficiency in the British car plants has been widespread and long lasting. Despite its small size Ford tended to be more profitable than either Austin or Morris. This was a function of its more efficient productive facilities and its more standardized and less fragmented model range.

36. Some firms were very small. A firm such as Allard made just 12 cars between 1936 and 1939, and another 1,700 between 1946 and 1959. Jensen took 32 years to achieve a total output of 1,000 cars (1935–67), which is less than its current annual output.

37. I am indebted to my former colleague George Maxcy of Hull University for clarification of this point.

38. Information kindly supplied by Mr Michael Sedgwick, the motor historian.

39. During the 1930s the average wage in manufacturing was £3 a week.

40. Rover, in the late 1930s, geared-up to make 200 cars a week. No slumps or booms in demand affected this, so the cost stability achieved produced good profits.

41. A point to note here is that following the Kennedy Round of tariff reductions, but before British membership of the EEC, the British customer in the 1970s had a choice of cars the like of which had not been available since the early 1930s. Over 25 makes were involved in the 'mass' and 'executive' car markets, without counting such exotic machines as Aston Martin or Ferrari. Oligopoly refers both to the number of firms and to the fact that each firm had to take account of its rivals' reactions to its own strategy. Collusive behaviour may be part of the story but as indicated earlier collusion has been absent during all stages of the motor industry's development.

42. The offer was made in November 1960 but the take-over was not completed until 1961.

43. Jowett's goal had been "100 cars a week, every week, and no overtime worked". During the 1930s this cautious conservatism allowed the firm to survive. In the 1930s Jowett found niches by producing the only viable 7 (fiscal) h.p. car, while the later Jowett 8 h.p. was larger and roomier than other 'eights', which partly offset the premium price of £158. The Singer Bantam 9 h.p. of 1938 at £139 10*s.* (£139.50) although dearer than the 'eights' made by the Big Six, offered 1 extra h.p. and fitted into a niche between the 8 and 10 h.p. cars shared only with Standard. This, and production of sports cars, helped the firm to survive by avoiding head-on competition with the Big Six as much as possible.

44. This was during the post-war steel shortage when Pressed Steel, Briggs, etc. concentrated on supplying their larger and more powerful customers.

45. However, Citroen had changed hands during this period, being 'saved' from insolvency by the Michelin tyre company. Citroen himself knew nothing of the details of car manufacture, or about cars themselves, but he had a feel for general principles. His production methods and car designs were excellent but expensive, and his willingness to finance such expense meant that Citroen was always in debt. The depression of the early 1930s spelt disaster.

46. By 1970–4 the low profitability and excess capacity of many firms indicated that too many large firms remained in the European-wide industry. Compared with the U.S.A.'s Big Three, the increasingly

unified West European car market had 14 major large and medium-sized 'domestic' suppliers in a market the same size as the American one. This illustrates the crucial importance of exports to European-based firms.

47. However, even in 1974 BLMC was still largely a 'one-man band' and such a structure can lead to problems. A successful internal shake-out, however, of the sort needed by BLMC may have required a dictatorial approach. Once securely established, one would have hoped that BLMC would have a decision-making structure of a more corporate kind.

48. Indeed, not only did the four smaller firms within the Big Six gain in importance but as late as 1934 the 'other' makers held as much as one-fifth of the car industry's output.

49. By contrast, Ford failed in its attempt to enter the French market, while in present-day Germany Opel (GMC) and Taunus (Ford) find it difficult to do well at the same time, i.e. there appears to be room for only one firm making straightforward conventional cars. The survival of Rootes as a marginal producer (in terms of profits) until the 1960s gave Chrysler the chance to establish a foothold in the British car industry.

50. As steel allocations in the early post-war period were largely based on pre-war performances the smaller firms were insulated from competition by the larger producers. In a seller's market firms like Singer and Standard were able to do well, while at the same time those market conditions did not allow Austin, Morris, or Ford to grow to a position of absolute dominance: they simply did not have the steel supplies to make use of their full potential, although it *was* Ford that benefited most from the output race due to its very efficient Dagenham facilities. In short, as demand for cars exceeded supply at the prevailing prices, some people were willing to pay the higher prices charged by Jowett or Rootes rather than go without a car. As excess demand disappeared, or as output freed itself from supply constraints, price became a more important variable. Therefore to match Ford's price and quality Rootes and Standard accepted marginal profits, but Singer lost its independence.

1. In 1936 Hillman and Standard introduced new 'advanced styling' models at the same price as those charged for the replaced box-like models. Ford, Morris, and Austin did not follow suit until 1937, while Vauxhall's riposte was in 1938. This ability to steal a march on larger rivals by product improvement was the key to these two firms' success in the 1930s.

2. It must be remembered as well that the £100 Ford was a stripped-down and rather austere version of the £120 Ford 8 Model Y. Consequently the well-appointed 1937 model in effect represented a price reduction of £5.

3. Even so a mass-produced 10 h.p. car priced around £140–£160 was much cheaper than those made by specialists such as Crossley or Triumph in the mid-1930s: their prices were around £270–£320. Few customers felt that the quality or exclusiveness obtained by purchasing such vehicles was worth the price difference, most of which was due to higher unit costs stemming from sub-optimum output levels. In the 1970s the quality-orientated producers, e.g. Peugeot, Triumph, or Volvo have to price their products within about 30 per cent of comparable mass-produced vehicles if they wish to obtain tolerably efficient output levels. Few of the pre-war specialists could profitably price their products within this range while still giving superior quality. As a result they disappeared from the market.

4. Rootes, by purchasing most of its bodies from Pressed Steel, also enjoyed external economies.

5 *From trestles to tracks: the influence of the motor car manufacturing process on the design of British car factories*

PAUL COLLINS AND MICHAEL STRATTON

Most studies of the development of the British car industry have concentrated upon its broader economics and personalities, with more recent works also considering labour organisation and the role of trade unions.[1] Yet the organisation of production and the layout of workshops and factories was a major contemporary issue as evinced by the column space given to it both in automobile engineering journals and the more popular magazines such as *The Autocar*. This study is based on these sources, together with company photographic archives, deposited building plans, and collections of press cuttings and other material held by local libraries in Birmingham, Coventry, Wolverhampton, Manchester, Guildford, and Sheffield.[2]

The developing motor industry is considered during its first forty years; years which can be divided, somewhat arbitrarily, into three periods, each characterised by a style of car manufacture and ended by an event which, although not of immediate significance, was to set the predominant style for the succeeding period.

To 1914: hand production in workshops and early factories

The early development of plants for accommodating car production centred upon the use of modest workshops. The few purpose built factories established by 1905 were an exception; car making being accommodated as an adjunct to the production of cycles or other engineering.

Britain's first car factory, the Motor Mill in Coventry (see figure 1), was also untypical. Each of its four storeys was allocated to one of Henry J. Lawson's companies,[3] and a description of the Daimler Company's plant, housed there in 1897, recorded that as far as possible all operations were consecutive, with raw material going in at one end and finished cars coming out at the other.[4] The volume and speed of manufacture were also unimportant at the Motor Mill as it

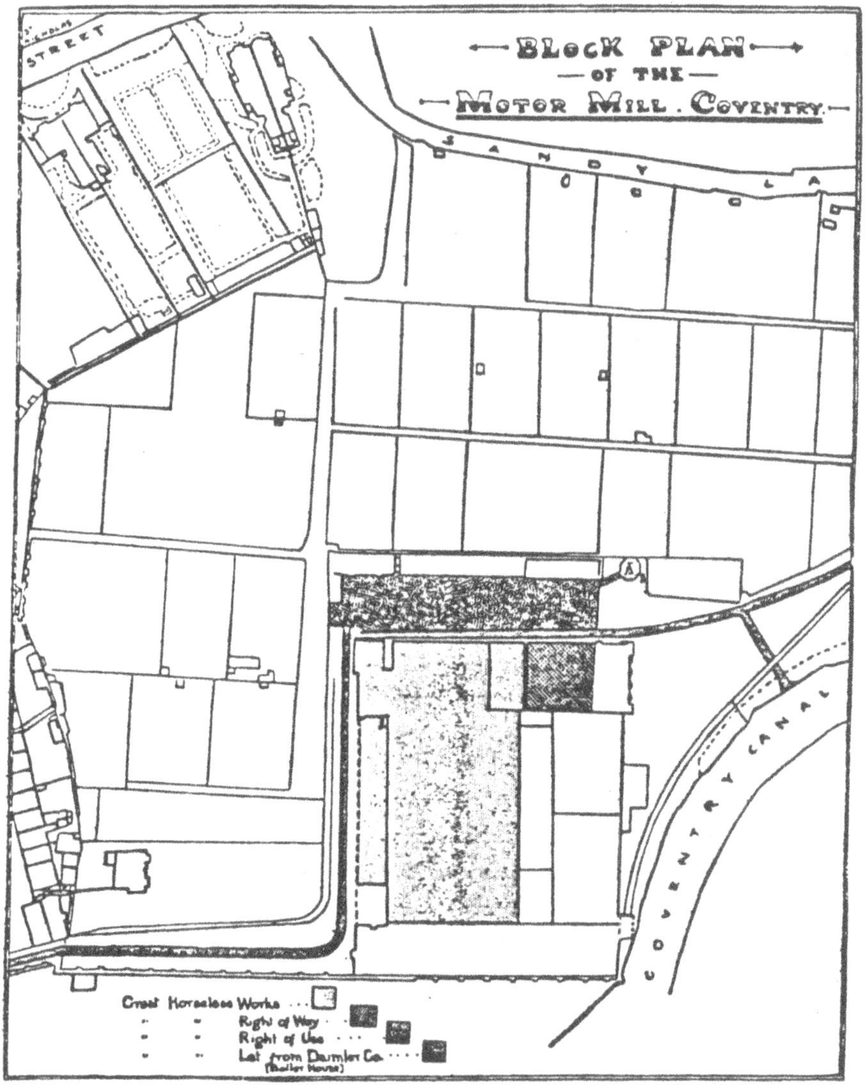

Fig. 1. A block plan of the Motor Mill, Coventry. From St J. C. Nixon, *Daimler, 1896–1946* (London, 1946), p. 36, by courtesy of Haynes Publishing Group.

was said at Daimler's AGM in 1897 to be 'impossible however well-equipped and managed a factory might be to produce a motor car complete with a body etc., in less than two or three months'.[5]

Britain's first cars were built by hand, often by small engineering firms in specially cleared or unused parts of their works. With a modest injection of capital such firms were well equipped both to develop prototype vehicles and to make an easy transition to low volume production.

The modest workspace required at the stages of experimentation and initial production is demonstrated most vividly by Morris in Oxford, whose business expanded from a cycle and motor cycle shop into a purpose built car hire garage, where the Bullnose Morris prototype was erected in a small workshop in 1912. Needing greater space, Morris purchased the former Oxford Military College at Cowley: a three storey building of 1882, with suitably open interior spaces. Car parts were received and machined on the ground floor; the first floor being for assembly of the chassis frame and fitting the engines and wheels; the second floor being for fitting the bodies; while the loft was used for storage and painting the wheels. Only once demand started to expand dramatically, just before the outbreak of the First World War in 1914, did Morris decide to invest in new buildings.[6]

Full car production normally necessitated new building, as did the manufacture of existing products in tandem with cars. The eastern industrial area of Coventry retains several examples of the type of bicycle and sewing machine factory that accommodated a modest level of car production, such as Swift of Coventry, who commenced car production as an adjunct to making sewing machines around 1899. The works developed so that by 1908 there was a two storey front range with an archway providing access to a series of single storey north-lit sheds.[7]

Two factories completed in 1901 were probably Britain's first purpose built car plants of any scale, and exemplified the two design approaches adopted in the Edwardian period: a series of single storey workshops following the traditional courtyard pattern, or multi-storey factories where sites were more constrained.[8] An example of the former was the Wolseley Works at Adderley Park in Birmingham. Planned from 1899 and opened in 1901 on an extensive site, its plan (shown in figure 2) is typical of many early purpose built car factories. Each shop was housed in a separate building or in a sectioned-off part of a larger building, containing the machinery and equipment necessary to produce a specific component or larger sub-assembly of components.

Production flowed towards the assembly and erecting shops in the centre of the site; machined parts going via their respective assembly shops, and car bodies coming from adjacent shops. It should be noted that foundry castings, notably engine blocks, had to travel the entire half mile length of the site to be machined.

The major drawback to this 'fixed shop' arrangement was that much effort

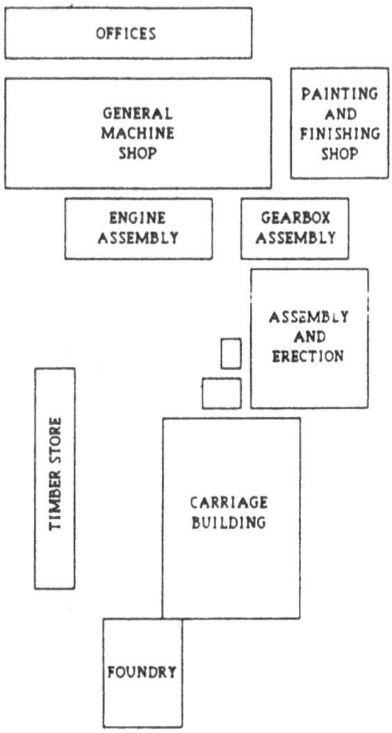

Fig. 2. A plan of the Wolseley works at Adderley Park, Birmingham, opened in 1901.

was expended in moving car components from shop to shop. It also meant that, even when areas were left for future building, the site was often too cluttered to allow for expansion when production of each additional car meant finding space to accommodate an extra chassis and body on their respective trestles.

The multi-storey approach and its inadequacies are represented by Dennis Brothers at Guildford. They expanded from making bicycles and motor tricycles in 1901, and moved into a three storey factory whose iron columns and deep iron-framed windows created large well-lit spaces for fabrication, a lift being used to move the chassis and completed cars, with final assembly taking place on the top floor. The ground floor housed a showroom, offices and an engine room; most of the first floor was an open workspace with a blacksmith's shop, and the top floor was partitioned into polishing and plating rooms, and an enamelling room. Almost upon completion Dennis Brothers' factory proved too small and it was extended in 1903. But by 1905, this too had become inadequate, and a fresh start was made on a green field site nearby.[9]

Many different arrangements of workshops were tried. One of the most striking and revolutionary was at the Clement–Talbot works off Ladbroke Grove in

London, completed in 1904, and described as marking 'a distinct epoch in the course of the automobile industry in this country'.[10] Production was ordered on a 'flexible shop' arrangement, in a large rectangular north-lit single storey machine and erecting shop. This massive space housed various processes, and could quite easily be reallocated as required. Bodymaking and trimming were done in a long row of buildings to one side of the works, and the back of the site contained a large plot for future building. A test track circumnavigated the main building, separating it from the offices, which were lavishly designed and appointed. A *porte-cochère* led to the main entrance hall and to a grand hall, 'with its mosaic pavement and rich and tasteful marble decoration . . . (which) is also the showroom'.[11]

Equally impressive architecturally, and overpowering in scale, was the 'huge and pretentious' works of Argyll Motors at Alexandria by Glasgow, opened on 26 June 1906.[12] The 60 acre site boasted 15 acres of buildings and a productive capacity of 60 cars a week. The works' outstanding feature was its terracotta-clad administration building with a massive central gilt dome, surmounting a central clock tower. The rows of north-lit sheds behind were allocated to various processes, with castings and other components being supplied from the company's other factories. The works showed a slightly bizarre attention to the care of the work force, each man being allocated his own numbered wash basin.[13] Criticised for their extravagance, Argyll retorted: 'the few extra hundreds required to provide a motor factory second to none in the world have been repaid already, and with interest, by the very advertisement that such a building is in itself'.[14] Unfortunately the critics were right. Predicted production levels were never attained, and the company failed to recover from the vast capital outlay which their impressive new works represented. By 1914, despite considerable success in motor rallies, they were bankrupt.

The late Edwardian period saw considerable attention being given to organisation of workshop practice. Typical machine shops worked to a batch production system, where a number of parts were processed on one machine, then moved to another for the next process. Each machine needed a 'batch' of parts to work on (hence the name), and one worker was usually needed per machine, which had to be stopped and retooled repeatedly to perform each different operation.[15]

Ford's plant at Trafford Park opened on 23 October 1911, initially for the assembly of cars from imported American components. From the start they employed a flow production method, in which bare chassis frames were pushed down a production track to a series of 'stations' where gangs of workers in pairs, one each side of the track, added a component or sub-assembly. Spending about five minutes per station, completed chassis assemblies rolled off the line to be united with a fully trimmed car body.[16] However Trafford Park did not begin an immediate revolution in car factory design as the works were established in the former premises of a carriage builder; the chassis line and its automated component supply being housed in newly built large sheds providing clear spans more akin to a railway terminus than a factory.

1914–1926: reorganisation without new building

The period 1914–26 was not marked by the building of any major new car factories in Britain; instead established works were reorganised and extended around the principles of flow production and to accommodate overhead conveyor systems.

The First World War halted investment in plants for car production, their capacity used instead to assist the war effort. To facilitate this the productive capacity of the larger works was increased by adding further single storey sheds. After the war, government contracts (some of which ran until the early 1920s) lapsed, and the buildings were given to the car firms. Some companies utilised these wartime extensions. Wolseley converted theirs to the production of machine-worked wooden body members. At other firms, like Austin, the extensions were not where the company wanted them, so were demolished and replaced by more suitable buildings for mass production processes.[17]

Lessons in working practices had also been learned through attempting to meet Ministry of War production quotas, notably in machine shop organisation, which were continued when car production resumed. A measure of flow production was also introduced by a number of companies. The layout of a car factory employing a production flow reorganised thus is shown in figure 3. Work passed through the factory following roughly the profile of a letter 'U'; raw materials entering at the top left-hand corner and the finished cars being despatched from the top right-hand corner.

However, the car industry's problems following the First World War necessitated more than the mere reshuffling of machines in workshops. There were three main problems: the plant was outdated and unbalanced, having grown piecemeal often in response to influences which no longer existed; the component industry was still not adequate to meet the demands placed upon it; and there had been no development in car body production, the shops for which had largely disappeared in those factories given over to war work.[18] One of the first to extend their works was Sunbeam at Wolverhampton, who opened a new pattern shop, pattern store, foundry, and machine shop complex in 1921; they were noted as being 'essentially time-saving as to the layout', and justified by 'war-time experience'.[19] Wolseley's use of wartime extensions at their plant began early in 1922, accompanied by a general works reorganisation, and Morris introduced 'time-saving methods' at both his newly acquired Coventry engine works and his main works at Cowley in 1923, including installation of a chassis assembly track.[20]

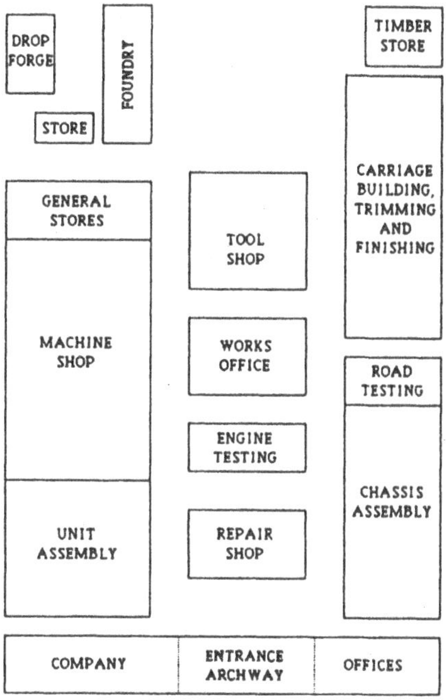

Fig. 3. Plan of a car factory having a 'U' profile production flow (about 1920).

Public taste was changing too. Fed by the design of sports and racing cars, it began to favour lines and curves hard to reproduce in wood. Steel had long been used for bonnets, wings and running boards, and increasingly for body cladding; but all fixed to an ash frame. Body making was a time-consuming process, having more to do with cabinet making than a modern industry. Problems were manifold. Production could not be increased because however many chassis assemblies could be made, it still took almost the same length of time to produce an ash body frame even with machine working of the basic members, and body production could not be stepped up without first laying in sufficient supplies of seasoned wood.

William Morris saw an answer to this problem in the USA and on his return persuaded the firm which patented these new processes, Edward G. Budd of Philadelphia, to join with Morris Motors in setting up a plant next to their Cowley works. They agreed, and formed a new company in 1926 to run the plant — the Pressed Steel Co. Ltd.

1926–1939: rebuilding for mass production

The years 1926–39 saw the construction of some new car factories, and wider reorganisation and extension by the larger firms who were introducing track production. Others resisted change. In October 1925, Vauxhall claimed to have incorporated some of the best features of mass production while preserving the individuality associated with the hand-built era. These included abandoning overhead line shafting in favour of each machine having its own electric motor. But all in all this was just like spitting into the wind. Within three months Vauxhall became part of the American General Motors combine.[21]

In 1926 a major series of investments were completed at Morris's Cowley plant, the most significant being the addition of a large new erecting shop. This marked a new chapter in the development of British car factories. A contemporary account noted:

> The new chassis erecting shop is at the farther end of the factory from the general offices and measures 500′ × 250′, the main chassis line traversing almost the entire length of the shop. Parallel with this shop is the chassis store. Two separate shops for body mounting, one for closed bodies and the other for open bodies, are arranged in line with the chassis store and chassis erecting departments respectively.[22]

It was the scale of these buildings that made them different, not their construction, which followed the then 'traditional' north-lit pattern, built taller to accommodate overhead conveyors. The following year Austin installed a similar chassis shop, accommodated within modified existing buildings. The need for height forced Hillman to build a pit for completed chassis to be set in as each gained its body. They also made use of a natural fall in their site which allowed parts to run to their stores on gravity roller conveyors.

In contrast to the adaptation and extension of plant, a completely new start was made with Ford's new works at Dagenham, which opened in December 1931, and continued to develop throughout the decade until it became an entirely self-contained plant, the biggest in Europe. Many of the principles of its layout were drawn from the parent company in Detroit. The quayside cranes for unloading iron ore and coal, and the blast furnaces and foundry to the side of the works were the dominant features of the plant, whose uniform north-lit sheds covered 14 acres with glass roofing. This open layout permitted a logical progression of materials and parts through to the main assembly lines.[23]

The great boom in the British car industry in the 1930s saw indigenous firms rivalling Ford in the scale of their investment. Morris commissioned a newly reorganised assembly plant late in 1934. The work cost £250,000 and included 12 miles of conveyors and five parallel chassis tracks, each producing a different chassis with stores acting as buffers between production of sub-assemblies and the main chassis lines. Completed chassis left the assembly shop to enter the body shop, where the two halves were united and placed on one of six trimming lines equipped with overhead runways, again acting as buffer stores.[24]

During the spring of 1936 the Ministry of Aviation approached some of the leading firms in the British motor industry to sound their interest in a scheme to produce components for the Bristol air-cooled aero-engine: the 'shadow' factory scheme. Under the proposals, the Ministry of Aviation would provide the capital cost of new factory buildings and plant, each company being allowed a large measure of freedom as to the type of factory, its siting and plant.

In November of that year it was announced that Austin, Daimler, Rover, and Standard were to join the scheme: Austin and Bristol would assemble the engines; and Austin and Rootes Securities Ltd would also manufacture airframes. The output of components and completed engines would be carefully co-ordinated, or, in other words, they would 'shadow' each other — hence the scheme's name. Construction began early in 1937 and they were in production by the end of the year.[25]

The scheme worked well to the outbreak of war, when, quite quickly, the shadowing fell apart, and delays in production, often at only one of the factories, caused work at the remainder to cease. In response it was agreed that the two Coventry makers (Daimler and Standard) and the two Birmingham makers (Rover and Austin) would each produce one complete engine between them, ensuring that at least one supply of aero-engines should remain in production at any one time.

The complete plant and services of the shadow factories were housed under one roof in conventional steel sheds with symmetrical rooflines.[26] Each featured a two storey office block, running the entire width of the factory, of modernistic design, using metal window frames, concrete lintels, and courses of coloured and decorative brickwork or rendering. Some of the corners of the offices were rounded to give a mildly streamlined imagery. After the war each firm acquired its shadow factory for car production.

The most fundamental transformation to affect car construction, introduced in the late 1930s, had few ramifications for the architecture of the factories. Chassisless or monocoque construction offered a 3 cwt or 14 per cent saving in weight and was introduced at Morris's Cowley plant in 1938 by the internal modification of the existing erecting shop rather than any substantial new building. The plant layout shown in figure 4 largely reflects the restructuring that took place in 1934. When monocoque construction was adopted, initially on two of the five chassis assembly lines, the detached shop formerly used for mounting the body on the chassis became a supply point for an overhead dual-duty conveyor. The bodies were carried the length of the old chassis assembly lines, to be united with running components as they progressed through the building.

Morris's monocoque bodies, along with those used by many other manufacturers (such as Austin, Commer, Daimler, Ford Commercial, Rover, Singer,

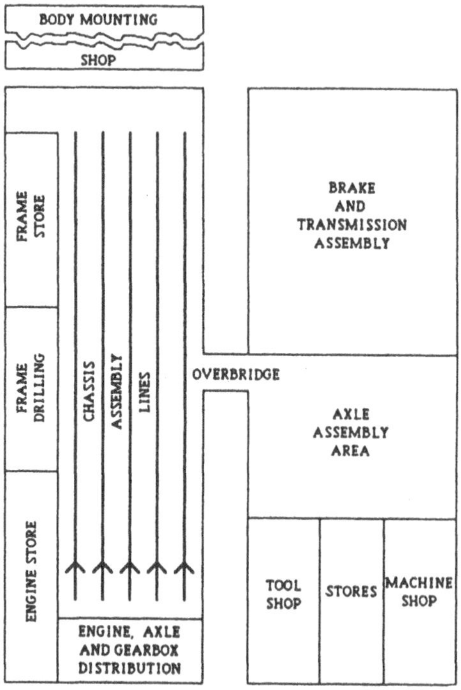

Fig. 4. Plan of the Morris assembly plant at Cowley (about 1938).

Standard, Talbot, Vauxhall, and Wolseley) were now made in the massive plant of the Pressed Steel Company at Cowley. The bodies were pressed and part assembled using automatic spot welding machines before despatch to their respective manufacturers. Within the one main building of the Pressed Steel works, covering most of its 35 acres, the location of the machinery and, hence, the path of the production lines were decided from drawings with precise datum lines.[27] The building had become little more than a protective shell. It marks the final phase of the major transformation in the design of car factories, from fixed to flexible shops, to the importance of tracked assembly lines fed by overhead conveyors and to a preoccupation with the linear arrangement of the stages of production. These processes were now, almost without exception, accommodated by being zig-zagged into a rectangular and high but single storey building, built largely of steel, with brick curtain walls and north-lit. It was the detached offices and the surviving earlier parts of many plants used as drawing offices or for peripheral processes that provided the relief to these near standardised hangars for mass production.

Notes

1 For example, G. Maxcy and A. Silberston, *The Motor Industry*, London (1959). R. Church, 'Markets and marketing in the British motor industry before 1914, with some French comparisons, *Journal of Transport History*, 3(1), (1982) pp. 1–20 (p. 13). D. Thoms and T. Donnelly, *The Motor Car Industry in Coventry Since the 1890s*, Beckenham, Kent (1985).

2 The early stages of the research for this article benefited greatly from assistance given by Peter Brockes and Michael Ware of the National Motor Museum, Beaulieu; and CRIBARTA, the Council for the Registration of Important Buildings connected with the Road Transport and Aircraft Industry. Interest in car factories was first prompted by a request from English Heritage, and its Chairman, Lord Montagu of Beaulieu, to study the evolution of British car factories.

3 W. B. Stephens (ed.), *The Victoria History of the Counties of England: a History of Warwickshire*, VIII, London (1964), p. 177.

4 M. E. Ware, *Making of the Motor Car 1895–1930*, Moorland (1976), description to plate 12.

5 Stephens, *op. cit.*, p. 180.

6 We acknowledge assistance received from the Nuffield Press; the Rover Group, and Oxford City Council concerning the various sites occupied by Morris.

7 The Planning Department of Coventry City Council and Mr A. B. Price of Lea-Francis Cars provided valuable assistance regarding car factory sites in Coventry.

8 *Automobile Engineer*, January–March 1919.

9 Information was provided by D. Mirylees, Local Studies Librarian, Guildford, and Matthew Alexander of Guildford Museum.

10 *The Autocar*, 16 January 1904, p. 68.

11 *Ibid.*

12 G. N. Georgano, *The Complete Encyclopaedia of Motorcars 1885–1968*, London (1968), p. 49.

13 D. Burgess-Wise, *Automobile Archaeology* (Cambridge, 1981), p. 24.

14 Ware, *op. cit.*, description to plate 14.

15 Maxcy and Silberston, *op. cit.*, p. 56.

16 Local Studies Department, Manchester City Library; D. Burgess-Wise, Ford Motor Company. On the history of the city's motor industry, see A. D. George, 'The industrial archaeology of motor works in Manchester', *Industrial Archaeology*, 17 (1983) pp. 161–5.

17 Thoms and Donnelly, *op. cit.*, p. 95 also acknowledge the problems created for some firms by late payment from the Ministry of War for work done under government contracts.

18 *The Motor*, 18 January 1922, pp. 1151–2.

19 *Motor Commerce*, 3 September 1921, p. 206.

20 *The Motor*, 17 July 1923, p. 1016.

21 *Automobile Engineer*, October 1925, p. 341.

22 *Automobile Engineer*, September 1926, p. 323.

23 Ford Motor Co. publicity department, *A Tour through Ford's Works, Dagenham, Essex*, Dagenham (1937). Further information on Dagenham was gained from a series of promotional films produced by Ford and now held at the National Motor Museum, in particular *By the Waters of the Lea*.

24 *Automobile Engineer*, October 1934, pp. 359–65.

25 The Midlands Shadow Factories administered by car firms were: Rootes Securities Ltd, (Humber), Coventry, 35 acres; Daimler Co. Ltd, Coventry 3 acres; Standard Motor Co. Ltd, Coventry, 3·5 acres; Rover Co. Ltd, Acocks Green, Birmingham, 2 acres; Austin Motor Co. Ltd, Longbridge, Birmingham, 15 acres, plus engine assembly shop, machine shop.

26 *Automobile Engineer*, November 1937, p. 444. These shadow factories bear close relation to plant erected for aircraft manufacture. See A. D. George, 'The industrial archaeology of the aircraft factory', *Industrial Archaeology*, 17 (1983), pp. 214–21.

27 *Automobile Engineer*, February 1939, p. 42.

6 *The British motor-cycle industry during the 1930s*

STEVE KOERNER

In December 1934 a special issue of the popular journal *The Motor Cycle* was devoted to the theme of 'British Supremacy'. The issue was a celebration of the ascendency of the British motor-cycle industry over all international rivals. This supremacy was manifest, various articles in the issue claimed, in a number of ways. Not only were British motor-cycle companies producing more than anyone else but they were also represented as being ahead of all others in terms of design and workmanship. In the sporting field, especially, British products were particularly successful, winning race after race, on both home and foreign tracks.[1]

Was there any truth behind these claims, or were they merely the puffing of some over-enthusiastic or perhaps xenophobic trade journalists? This article examines whether Britain really deserved its reputation as the world's premier motor-cycle producer, as its proponents so proudly claimed. It reviews the structure of the industry during the 1930s and provides a brief historical background to its growth. It also investigates the state of the major international competitors as well as the challenge that cheap, lightweight cars posed to the popularity of motor cycles on the home market. Finally, it advances the argument that the way the motor-cycle industry tried to cope with its underlying problems at this time determined its subsequent progress and formed the basis of the ultimate collapse several decades later.

The motor-cycle industry had emerged from the bicycle industry at around the turn of the century and, for a time, evolved alongside the motor-car industry. Until 1924 there were more motor cycles on British roads than motor cars (see Tables 1 and 2). During the Great War the industry suffered a setback when much of its production capacity was diverted to munitions work. After 1919 production grew rapidly, and by 1925 Britain was the world's undisputed volume producer (see Table 1) and the biggest exporter, shipping abroad more motor cycles than all other rivals combined. Indeed, such was the formidable

Table 1 *Production totals for the three major motor-cycle manufacturing countries*

Country	*1925*	*1929*	*1933*	*1935*	*1937*
Britain	120,000	146,700	52,200	63,100	82,014
Germany	55,980	201,000	53,400	123,100	171,239
USA	45,000	31,900	7,400	14,110	17,700

Sources. BCMCMTU, *Review of the British Cycle and Motor Cycle Industry* (Coventry, 1925); Imperial Economic Committee, Thirtieth Report, *Survey of the Trade in Motor Vehicles* (London, 1936); US Strategic Bombing Survey, *German Motor Vehicle Industry* (Washington, D.C., 1947); Harry Sucher, *Harley-Davidson: the Milwaukee Marvel* (Sparkford, 1990), and *The Iron Redskin* (Sparkford, 1990).

reputation of British motor cycles that they overshadowed the domestic competition in Continental trade shows. In Italy, for a time, even Il Duce was accompanied by an escort of British-built motor cycles.[2]

Moreover, although the British motor-cycle industry produced far less than its motor-car counterpart — 61,767 units compared with 160,266 (worth £32,869,000, compared with £5,161,000 for the former) — at the beginning of the 1930s it was arguably a more successful industry in terms of international acceptance and prestige.[3] While motor-car sales tended to be concentrated in the home, empire and dominion markets, British motor cycles sold in many areas where the former did not, a point that was remarked upon at the time.[4] In 1927 a reporter with the *Daily Telegraph* was moved to write:

> It is depressing to the motorist travelling on the Continent to meet so rarely a British-made motor-car, but everywhere the British motor-cycle is upon the roads, and the foreigner willingly concedes its superiority. In design, lightness, and efficiency it beats everything.[5]

In terms of the proportion of machines exported, the motor-cycle industry far outdid its motor-car counterpart. In 1929, for example, 62,377 out of a total 147,000 motor cycles, or approximately 42 per cent of production, were sent abroad (see Table 2). By comparison, that same year, the motor-car industry exported only 23,891 out of a total of 182,347 cars, or 13 per cent of production (see Table 3). The contrast between international motor-cycle and motor-car producers was striking. Although the Americans overwhelmingly dominated car manufacture, making over 5 million units in 1929, compared with barely 200,000 units by the No. 2 producer, Britain — even when American production dropped to just over 4 million in 1935 it was still ten times that of Britain — the situation was reversed in respect of motor cycles. With 147,000 units manufactured in 1929, compared with America's 31,900, Britain was well ahead.[6]

Table 2 *British motor-cycle registrations, production, imports and exports, 1919–39*

Year	*Registrations*	*Production*	*Exports*	*Imports*
1919	114,722	65,000	8,330	1,481
1920	287,739	100,000	21,304	4,277
1921	373,200	80,000	8,104	2,130
1922	377,943	60,000	7,280	965
1923	430,138	80,000	16,156	1,011
1924	495,579	110,000	37,911	402
1925	558,911	120,000	47,114	867
1926	628,955	120,000	48,121	75
1927	681,410	160,000	53,000	149
1928	712,583	145,000	59,906	76
1929	731,298	147,000	62,377	103
1930	724,319	126,500	42,689	236
1931	626,649	74,700	23,247	108
1932	599,904	70,400	19,537	16
1933	562,656	52,200	17,731	16
1934	548,461	58,500	16,807	20
1935	521,128	64,700	18,000	0
1936	510,242	55,200	20,500	0
1937	491,718	82,014	25,400	200
1938	499,265	65,100	19,800	200
1939	n.a.	66,400	18,900	100

Sources. BCMCMTU, *Review of the British Cycle and Motor Cycle Industry* (Coventry, 1935); Michael Miller, 'The British Motor-Cycle Industry before 1939' (unpublished); SMMT, *The Motor Industry of Great Britain* (1939).

It was also true that the motor-cycle industry was far more secure in the home market. Although both industries were protected by the McKenna duties, the motor car firms had more need of the tariff wall. In 1929, for example, a mere 103 foreign motor cycles entered Britain, or less than one per cent of total domestic production. In contrast, that same year 21,520 foreign motor cars were imported, or nearly 12 per cent of total domestic production. By 1937 the differential had narrowed, but remained in favour of the motor-cycle industry. Some 200 foreign motor cycles, again less than 1 per cent of home production, were imported. Motor-car imports had dropped to 18,609, or a little less than 5 per cent of production, but still proportionately higher than the two-wheel sector.

What was the structure of this highly successful industry during the period in question? In certain respects the motor cycle industry shared some common characteristics with its motor-car counterpart, having started with a vast number of firms of varying sizes which was slimmed down by the late 1920s

Table 3 *British Motor car production, registrations, exports and imports, 1919–38*

Year	*Registrations*	*Production*	*Exports*	*Imports*
1919	109,715	n.a.	n.a.	n.a.
1920	186,801	n.a.	4,294	n.a.
1921	245,882	n.a.	1,966	n.a.
1922	319,311	n.a.	1,338	12,992
1923	389,767	71,396	3,256	14,429
1924	482,356	116,600	11,007	10,800
1925	590,156	132,000	17,771	31,781
1926	695,634	153,500	14,858	10,923
1927	800,112	164,553	16,139	18,194
1928	900,557	165,352	18,192	22,582
1929	998,489	182,347	23,891	21,520
1930	1,075,081	169,669	19,226	9,751
1931	1,103,715	158,997	17,104	2,118
1932	1,149,231	171,244	26,942	2,762
1933	1,226,541	220,779	33,802	3,619
1934	1,333,590	256,866	34,877	10,851
1935	1,505,019	311,544	44,193	13,563
1936	1,675,104	353,838	51,173	12,323
1937	1,834,248	389,633	53,655	18,609
1938	1,984,430	342,390	44,130	n.a.

Source. SMMT, *The Motor Industry of Great Britain*, 1939.

and throughout the 1930s. For example, in 1925 there were approximately 120 firms in Britain manufacturing motor cycles; by 1939 the total had shaken down to thirty-two.[7]

In common with the motor-car industry, several of the larger motor-cycle companies, a so-called Big Six, dominated the industry, followed by a number of medium-size firms, several of which made extensive use of proprietary bought-in parts (mainly engines). There were also specialist firms which built expensive sports and touring machines, as well as three major proprietary engine manufacturers. Although there were firms which built cars as well as motor cycles at the turn of the century, by the 1930s such links had largely been severed.[8]

The Big Six accounted for a very large proportion of the industry's production; it has been estimated that two firms alone manufactured slightly over 60 per cent of gross output.[9] Of the Six, BSA was the clear market leader (a position it had held since the early 1920s) producing 12,000 to 18,000 machines per year for much of the decade, or around 20–5 per cent of total British motor-cycle output.[10] As for the others, they continually jockeyed for the No. 2 spot, which regularly changed from year to year.[11]

All the Big Six were located in the Birmingham–Coventry–Redditch area, with the exception of Matchless (Associated Motor Cycles — AMC — after 1937) which was based in London. BSA (Birmingham Small Arms), originally an armaments maker, had expanded into bicycles and then cars (Daimler and Lanchester), steel, machine tools and other businesses which gave it access to resources not available to the other firms.[12] Triumph simultaneously built bicycles, motor cycles and cars until 1936, when, after suffering serious financial trouble, it was split three ways.[13] The others continued to build motor cycles and sometimes bicycles to the end of the decade.

The remaining companies were a mixed bag. Many of the medium-size firms produced a fairly extensive product line in their own right, albeit often at a higher price than those of the Big Six. A number of firms were heavily dependent on several proprietary engine manufacturers. The existence of these specialist firms had been very significant in terms of easing access to the industry during its formative years. Throughout the 1930s they made it possible for smaller firms to hold their position in the market.

Most of the firms in the industry were privately owned, and only a few were quoted on the stock market. In marked contrast with the motor-car industry, ownership and management were exclusively British. The industry also shared a number of general supply and accessory firms with its motor-car counterpart, such as Dunlop tyres and Lucas electrics, although the motor-cycle factories were capable of a great deal of in-house work.[14]

The industry was represented by a trade association, the British Cycle and Motor Cycle Manufacturers' and Traders' Union ('the Union'), whose membership included virtually all enterprises connected in one way or another with the production of bicycles and motor cycles. The Union, which was based in Coventry, had a number of functions, including organising the annual show (open only to its members for display purposes), representing the views of the industry with regard to legislation, taxation, general parliamentary activity and other dealings with government, including tariffs and import duties. The Union organised intelligence reports on overseas markets and general advertising campaigns, as well as technical co-ordination through bodies such as the British Motor Cycle and Cyclecar Research Association. The Union also worked closely with the Auto Cycle Union (a branch of the RAC) to regulate approved sporting events.

At the heart of the Union's authority over the industry was the bond that all members had to sign as a condition of membership. The bond required all members to follow strictly the rules of the Union, which prevented them from participation or support of any advertising, commercial shows or sporting activity not officially sanctioned by the Union. Infractions of Union rules would invariably result in stiff fines and other penalties, which were enforced through the offices of an associated organisation, the Cycle Trade Union.[15] The bond also set the terms and conditions of the discounts and rebates that could be offered by manufacturers to their retailers and by the retailers to the public.[16]

In essence this system, reinforced by a set of agreements between the Union, the manufacturers, component makers and factors, prevented any motor cycle, once the price had been set by the manufacturer, from being sold at a lower price by any retailer. Among other things, it also prevented a retailer from selling any motor cycle acquired from a manufacturer who was outside the Union, and vice versa.

Was this price maintenance in fact price-fixing? The Union did not think so, and vehemently asserted that price maintenance was fair and voluntary, created in the best interests of all concerned, be they manufacturers, retailers or consumers.[17] Although the Union's files do not contain much material directly relating to price-fixing, there is strong circumstantial evidence that it did take place.[18]

The Union was a profit-making institution in its own right, thanks to its sponsorship of many successful Annual Motor Cycle Shows. Union bank balances were always well in the black, and throughout the decade it possessed financial resources measured in tens of thousands of pounds, which continued to grow year by year. For example, in 1934 its balance was £69,561, a total which had risen to £77,888 by 1939.[19]

Public interest in the industry was catered for by a popular motor-cycle press aimed primarily at enthusiasts. Two magazines, *The Motor Cycle* and *Motor Cycling*, dominated the market, although there was also a weekly industry journal, *The Cycle and Motor Cycle Trader*, its circulation restricted to manufacturers and retailers, a fact which makes its pages echo with opinions a little more open than one finds in the other two.[20] The two popular journals enjoyed a close relationship with the industry. It was not uncommon, for example, for their editors to be invited to important Manufacturers' Union meetings in order to put their views forward. Nor was it unusual for members of the press to move into the industry or back again.[21]

What was the industry producing during the 1930s? British motor-cycle companies were notable for their varied and extensive product line. British consumers had the widest choice of motor cycles anywhere in the world, ranging from small single-cylinder machines up to large-displacement twin and even four-cylinder models.[22] British consumers seem to have had a marked preference for the big single-cylinder machines in the 350 cc and 500 cc displacement classes (see Table 4), a point which is suggestive of sports and touring use. The larger machines were also necessary in order to haul the many sidecars on the road.[23]

There were two major international competitors, the Americans and the Germans, who offered their clientele very different products. The American industry, robust until the First World War, had been devastated by cheap cars,

Table 4 *Motor cycles on the road, 1933–38, by displacement class: number registered in Great Britain during the year ending 30 September*

Displacement class (cc)	*1933*	*1934*	*1935*	*1936*	*1937*	*1938*
Solo motor cycles:						
Up to 150	21,068	25,703	27,124	30,703	31,809	32,867
150–250	131,706	137,193	134,904	136,500	135,469	131,620
Over 250	244,554	220,608	197,319	188,913	182,873	172,964
Motor cycle and sidecar combinations:						
Up to 150	24	13	27	45	58	51
150–250	1,315	1,634	1,241	1,295	996	930
Over 250	144,636	140,589	131,041	124,159	114,999	105,219
Tricycles	19,353	22,716	24,911	24,165	21,374	18,724
Total	562,656	548,456	516,567	505,780	487,578	462,375

Source. Ministry of Transport Return showing the Number of Mechanically Propelled Vehicles registered for the first Time under the Roads Act, 1926.

notably the Ford Model T, which had flooded on to the roads after 1913.[24] By the late 1930s only two companies, Harley-Davidson and Indian, had survived. The American motor-cycle market had shrunk drastically, although the two companies had some success in the export market, mainly in the Americas and in certain British dominions. American motor cycles were invariably large, powerful machines designed for long distances and rough roads.

The German industry, a leader before 1914, gradually progressed during the 1920s and, in terms of overall production, had overtaken the British industry by 1929. However, aggregate figures are misleading, in so far as much of Germany's powered two-wheel production was in small-capacity machines or what were called 'auto-cycles' (mo-peds), primarily in the 50 cc to 100 cc range, which was in turn a reflection of lower domestic purchasing power.[25] The German industry comprised a greater number of firms than the American, and offered a more diversified although less extensive product line than the British. Devastated by the 1929 Crash, it quickly recovered after 1933, thanks to the supportive nature of National Socialist transport policies. German production overtook Britain's once again in mid-decade, although the machines were, as before, in the main cheaper, small-capacity ones.[26] Japanese production, incidentally, was virtually negligible during this period.

If there was real substance to the claims of 'British Supremacy' in the motor-cycle world, the industry also suffered from a number of serious weaknesses that could not be glossed over. Indeed, its supremacy had been undermined from the late 1920s onwards, and by 1935 the industry found itself in the middle of a severe crisis.

Home and export markets suffered a massive drop in both sales and motor-cycle use. Between 1929 and 1934 overall production slumped from 120,000 to 60,000 units, the number of motor-cycle registrations (the index of the number of motor cycles in use in Great Britain) declined from an all-time high of 790,000 to 540,000, while exports virtually collapsed, falling from 62,377 to 16,807 units over the same period (although Britain's exports still remained greater than those of her rivals). Some of the drop can be attributed to the world-wide depression which hit other businesses equally hard. Yet the motor-car industry, while suffering initially, had recovered by 1935 and was enjoying record sales. Why had British consumers stopped buying motor cycles at the same rate as hitherto?

Two major factors underlay this shift in consumer preference with regard to personal transport. One was that while the prices of motor cars, especially the lightweight or 'baby' cars produced by Austin and Ford, had continued to drop during the 1920s and 1930s, those of motor cycles had remained relatively constant. Until then there had been a marked difference in price between cars and motor cycles.[27] The second factor was the continuing technical improvements typical of the motor-car industry: electric starters, all-metal bodies for better weather protection and vastly improved suspension systems were only some of the features now frequently found as standard even on economy cars.

By comparison, motor cycles had remained technologically stagnant and continued to demand more of their riders. They had to be kick-started, there was no effective protection against the weather, suspension systems were questionable and they were inherently unstable.[28] Carrying capacity, even with a sidecar, was still less than the smallest standard motor car offered. Despite the best efforts of designers, motor-cycle riders and their pillion passengers remained far more vulnerable to injury than anyone in a motor car should they be involved in an accident, whether another vehicle were involved or not.

However, the matter of price may have been the most important determinant of the choice between a car and a motor cycle, notwithstanding hire-purchase schemes and low deposits. As the motor-car industry adapted more and more to American-style mass production and as prices continued to drop there was also a concurrent development which was probably just as, perhaps even more, damaging to motor-cycle sales. This was the growth of the used car market, which seriously undercut the economy appeal of the motor cycle (see Table 5).

This comparison was especially acute in the competition between motor-cycle sidecar combinations and light cars such as the Austin Seven. (Users of solo motor cycles were less likely to switch to a four-wheel vehicle.[29]) In the late 1920s a 350 cc motor cycle combination still enjoyed a distinct price advantage over a used 8 h.p. car; ten years later, however, the difference had nearly

Table 5 *Prices of new motor-cycle and sidecar combinations compared with those of second-hand cars; selected years (£)*

Sales season	*1929/30*	*1932/32*	*1934/34*	*1936/37*
Comparison I				
1 Price of a new 350 cc combination	63·3	64·7	66·0	68·1
2 Price of a two-year-old 8 h.p. car	81·2	73·1	66·1	66·6
Comparison II				
1 Price of a new 500 cc combination.	–	72·9	74·7	79·3
2 Price of a three-year-old car not exceeding 10 h.p.	–	72·2	65·4	68·5
Ratio 2:1	n.a.	0·99	0·88	0·86

Source. M. Miller, 'The British Motor Cycle Industry before 1939'.

vanished. Indeed, registration figures for motor-cycle combinations show a consistent deterioration, far more acute than those for solo motor cycles.[30]

While motor-cycle manufacturers saw the 'top end' of their market eaten away by cheaper cars, they also encountered a similar problem at the bottom end. During the late 1920s and the 1930s there had been a phenomenal increase in bicycle use throughout Britain, and by mid-decade there were thought to be anything up to 14 million cycles in use.[31] At an average price of £3 to £5 the bicycle met a need for personal transport among those in urban or suburban areas which was not satisfied by public transport. No doubt the people who used it could afford neither a car nor a motor cycle.[32] What did critics of the industry have to say and what were their remedies for this crisis?

The critics were found in three general groupings. There were those inside the industry, working in particular firms or in the retail end of the business, who thought that more motor cycles could be sold with a change of attitude on the part of those who manufactured and distributed them. There were technical people such as engineers and press commentators who were disturbed by the industry's lack of progress, comparing unfavourably with those of Italy and Germany. Finally there were those who were affronted by the fundamental character of motor cycles, especially their noise and the manner in which they were ridden. The latter type of critic tended to be an ordinary citizen, a member of organisations such as the Anti-Noise League and the Pedestrian Association, although it also included members of the (trade and business) press, the judiciary and parliamentarians.

The criticism boiled down to two main issues. Growing sections of the public had become increasingly irritated by the amount of noise motor cycles created at sporting events, never mind in normal use or in the hands of over-enthusiastic riders. Government officials received complaint after complaint about the noise and disruption caused by motor-cycle events such as rallies, trials, beach racing and so forth. There was also public uproar about the hazards of pillion riding, the high fatality rate among young motorcyclists and the danger to other road users of reckless riding.[33]

More fundamental to the future of the industry, however, was the debate over the economy motor cycle, and its attendant theme, the potential of female consumers, which had been a subject of controversy for years. This criticism really turned on the issue of what the market was — or, rather, of what it could become. Critics maintained that it could be much enlarged if only the industry would adopt a more progressive approach to what it made and how it marketed its products. This was especially true of the manufacturers of 'economy' motor cycles and press commentators, who saw small machines as the salvation of the industry.[34]

The problem was that, in the absence of any effective marketing surveys, no one in the trade really knew exactly who was buying motor cycles and why.[35] There were two schools of thought on the question.

Publicly spokesmen for the industry asserted confidently that theirs was a market made up of mostly young working-class males, who used motor cycles primarily to commute to and from work.[36] The growth of suburban housing estates and new factories outside town and city centres had facilitated this development. Some within the industry regretted the association between the working class and the motor cycle. As one journal observed, the industry had slipped down market by comparison with its motor-car counterpart: 'Cars are Harrow, bikes are Borstal.'[37]

The critics remained unconvinced. Was a large 350 cc to 500 cc motor cycle, the industry's biggest-selling product, really necessary for day-to-day commuting? It was as easy to get to work on a 150 cc (or less) machine. Nor did the argument take account of the fact that motor-cycling had a strong appeal to many who were hardly working-class commuters, even if they were only a minority of the market. Throughout this period *The Motor Cycle* regularly carried news about the Public Schools' Motor Cycle Club as well as kindred groups such as the Oxford University Motor Cycle Club. These associations are unlikely to have been bastions of proletarian membership. Nor could T. E. Lawrence, Lawrence of Arabia, then probably Britain's best-known motor-cycling enthusiast, have been thought of as a typical factory commuter.[38]

Sporting events were often the focus of attention for large groups of motor-cycle enthusiasts, and these too attracted spectators from a variety of social backgrounds. The *New Statesman* reported that at the Isle of Man Tourist Trophy (TT) races 'universities and public schools vie with the garage hands and Birmingham stockbrokers in their interest'. The crowds there were said to be teeming with 'thousands of youngsters in Harris tweeds with club ties; as many North Country artisans with their sweethearts; and the greedy efficient people who sell cycles in every city and town from Land's End to John o'Groats'.[39]

The TT races attracted much of the critics' ire. Detractors pointed to the industry's near obsession with sports functions such as the TT races, events characterised by their emphasis on speed and good handling that generally required large and high-powered motor cycles. This emphasis had in turn a corresponding and, some thought, detrimental influence on motor-cycle design and expended resources that could have been used to develop more utilitarian models.[40]

The industry was truly at a crossroads. As one correspondent wrote in *The Cycle and Motor Cycle Trader*, the industry could not have it both ways. It would have to chose between building the big, often sports-oriented, motor cycles or the smaller commuting machines. 'You can make your sporting machine, you can make it fast, but so far you can't make it quiet. You can make your motor cycle for the million, but the million just isn't there for a single-track vehicle.'[41] Such was the choice: either the industry would continue to stagnate, catering to its traditional market, or it could attempt to break into a new stratum of potential customers. How did the industry and its constituent members respond to the crisis and attempt to confound the critics?

On 9 July 1935 the Union scheduled a special management committee to discuss the alarming drop in motor-cycle registrations and exports. A brief was tabled by the vice-president of the Union, Eric Barnett, which summarised the problem and suggested counter-measures.[42] After lengthy discussion on the issues the committee resolved to set up two sub-committees to study points raised by the critics, especially the noise and safety problems, and ways of increasing motor-cycle sales.

With regard to the technical matters, the Union did devote some of its financial resources to scientific research to discover better ways of silencing motor cycles. By the late 1930s the Ministry of Transport seemed to be satisfied with the progress that was being made. In the commercial field, however, the Union had less success, even though some efforts were made to co-ordinate advertising and to launch a co-operative insurance scheme to counter high premiums. These efforts were initially successful but they seem to have mostly ended inconclusively by 1937, a development which prompted further criticism from within the industry.[43]

Most of the Union's efforts to enlarge the market took the form of attacks on the government's formula of taxation by weight and engine capacity, which, it claimed, discouraged the public from buying smaller motor cycles and was therefore a serious barrier to increased sales. Another point of contention was recently implemented legislation which required motor-cycle driving licences, tests and compulsory third-party insurance. The last of these was thought to be the cause of the high insurance premiums. The government might have set these requirements out of concern for the public interest but, as far as the industry was concerned, they were simply a further deterrent to sales. The Union's solution was for the British government to follow the example of its French and German counterparts and either substantially reduce or simply remove all tax and regulations for motor cycles of less than 200 cc engine capacity.[44]

This much was being done at industry level. What steps did individual firms take to increase sales? Did they try and respond to the proposition that there was a wider market waiting to be tapped if only the right kind of motor cycle was on offer? Barring several notable exceptions among smaller firms, it appears that they virtually ignored the critics' suggestions.

BSA, for example, was not only the industry's largest producer but also offered the most comprehensive model line-up available in Britain or anywhere else. The breadth of its production, covering machines from 150 cc to 1,000 cc capacity, was a point of some pride. BSA's chairman had once informed shareholders that the secret of the group's success was the ability to provide 'a thoroughly reliable range of machines of almost every kind, fit for any purpose, by any person of any age in any country and at almost any price'.[45]

Yet when it came to promoting the newest offering for the 1935 season, the company chose to emphasise not an economy machine but its new medium-weight sports/enthusiast model, the Empire Star, a high-performance 500 cc single-cylinder machine which had made a sensational debut on the race track and which cost £65 10*s*. In 1939 the company actually dropped its only small-capacity machine (150 cc) from the catalogue.[46]

Constructive responses to the critics were restricted to the smaller firms, such as Coventry-based Francis-Barnett. For the 1935 season Francis-Barnett offered seven motor cycles ranging from 150 cc to 250 cc, two of them variations of the Cruiser model. The Cruiser incorporated many of the features that critics of the industry were calling for. It had a 250 cc engine capable of speeds of up to 50 m.p.h. which was enclosed in order to prevent oil from soiling the rider. It had a form of weather protection to keep the rider dry, a silencer system better than most, and was priced at a modest £37 5*s*. Although selling reasonably well, it never became the breakthrough to a new market that some had hoped.[47]

By the 1938/39 season a number of companies (none of them from the Big Six) were offering auto-cycles. British consumers seem to have reacted favourably, and there was modest interest in the small-capacity machines. The outbreak of war made it impossible to determine how successful they might have become.[48]

Some thought the manufacturers' cautious approach had been vindicated when in the late 1930s sales stopped falling and even picked up slightly. But registrations continued to drop. This seeming contradiction was difficult to interpret. Some suspected that committed motorcyclists were still buying new machines while others simply discarded theirs, which in turn were unable to find a place in the used motor-cycle market. Others in the industry were inclined to dismiss the validity of government statistics.[49]

Even as the home market began to stabilise, the industry became aware of a major threat to what remained of its export market. Spurred on by government incentives, the German motor-cycle industry launched a vigorous and successful campaign to sell its products in traditional British markets, especially Holland, South America and parts of Asia, much to the alarm of the British industry (see Table 6).[50]

Table 6 *British and German motor-cycle exports, 1933–37*

	British		*German*	
Year	*No.*	£	*No.*	£
1933	17,731	670,712	2,006	64,090
1934	16,497	648,998	1,904	75,999
1935	18,074	701,938	5,702	179,682
1936	20,460	799,414	14,612	377,736
1937	25,350	1,026,776	31,708	596,246

Source. Memo 47/38, 'Germany: Export Trade in Bicycles and Motor Cycles', BCMCMTU guard book, MSS 204/3/1/44.

The Manufacturers' Union complained bitterly to government Ministers that they were unable to compete effectively with their German rivals because of legislative handicaps. Not only did the Germans receive government subsidies which enabled them to sell their products at prices the British found difficult to match, but the lack of regulations affecting the German motor-cycle market (compulsory insurance and driving licences for lightweight motor cycles had been waived) enabled them to concentrate on fewer models and benefit from larger and longer production runs, thus reducing their unit costs.

However, as civil servants reminded industry representatives, German exports were predominantly in the 'ultra-light' (auto-cycle or mo-ped) category, in contrast to the larger and more expensive British motor cycles. The real problem, one of them confided, seemed to be that 'Germany has produced a motor cycle which the world wants and we appear to have lagged behind.'[51]

In order to counter the German incursions, British manufacturers began cutting prices to maintain competitiveness. The Germans responded with cuts of their own, and so commenced a price spiral which both sides came to see as mutually destructive. The motor-cycle industry was not alone in this struggle; many other industries also faced fierce competition from German rivals, a fact which quickly came to the attention of the Federation of British Industries and the Board of Trade. The outcome was a complex series of negotiations between British and German industries, conducted under the sponsorship of both governments, with the aim of reaching what amounted to a set of international cartels. This process culminated in the Dusseldorf agreement of March 1939. Although the British and German motor-cycle industries, which were an integral part of these negotiations, reached agreement in principle with regard to pricing and market share, events later that year prevented its consummation.[52]

So why did the small economy motor cycles not sell in the numbers they were supposed to? Or, to put the question differently, were the circumstances right for the industry to vastly increase its production capacity, a pre-condition of any decision to start manufacturing and marketing small motor cycles?

Part of the problem can be traced back to the debacle the industry had suffered when it tried to sell scooters and other innovative machines in the early and mid-1920s.[53] Industry leaders may have believed that such designs had been tried out before and had been a failure; they were not willing, especially in the economic conditions then prevailing (compared with the expanding market of the 1920s), to take another gamble. It must have seemed far better instead to stick with the tried and true. The other problem was that, failing volume production, the small-capacity machines by definition meant small profits, a point of great concern to the industry.[54]

Assuming that the industry wished to change its overall orientation, perhaps the only way to deal with the dilemma would have been to narrow down the number of models on offer and reap the benefits of larger and longer production runs, following the German example. But that would have been a difficult strategy, for a number of reasons.[55]

To begin with, many in the industry simply did not believe they should be building motor cycles on any kind of larger-scale production basis, and indeed the sentiments of BSA's chairman, quoted above, about catering to all segments of the market, seemed typical.[56] The major firms were quite happy to continue building their bigger single-cylinder machines in comparatively limited numbers, even if it meant under-utilising factory and plant. Moreover the industry was already having great difficulty with quality control and there is some doubt whether it possessed either the facilities or the skilled management that would have enabled it to expand to the volume necessary to service a larger market.[57]

BSA, for example, had already been criticised by *The Automobile Engineer* for being slow to introduce modern production techniques, and Triumph's Coventry factory layout reminded new owner, Jack Sangster, of 'rabbit warrens' when he bought the company in 1936.[58] The presence of a foreign-owned competitor in Britain, a motor-cycle equivalent of Ford, might have exerted the kind of pressure that forced the car manufacturers to revamp their factory practices.[59]

Was labour militancy ever an impediment to retooling or reorganising the factories? Certainly organised labour was no obstacle to change in the industry at the time. Although trade unions had been strong in some motor-cycle factories before and after the First World War, they had been gravely weakened by the slump. For example, when Jack Sangster took over Triumph he immediately instituted a pay cut on a 'take it or leave it' basis which met with no resistance. Previously, Triumph workers had been among the most militant in the industry. There is no record of labour unrest at all during the 1930s, although there were disputes in some of the component industries such as tyre manufacturing.[60]

Did the industry have the financial resources to do what the critics urged it to do? It is true that BSA, AMC and Enfield reported rising dividends at the end of the decade and the private companies were almost certainly profitable. For example, after years of paying their shareholders no dividends, BSA paid out 10 per cent on the ordinary shares in 1938, while AMC's dividends jumped from 5 per cent to 10 per cent between 1937 and 1938. Much of the increased profitability was due to the rearmament programme, which resulted in many lucrative military contracts, some of which involved motor cycles, although others required component manufacturing for the aircraft and armament industries.[61]

The industry easily identified the root cause of its inability to increase the motor-cycle market. Government legislation was obviously the main culprit. But was there any truth in the complaint that the industry was over-taxed and over-regulated? Could the government, lacking hard evidence from the industry that relaxing the legislation would increase sales, and under pressure from other quarters to retain the laws, have done anything else?

Neville Chamberlain, who was either Chancellor of the Exchequer or Prime Minister for much of the 1930s, had been managing director of BSA Cycles during the early 1920s. Surely he would have had some understanding of (and perhaps sympathy for) the industry's problems. Yet the legislation remained fundamentally unchanged. Although the 1932 budget altered the tax structure, to favour sales of motor cycles under 150 cc capacity, it was not sufficient to satisfy the industry.[62]

Perhaps most important, there were those in the industry who did not believe there was a market for anything other than what was already being produced, and they could point to the types of motor cycle that were moving off the showroom floors to substantiate their case. When the public were offered small motor cycles they did not buy them in any great numbers. On the other hand the big 350 cc to 500 cc models remained consistent best-sellers.

Did the companies do all they could to expand their market? How much were they spending on advertising, and where? The industry was particularly disappointed by its failure to induce women, among other non-traditional consumers, to buy its products. This could be done only by reaching out to the kind of people who had never thought of buying a motor cycle but might if they were pitched a convincing case. On the evidence available, it is not at all clear that the industry was prepared to take such steps to widen its market.

Neither the Union nor the individual firms increased their advertising budgets, which lagged far behind the car and even the bicycle industries (see Table 7), nor did they advertise beyond the enthusiast press.[63] There was certainly money available to them at the time. On this point at least the critics were not adequately answered.

Table 7 *Advertising expenditure by the cycle, motor-cycle and motor-car industries, 1935–38 (£)*

Industry	*1935*	*1936*	*1937*	*1938*
Bicycles	160,985	200,446	223,335	173,912
Motor cycles	36,441	38,821	39,206	34,823
Motor cars	901,089	877,141	911,726	853,799

Source. Statistical Review of Advertising, 1935–38.

In summary, how should we assess the history of the motor-cycle industry during this time? Did it respond effectively to the crisis brought about by the drastic fall in demand, or is this yet another example of entrepreneurial failure?

The industry had effectively dealt with the circumstances it faced. The strategies seem a fairly rational response to the crisis, and the industry was able to hold on to a stable, if traditional, market and, most important, continued to make money. By 1939 the industry, helped by its restrictive trading rules as well as by its incipient commercial agreement with the Germans, had created a cosy environment for itself which removed any real pressure, external or internal, for change.

It is difficult to know whether or not there was ever a serious possibility of cultivating a large-scale economy motor-cycle market in Britain during the 1930s.

The industry was simply not committed to finding out whether it existed. The crucial point which emerges from this period is how the decisions made then affected the industry in the coming decades. For the 1930s were a watershed in the history of the industry. Thereafter it was arguably committed, perhaps irreversibly, to a policy of building mostly large displacement motor cycles for a market composed essentially of enthusiasts.

Other variants of the economy motor cycle were launched, but the major development of the post-war era was that the industry became more and more oriented to the North American market, the one that remained most loyal to the type of motor cycle Britain specialised in building.[64] By the late 1960s, in a complete turn-round from the situation during the 1930s, when Australia was the major export market, a high proportion of output went to either the United States or Canada.[65]

Nor was the industry ever to get nearer to large-scale production before it finally crashed into bankruptcy in 1973, although there was some modernisation of plant. Indeed, there was to be only a slight expansion in output. In 1959, its best year ever, the entire British industry produced a total of 127,500 motor cycles.[66] Yet in 1929 it was already capable of producing 147,000 machines. During the 1930s a degree of security was purchased at the cost of long-term failure.

Notes

1 *The Motor Cycle*, 13 December 1934; the Isle of Man TT (Tourist Trophy) race results are provided in detail, along with the nationality of the participants, in Nick Harris, *Motorcourse History of the Isle of Man TT Races, 1907–89* (Richmond, Surrey, 1990).

2 See Cyril Ayton, Bob Holliday, Cyril Posthumus and Mike Winfields, *The History of Motor Cycling* (Norwich, 1979), pp. 109–10. A photo of British-built motor cycles in use at an Italian fascist rally was published in *The Motor Cycle*, 14 November 1929, p. 733, and again on 6 June 1935, p. 777. The *Midland Bank Monthly Review* also commented on the popularity of British motor cycles among Italians in its March/April issue of 1933, at p. 5. The *Manchester Guardian Commercial* of 24 March 1927 remarked how British-built motor cycles dominated Continental trade fairs.

3 The motor-cycle and motor-car output figures are derived from the 1930 *Census of Production, Part 2* (1931), p. 334. By way of comparison, that same year the British bicycle industry produced 882,105 units worth a total of £3,177,000.

4 See various Board of Trade memos, including one by C. E. House entitled 'Motor Cars', regarding British car and motor-cycle sales, dated 13 September 1938. Public Record Office (PRO), BT 59/24/489/20, BT 59/24/589.

5 *Daily Telegraph*, 22 August 1927, in the press clipping books of the British Cycle and Motor Cycle Manufacturers' and Traders' Union, MSS 204/10/1/2, Modern Records Centre (MRC), University of Warwick.

6 The figures are from *A Survey of the Trade in Motor Vehicles*, Report of the Imperial Economic Committee, Thirtieth Report, (1936), pp. 7–9, 101. The difference between the two industries was noted in G. C. Allen, *British Industries and their Organization* (1959), p. 181.

7 A large proportion of these firms were simply back-yard or small garage-based enterprises which had dropped out of the market by the end of the 1920s. *The Cycle and Motor Cycle Trader* thought the depletion of firms owing to the Depression was a positive development in so far as it 'weeded out' what were termed 'mushroom concerns'. See 'Promise of prosperity', 4 March 1938. C. J. Ayton, *Guide to Pre-war British Motor Cycles* (Feltham, 1985), p. 9.

8 In alphabetical order the Big Six were Ariel, Associated Motor Cycles (formerly Matchless) BSA, (Royal) Enfield, Norton and Triumph.

9 See Michael Miller, 'The British Motor Cycle Industry before 1939' (unpublished), p. 1. A copy of this paper was kindly provided by the author. According to one post-war survey these two unnamed firms produced 63 per cent of all output. See H. Leak and A. Maizels, *The Structure of British Industry* (1945), p. 52. Lack of sufficient documentation prevents a more precise calculation of market share.

10 BSA's best pre-war year was 1926, when it manufactured a total of 29,099 motor cycles. By 1933 production had dropped to a low of 10,979 units and thereafter it fluctuated from year to year, with a high of 18,563 in 1937. See BSA's Report on Accounts, Twelve Months ended July 1938, in the BSA Collection, MRC, MSS 19A/2/37, p. 4.

11 This is the assessment of Mr Jock West, who became AMC's sales director after World War II and who had been active in the industry as a TT racer during the late 1930s. Communication with the author in June 1991.

12 Car companies such as Hillman, Humber, Rover, Singer and Triumph all began as bicycle manufacturers and subsequently branched out into either cars or motor cycles, or occasionally both. The careers of such leading motor industry figures as Lord Nuffield and John Siddeley began in the bicycle trade. In his speech to the 1922 AGM, BSA's chairman specifically noted that the recent acquisition of Jessop & Sons' steel company was designed in part to give the parent firm greater control over raw material supplies. See Chairman's Speech, delivered on 25 April 1922, copy in the BSA papers on deposit at the Birmingham Central Reference Library, MS 321/A (Reports on Accounts).

13 Triumph cars ultimately became part of Standard Motor; Triumph bicycles was bought by Raleigh Industries; the entrepreneur Jack Sangster picked up the motor-cycle end of the firm and created Triumph Engineering Company, a dedicated motor-cycle producer. See Ivor Davies, *Triumph: the Complete Story* (Swindon, 1991).

14 See Alfred Plummer, *New British Industries in the Twentieth Century* (1937), p. 95. A thorough description of the wide range of the services that the Triumph factory in Coventry was capable of can be found on Jack Wicks's tape of reminiscences on deposit at the Coventry Record Office. Wicks was a staff designer who began work at Triumph in the late 1930s.

15 The guard books of the CTU contain a number of case files relating to various miscreants who had broken Union rules and suffered the appropriate punishment. See MSS 204/CT/3/1/1–5.

16 See, for example, the 1935 Bond, on deposit with the Union papers in the MRC at MSS 204/4/4/1. The agreements were renewed annually.

17 A point repeatedly made by the Union's Director, Major H. R. Watling, when he testified before the Committee on Resale Price Maintenance in July 1948. See PRO, BT 64/540, file 376/1949.

18 In one instance, during a meeting of the Motor Cycle Manufacturers' Section of the Union on 5 April 1937, there was what was recorded as 'a full discussion in which all members represented at the meeting took part', resulting in unanimous agreement to raise retail prices by at least 30*s* the following month. See the Union Minute Book, MSS 204/1/1/14, p. 2482. An article in the 19 April 1937 edition of *The Cycle and Motor Cycle Trader*, refers to the meeting and identifies it as having been held for the purpose of discussing a price increase.

19 See the Annual Report and Balance Sheet for 1934 and 1939, in the Union's papers, MSS 204/4/3/2, MRC.

20 In 1934 the circulations of the three journals were estimated as follows: *The Motor Cycle*, 126,004; *Motor Cycling*, 39,160; *The Cycle and Motor Cycle Trader*, 8,550. The figures are provided in the minutes of the Management Committee meeting of 12 March 1935, on p. 2146 of the Union's Minute Book, MSS 204/1/1/12.

21 Graham Walker, for example, was an executive with the Rudge-Whitworth motor-cycle company before going on to become editor of *Motor Cycling*.

22 See an untitled briefing minute prepared for the Minister of Overseas Trade (n.d. but probably November–December 1938), in PRO, BT 59/24, sub-file 589, and labelled 'Department of Overseas Trade, Discussions with UK Trade Organisations, No. 25, Motor Cycles'. For the best consolidated guide to the various models being produced by the industry in the 1930s see Roy Bacon, *British Motorcycles of the 1930s: the A–Z of Pre-war Marques* (1986). See also Bob Currie, *Great British Motor Cycles of the Thirties* (1991), for a more general description.

23 See Phil Schilling, *The Motorcycle World* (New York, 1974), p. 54.

24 According to statistics maintained by the Manufacturers' Union, in 1934 the number of registered motor cycles on American roads totalled 95,643 machines, although there had been 210,000 machines registered in 1923, a figure which slipped to 126,850 three years later. See *Review of the British Cycle and Motor Cycle Industry* (third edition, Coventry, 1935), p. 8.

25 The proportion of motor cycles under 200 cc in Germany had grown to 60·5 per cent of all registrations by 1936 and jumped to 72 per cent in 1938. See Fritz Blaich, 'Why did the pioneer fall behind? Motorisation in Germany between the wars', in Theo Barker (ed.), *The Economic and Social Effects of the Spread of Motor Vehicles* (1987), p. 151.

26 *The Motor Cycle* had already noted the 'amazing growth' of the German industry during the late

1920s. See the 18 April 1929 issue, p. 602. This was a view also shared by the *Times* in an article entitled 'German motor cycles — bid for supremacy in production', 5 August 1929, p. 9. For an explanation of the slow growth of the German motor industry during the 1920s see I. D. Turner, 'British Occupation Policy and its Effects on the Town of Wolfsburg and the Volkswagenwerk, 1945–49', unpublished Ph.D. dissertation, UMIST (1984), pp. 48–52, and R. J. Overy, 'Cars, roads and economic recovery in Germany', *Economic History Review*, second series, XXVIII (1975), pp. 466–83.

27 By the calculations of the Society of Motor Manufacturers and Traders (SMMT), taking 1924 as a benchmark of 100, prices had dropped to 49·8 by 1935. See SMMT, *The Motor Industry of Great Britain* (1939), p. 47. The question of motor-car prices during the inter-war period is addressed in Roy Church and Michael Miller, 'The Big Three: competition, management, and marketing in the British motor industry, 1922–39', in Barry Supple (ed.), *Essays in British Business History* (Oxford, 1977). The drop in car prices also eroded the advantage motor cycles had previously enjoyed in respect of maintenance costs. See Ayton *et al.*, *History of Motor Cycling*, p. 40.

28 In fairness to the motor-cycle industry, it should be noted that there had been great advances in the quality of tyres, brakes and steering mechanisms. These, however, were simply insufficient to counterbalance the natural disadvantages of the motor cycle compared with the motor car.

29 The experience of the family of future Prime Minister Harold Wilson is illustrative of this process. In 1918 his father bought, for £50, his first motor vehicle, a second-hand motor-cycle and sidecar combination. This was replaced several years later by a new combination unit. In 1925, the family's financial position having improved, he purchased an Austin Seven motor car worth £149. There is no record of any further motor cycles in the Wilson household. See Austen Morgan, *Harold Wilson* (1992), p. 13.

30 Miller explains the 'long-run extermination of combinations and tricycles' by the fact that they 'served as cheap substitutes for light cars and vans'. With 'their discomfort, exposure to the elements, and limited loads, they were poor substitutes, and only cheapness to run could allow them to compete'. All prices used here are derived from this source. See 'British Motor Cycle Industry', p. 6.

31 According to the Ministry of Transport's 1936 road traffic census, bicycle use had increased by 94·98 per cent from 1931 to 1935. See *Road Traffic Census, 1936 Report* (1937), p. 6.

32 The average price of bicycles is found in the *Census of Production* for 1935, at p. 377; see also Miller, 'British Motor Cycle Industry', pp. 5–6, for other perceived barriers preventing bicycle owners from upgrading to motor cycles.

33 Some of the complaints to various public officials can be found in PRO file HO 45, particularly sub-files 11100, 17413 and 456309. When giving evidence before a select committee of the House of Lords on 'The Prevention of Road Accidents' in May 1939, H. A. Tripp, Assistant Commissioner of Police, deplored the high level of motor-cycle accidents, which he thought was a consequence of the rashness and impulsiveness of youth. See BS 96, House of Lords Sessional Papers, 1937–38/4, *Report by the Select Committee of the House of Lords on the Prevention of Road Accidents, together with the Proceedings of the Committee, Minutes of Evidence and Index* (1938), pp. 49–50. There was evidently a widespread belief among motorcyclists that there was bias against them in the courts and among police forces. See 'Those anti-magistrates', *Motor Cyclist Review*, March 1929, p. 413.

34 There was considerable discussion in the motor-cycle press during the 1920s and 1930s about what kind of machines the manufacturers should build. See, for example, 'An "Everyman" prophecy' by 'Ixion', *The Motor Cycle*, 31 January 1929, p. 158, and 'Making motor cycle sales', *The Cycle and Motor Cycle Trader*, 29 January 1937, p. 80.

35 It seems that no systematic marketing surveys were conducted for the motor-cycle industry at this time. As one industry-based commentator remarked, 'Who uses motor cycles, and why? is a simple question, and the answer should not be too difficult to find if some attempts were made to discover it. And yet today there is no one in the country who can with accuracy provide that answer, because the job of finding it out has never been properly tackled.' See 'Who rides motor cycles — and why?', *The Cycle and Motor Cycle Trader*, 4 March 1938, p. 165.

36 This was the opinion of BSA's chairman, who in a speech to shareholders identified 'the wage-earning classes' as 'the backbone of the motor cycle market on which the prospects of your Birmingham factory depends'. See Chairman's Speech, 15 November 1932, copy on deposit in the BSA papers, MS 321/A (Reports and Accounts), at the Birmingham Central Reference Library. His words were later echoed by the chairman of AMC in his speech to the shareholders at the annual general meeting on 28 December 1939, when he identified the group's market as being 'principally comprised of young men'. See AMC Annual Report for 1938/39, on deposit at the Guildhall Library, London.

37 The opinion of 'Peeping Tom' in 'Hampered by the DU agreement', *The Cycle and Motor Cycle Trader*, 17 June 1938, p. 214. S. A. Davis of the British Motor Cycle Association was quite certain of the connection between the working class and the motor cycle when testifying before the select committee of the House of Lords on the prevention of road accidents on 19 May 1938. See pp. 337–8 of the proceedings. The *Economist* noted that the motor-cycle industry's main clientele 'tends to be restricted to workers living at a greater distance than the average from their employment. Week-end pleasure users, though numerous, tend to become proselytes to small-car ownership, and youthful lovers of speed find light sports cars more to their taste.' 'Cycles and motor cycles', *Economist*, 30 November 1935, pp. 1059–60.

38 Although many public schoolboys may have been devoted to their motor cycles, some headmasters were clearly disapproving. In 1923 there was an inter-school competition sponsored by the North West London Motor Club at Amersham. The match could not be prevented but, 'for some reason or reasons presently unknown', the headmasters forbade their boys to compete in the names of their schools. 'Motor cyclists in the making', *The Motor Cycle*, 12 September 1923, pp. 373–4. *The Motor Cycle* also produced a special volume entitled *The Motor Cycle Book for Boys* (1928) which, judging by the illustrations, was directed at the male offspring of middle-class parents. Philip Vincent, who went on to found the motor-cycle company Vincent-HRD during the late 1920s, was a pupil at Harrow during this period. When Lawrence died in a motor-cycle accident there was an obituary in *The Motor Cycle* of 23 May 1935, p. 708. Lawrence regularly rode — indeed, was killed on — a Brough Superior, undoubtedly the most expensive motor cycle in Britain at the time. A Brough could cost as much as a new higher-grade economy car, about £140.

39 'About motoring', *New Statesman*, 12 June 1926.

40 'Every credit must be given to those responsible for the advanced stage of development that the racing motor cycle engine has attained. Nevertheless, to put relatively expensive, heavy, noisy engines, difficult to start, and sometimes critically stressed, into commercial production and available to the general public is not in the best interests of the Industry.' 'The motor cycle industry', *Automobile Engineer*, January 1936, pp. 1–2.

41 See also 'Shall we scrap the TT?' by 'Exporter', *The Cycle and Motor Cycle Trader*, 26 April 1935, p. 60.

42 A copy of Barnett's memo, dated 9 July 1935, and entitled 'Review of the Situation in the British Motor Cycle Industry', is contained in the Union guard books at MSS 204/3/1/38, p. 12. Barnett was himself one of the directors of Francis-Barnett, a leading manufacturer of smaller-displacement motor cycles.

43 See the article entitled 'Showmanship', *The Cycle and Motor Cycle Trader*, 10 September 1937, p. 2225.

44 A copy of the Union's brief to the government on the subject of motor-cycle taxation is to be found in PRO, BT 59/24/589. The question of what position to take with regard to taxation was thoroughly canvassed in the pages of the Union's *Quarterly Journal*, especially in the February and August 1929 and June 1930 issues. Copies of the journal are on deposit among the Union's papers at the MRC, MSS 204/4/2/5. In contrast to the Motor Cycle Manufacturers' Union, the SMMT was unable to persuade its members to reach a unified position on taxation, despite repeated invitations from the government to do so.

45 See the BSA Chairman's Speech of 29 April 1924, *cit.*

46 See the BSA Chairman's Speech of 11 October 1934, which specifically mentions the launch of the Empire Star machines. According to the annual 'Buyers' Guide' published by *The Motor Cycle*, the 150 cc model was not available in 1939, although there were more 250 cc models for consumers to choose from. The company also continued to offer its 500 cc and 1,000 cc motor cycles.

47 For more on this machine see Peter Watson, 'Bridging a gap', *Classic Bike*, February 1985, pp. 45–8, and Jonathan Jones, 'Comfort with cleanliness', *The Classic Motor Cycle*, July 1991, pp. 22–6. I am indebted to Mr Peter Watson for bringing the history of this model to my attention.

48 At the 1939 show there were nine companies (none of them from among the Big Six) which had auto-cycles on display, compared with only several three years previously. See G. S. Davidson, *The Motor Cyclist's Annual, 1939–40* (1939). According to one history of the industry, the popularity of auto-cycles, nicknamed 'Wilfreds', after a well known cartoon character of the time, was based on the public's desire for very cheap transport in anticipation of wartime conditions. See Ayton *et al.*, *History of Motor Cycling*, pp. 170–1.

49 See 'Fewer motor cycles in use', *The Cycle and Motor Cycle Trader*, 1 January 1937, p. 62; 'False figures', *ibid.*, 7 May 1937, p. 95.

50 A correspondent informed the Union that the Germans were 'penetrating with the characteristic Teutonic thoroughness every country East of Suez'. Memo 16/37. 'India: German Motor Cycle Competition', 1 February 1937, in the Union guard books, MSS 204/3/1/41.

51 See Union memo dated 25 November 1937, entitled 159/37, 'Germany: Developments in the Bicycle and Motor Cycle Industry', which notes a 'striking increase' in German exports of motor cycles of less than 100 cc capacity. See also PRO, BT 59/24/589, 'Department of Overseas Trade, Discussions with UK Trade Organisations, No. 25, Motor Cycles', dated 26 October 1938. *The Cycle and Motor Cycle Trader* blamed the industry's fixation on sporting events for the erosion of its competitive position abroad. The problem was that 'Overseas buyers don't want what we want them to want. If the German national were placed as we are, and if cars in America were not so cheap as they are, our export trade in motor cycles would be worth a small packet of snuff.' The *Trader* advocated a change of emphasis in the industry's production line: 'Let us drop this power-bike idea. Let us make a car on two wheels.' See 'Shall we scrap the TT?', *The Cycle and Motor Cycle Trader*, 26 April 1935, p. 60.

52 A copy of the agreement negotiated between the Union and its German counterpart at Dusseldorf is attached to p. 2763 of the Union's Minute Book, MSS 204/1/1/15. An overview of the Anglo-German commercial talks is contained in C. A. MacDonald, *The United States, Britain and Appeasement, 1936–39* (1981).

53 The scooter craze of the 1920s, and two-wheeled vehicles like the Ner-a-Car, are well described in chapter four of Ayton *et al.*, History of Motor Cycling. See also a contemporaneous account, 'Can the scooter come back?' by Francis Jones, *The Cycle and Motor Cycle Trader*, 1 May 1936, p. 82. The question was also raised during a discussion which followed Triumph Engineering managing director Edward Turner's paper entitled 'Post-war Motor Cycle Development', delivered to a meeting of the Institution of Automobile Engineers. See *Proceedings of the Institution of Automobile Engineers*, XXXVII (1942–43), pp. 320–1.

54 For example, according to BSA's own financial records, the company made a profit margin of 27 per cent on the 150 cc size machines but made 45 per cent on their biggest machines, the G-9 1,000 cc V-twins. The 500 cc Blue Star machines earned a 39 per cent margin. This information is drawn from data in BSA's Reports on Accounts, MRC, MSS 19A/2/35, p. 16.

55 AMC's policy in respect of manufacturing and marketing ran directly counter to this strategy. When it acquired Sunbeam in 1932 the chairman assured shareholders that the company was now able to offer consumers, along with its existing Matchless and AJS line-ups, three separate and competing sets of motor-cycle models. This was considered a good thing in terms of consumer choice. See Matchless/AMC Annual Report for 1933, on deposit in the Guildhall Library, London.

56 In his testimony to the Committee on Industry and Trade in March 1925, Major Watling claimed that, because of the peculiarities of the British market, which required a large range of models, 'mass production' in the American sense of the term was simply out of the question. See *Minutes of Evidence*, Committee on Industry and Trade (1924–27), pp. 451–2. The Norton company, for example, was proud of the fact that it did not have a moving assembly track at its Birmingham factory. To convert to that type of production was, in its mind, to compromise with established standards of quality and craftsmanship. See 'Performance in the making', *Export Trader*, May 1938, pp. 192–3.

57 Evidently quality control was so poor, the editor of *The Motor Cycle* informed members of the Union's management committee, that he was afraid to publish all the some 10,000 letters he had received from irate customers, since 'publication would have a damping effect upon other readers' enthusiasm'. According to the editor, A. B. Bourne, the complaints focused on the general lack of dependability of the owners' motor cycles, indeed 'from our own point of view the present position is disheartening to say the least'. See Union memo 46/36, 'Motor Cycles: Criticisms by Users', dated 18 March 1936, in the Union guard books, MSS 204/3/1/39. This criticism was echoed by a disgruntled retailer, E. P. Huxham, in a letter to *The Cycle and Motor Cycle Trader* of 1 April 1938, p. 11.

58 See 'The works of the BSA Co. Ltd', *The Automobile Engineer*, November 1928, pp. 434–9; 'The Triumph rejuvenation', *The Cycle and Motor Cycle Trader*, 31 January 1936, p. 73. Both companies did reorganize and reinvest during the late 1930s but did not substantially increase their production rates.

59 Precisely the point made by the Motor Cycle Section of the Australian Association of British Manufacturers, which was sent to the Union's Coventry headquarters. Among other things, the association commented that the British motor-cycle industry 'sorely needs' the counterparts of Ford and Vauxhall to stimulate it to produce motor cycles for the 'vast majority, sensible vehicles at sensible prices'. See Union memo dated 22 January 1936, entitled 9/36 'Australia: Views on British Motor Cycle Design', in the Union guard books, MSS 204/3/1/38.

60 The background of labour relations in the motor-cycle industry is outlined in Steve Koerner, 'Trade Unionism and Collective Bargaining at two British Motor Cycle Factories: a Study of BSA/Small Heath and Triumph/Meriden, 1951–73', unpublished M.A. dissertation, University of Warwick (1990), chapter 3. As far as strikes in related industries are concerned, a dispute over wages at the John Bull tyre company's Leicester factory, which supplied various motor-cycle firms, was reported in July 1935. Some 400 employees were affected. *The Cycle and Motor Cycle Trader*, 5 July 1935, p. 2. By contrast, there is no record in the trade press of labour disputes in any motor-cycle factory during this period.

61 The fact that BSA was benefiting from the rearmament drive, primarily in its small arms division and at Daimler, was noted in the business press. The *Statist*, for example, reported that turnover had increased, owing to military contracts (19 June 1937, p. 965). The profits earned by BSA from this source were also remarked by the Labour Research Department in its *Dividends from Defence* (1939), p. 17. Other industry firms picked up similar work as well. Enfield Cycles, for one, reported military contracts, as did Matchless Motor Cycles. See *Stock Exchange Gazette*, 19 November 1938, and Directors'

Report, Matchless Motor Cycle Company, Tenth Annual General Meeting, 16 December 1938, copy on deposit at the Guildhall Library, London. By the end of 1938 Norton was so preoccupied with building motor cycles for the armed forces that it actually dropped out of racing, much to the dismay of many sports enthusiasts. See 'No Norton racing programme', *The Cycle and Motor Cycle Trader*, 9 December 1938, p. 199.

62 In fact the government had entertained the notion of further relaxing the regulations and taxes on small motor cycles (under 100 cc) but had decided not to because the industry had failed to produce sufficiently strong arguments to show that further concessions would increase their sales. Indeed, most of the industry's arguments seemed to be negative comparisons with the situation enjoyed by its Continental counterparts. Thus, it argued, if deregulation worked in France or Germany it would perforce work in Britain. However, as a minute written by a Mr Jones, dated 20 December 1938, put it, in the absence of more information from the Union 'We cannot offer an opinion on how far these regulations are an impediment to the use of the light-weight motor cycle in the United Kingdom.' To which the Comptroller General of the Department of Overseas Trade added, 'I agree. We have nothing to work on.' See minute from 'Jones' dated 5 December 1938 in PRO, BT 59/24, sub-file 589, 'Department of Overseas Trade, Discussions with UK Trade Organisations, No. 25, Motor Cycles'.

63 In a memo marked 112/38, and entitled 'Motor Cycle Propaganda', a dealer was quoted on the subject of the industry's failure to advertise in what he called the 'lay press'. The unnamed correspondent believed that if more motor cycles were to be sold it was important to advertise in the popular as opposed to the enthusiast press, as 'the people I have in mind are not likely to read motor cycle publications'. The memo is contained in Union guard book MSS 204/3/1/45 at p. 155. A columnist in the *Trader* who had recently attended the Motor Show remarked how much better its presentation was than that of the Motor Cycle Show. He also criticised the motor-cycle industry on the grounds that, unlike its car counterpart, it emphasised the sporting side of its products to the detriment of their utility function. See 'Motor Show musing' by 'F.J.', *The Cycle and Motor Cycle Trader*, 22 October 1937, p. 66.

64 The small-engine BSA Bantam, probably the single best-selling British model of the post-war era, is an honourable exception to this rule. It was, however, a German, not a British, design which BSA picked up by way of the war reparations programme. See Roy Bacon, *BSA Bantam, all Models, 1948–71* (Ventnor, 1989).

65 In 1935 Australia imported 5,060 British motor cycles, a figure that had increased to 8,568 by 1937 (out of totals of 18,000 and 25,400 respectively). In contrast only sixty-one machines were sent to the United States in 1935, although the figure had increased to 166 in 1937. However, during 1969–70 Triumph Engineering exported 33,320 motor cycles altogether, 21,428 of which went to the United States (65·8 per cent) and another 3,410 (8·5 per cent) to Canada. See memo 52/38, 'World Export Trade in Bicycle and Motor Cycle Products', dated April 1938, in the Union guard books, MSS 204/3/1/44; Triumph Engineering Company, Accounts Analysis, MSS 123/2/3/23/1, on deposit at the MRC.

66 For a summary of post-war developments see Barbara Smith, *The History of the British Motor Cycle Industry, 1945–75* (University of Birmingham, Centre for Urban and Regional Studies, 1981). Total production for 1959 was actually recorded as 248,900 units. However, 108,000 were small-displacement mo-peds and scooters mostly of German and Italian design built under licence. A further 13,500 were three-wheel machines. See *Business Monitor*, Production Series, *Motor Cycles, Three-wheeled Vehicles, Pedal Cycles and Parts* (1968). In contrast, in 1960, after the construction of a new factory in Suzuka City, Honda Motors of Japan alone could produce around 360,000 machines per year, albeit virtually all in the lightweight classes, but a figure well in excess of the combined output of the entire British industry at the time. See Tetsuo Sakiya, *Honda Motor — the Men, the Management, the Machines* (Tokyo, 1987), pp. 118–19.

Acknowledgements

This article is based on my Ph.D. dissertation, currently in progress. I would like to thank my supervisor, Nick Tiratsoo, for his comments and guidance. Thanks also to Richard Storey and the staff of the Warwick University Modern Records Centre, where much of the research for the article was completed.

7 The background to bus regulation in the 1930 Road Traffic Act: economic, political and personal influences in the 1920s

CORINNE MULLEY

The Road Traffic Act of 1930 marked the beginning of comprehensive State intervention in the control of omnibuses. The measure achieved lasting importance – for fifty years its provisions remained in force virtually unchanged. It was only in 1980 that the spirit of the Act was questioned by a Transport Act which has returned the inter-city bus and coach industry to its pre-1930 state.

Before 1930 the powers to regulate omnibuses were vested in the local authorities, by the Town Police Clauses Acts of 1847 and 1889. The Act of 1847 codified and consolidated those clauses which the local police had already found necessary or desirable to obtain, in special Acts, for the regulation of hackney carriages (or cabs). In 1889 the appropriate provisions of the 1847 Act were extended – with certain amendments – to omnibuses. These two Acts permitted the local authorities to impose a high standard of vehicle safety and to define routes and frequency of operation within their own boundaries. In addition, the Acts empowered the licensing authorities to make bye-laws to regulate the conduct of owners, drivers and conductors. These powers were, however, infrequently used. After 1930 a comprehensive new licensing system was set up by the Road Traffic Act, administered by an independent body, the Traffic Commissioners, who controlled vehicles, drivers and conductors, routes, fares and details of services for all public service vehicles.

In the 1920s both the tramway and the railway companies increasingly suffered from the competition of motor vehicles. Tramway receipts fell by just over 21 per cent in that decade[1] and railway revenues dropped by 17 per cent between 1923 and 1930.[2] However, it was the financial position of the railway companies which aroused most concern, as their capital had been a favoured mode of private investment, whereas, by 1920, the majority of tramways were owned by local authorities.[3] Sources antedating the Royal Commission on Transport of 1928 suggest that it was this competition which prompted the railways to obtain powers to own, operate or take financial interest in passenger-carrying motor transport (finally granted in August 1928). For example, K. G. Fenelon, writing in 1925, stated that 'the railways feel that the only effective reply to the challenge [of the development of road transport] is to be furnished by the provision of road services in conjunction with their railway system'.[4] In 1928 C. T. Brunner put the same point even more forcefully: 'the eagerness of the railways to obtain road powers seems to constitute a virtual admission that their own branch of transport is now antiquated and unsuitable in many cases for modern conditions'.[5]

The post-1930 literature attributes the quantity licensing provisions of the 1930 Road Traffic Act to two main causes: first, a belief that uncontrolled competition produces an unco-ordinated and wasteful transport system; and second, the combined pressure from railway and tram interests in an attempt to protect their own traffic, this pressure being exerted through their forceful evidence before the Royal Commission. C. E. R. Sherrington, for example, suggested in 1934 that while road competition led the railways to seek road powers it was uncontrolled competition leading to congestion and wasteful competition that initiated the quantity licensing restrictions.[6] Two years later D. N. Chester reiterated Sherrington's suggestion and argued that the 1930 Road Traffic Act was based on the belief that 'unfettered competition is certain to lead to an inefficient transport system'.[7] This idea was extended – to protect both railways and tramways, whose financial position was also deteriorating – and used to justify the control of omnibuses in competition with alternative forms of transport.

The more recent literature attributes the quantity licensing legislation to the same causes of wasteful competition and pressure. Philip Bagwell, for example, suggests that concern over the impact of motor transport on the railways led to the appointment of the Royal Commission on Transport 'to consider the co-ordination of all forms of transport'.[8] On the subject of wasteful competition, Barker and Savage comment, 'there was also wide agreement among those operators trying to provide regular services, as well as among a substantial section of the travelling public, that uncontrolled competition in road passenger transport was not in the public interest'.[9] Dyos and Aldcroft agree that unregulated competition was not producing the best results but argue that contemporary feeling in favour of regulation may not have been as unanimous as the report of the Royal Commission suggested.[10] The most contentious part of the 1930 Act's regulatory provisions has always been the route licensing sections. The intention here is to analyse the reasons for their introduction, and to examine both the economic rationale and the political influences that led to the enactment of this major piece of legislation.

As with the railways in the 1830s, the government's initial involvement in the road passenger industry arose out of a concern for public safety. However, the examination of safety requirements led, again as the railways had experienced, to a substantive review of other aspects – notably competition. It was concern for public safety which in the early 1920s provoked the first official investigation of the potential regulation of omnibuses. Concomitant with the fast growth of motor traffic after the Armistice was a rise in the number of fatal and non-fatal motor accidents. Official concern for public safety was aroused in 1920, when different pressure groups were seeking restrictions to contain this development. The most vociferous comments came from the lobby seeking regulation of all motor vehicles; they claimed that the growing number of vehicles on the streets, especially in London, was causing chaos, congestion and an increasing level of accidents. The omnibus, in particular, was heavily criticised for its threat to public safety, despite the fact that deaths and non-fatal injuries attributable to motor buses were rising at a slower rate than the growth of vehicles.[11]

Control of motor vehicles was difficult, however, since the existing laws were designed only to control the much more slow-moving horse-drawn forms of transport. Thus a special committee of the Ministry of Transport's Roads Department, the Taxation Committee, was created to examine the taxation and regulation of motor vehicles. The Ministry of Transport, since its inception in 1919, had had a pre-eminently railway administration. Both the first Minister, Sir Eric Geddes, and the Secretary, Sir Francis Dunnell, were former North Eastern Railway men.[12] The fact that a separate Roads Department existed at all was considered a victory for the roads lobby, who feared that, without it, the railway bias in the Ministry would seek only to strengthen and protect the railways at the expense of the increasingly competitive road industry. A consequence of this struggle for independence was that each department within the Ministry acted in a totally unco-ordinated fashion so far as policy developments in other modes of transport were concerned.

The question of omnibus licensing and regulation fell originally within the terms of reference of the Taxation Committee, which was under the chairmanship of Sir Henry Maybury, Director General of Roads. However, early in 1922, a departmental Committee on Hackney Vehicles – with greater local authority representation – was appointed specifically to look at this problem. Representation on the committee was divided between official representatives (two), motoring organisations (six) and local bodies (seven).[13] The terms of reference were quite explicit and referred solely to passenger-carrying vehicles.[14] The creation of this separate committee did not appear to have political implications: it was conceived during the office of Lloyd George's coalition, although it first met after Bonar Law had formed his Conservative government. Ideas of restrictive regulation at this time were not in line with either government's view and would have taken lengthy justification (as with the railways).[15] The non-party status of the committee reinforces the view that its primary concern was with road safety. The evidence before the Hackney Vehicle Committee and its recommendations must be examined first if we are to explain how the idea of quantity licensing regulation arose.

Successive governments in the 1920s claimed to recognise the need for legislative provisions for road transport, but their time was fully occupied with other measures. The only exception was the London Traffic Act of 1924, a hasty measure which attempted to relieve the city of the 'chaos' caused by the free market in road passenger transport. The London Traffic Bill relied heavily on the evidence and interim recommendations of the Hackney Vehicle Committee, although the Act was on the statute book long before the committee produced its own report. By this Act London became a special case and, for that reason, is not discussed here.

Renewed political and public pressure in 1927, in the form of private Bills before Parliament, stirred the Baldwin government into action. In 1928 a Royal Commission on Transport was appointed to examine the whole 'transport problem' after a final realisation that all transport modes needed to be considered together rather than in isolation by the different departments within the Ministry of Transport. The appointment of the Royal Commission marked the beginning of co-ordination between the internal departments of the Ministry; this is reflected in their evidence before the Royal Commission. This evidence, together with the Royal Commission's recommendations, is analysed in the second part of this article.

The reports and evidence of the Royal Commission and the departmental report have long been available in print but important additional sources of information are the files of both the Hackney Vehicle Committee and the Royal Commission (Ministry of Transport), and the Cabinet papers of the 1920s. These encourage a reinterpretation of the contemporary view that pressure from railway and tram interests was the original cause of restrictive regulation on omnibuses.

The evidence (I): the Hackney Vehicle Committee

The first meeting of the Hackney Vehicle Committee concentrated, initially, on safety considerations and the replies which Pool Godsell, secretary to the committee, had received from the various licensing authorities. He had asked them, in letters sent in July 1922, for their comments on 'the necessity for and method of control . . . from a public safety point of view' together with information 'as to the manner in which constraint . . . is exercised in the larger County Boroughs at the present time'. The discussions centred on the reply from Newcastle upon Tyne. This commented not only on the extent of public safety control but included the borough's opinion on possible regulation to ensure the adequate provision of 'public service':

> The public service extends to cover such questions as routes, fares, regularity and frequent service. The question at once arises whether these are matters for control except to quite a limited extent. Control is not associated with financial responsibility, but upon all these questions the financial position and stability of the carrier depends. The principles of control under this head need definition at an early stage.
>
> As suggestions, the following two points have been raised:
>
> (i) a regular service. This to prevent two things,
>
> (a) the with-holding of a reliable public traffic facility, and
> (b) irregular intervention in the working of routes by irresponsible carriers;
>
> (ii) a published scale of fares. This to prevent variable charges.

> Any proposal for limitations must be accompanied by some advantages to the carrier. The obligations laid on the carrier to supply and maintain a public service must be accompanied by corresponding rights of some sort.[16]

It was unanimously agreed by the members of the committee that some sort of regulation was desirable, but a mixed reception was given to the idea that a uniform standard such as 'certificate of fitness' should be enforced. For example, Sir Robert Fox, the Town Clerk of Leeds, argued, along familiar lines, that there would be no guarantee that the vehicle would be maintained in the state in which the test was passed. Arguments at the other extreme put forward the view that, unless some sort of national standard were set, the ridiculousness of the current licensing procedures might be perpetuated: for example, more stringent vehicle tests might be required by differing, yet adjacent, licensing authorities, and the contemporary system of control would not be improved. An example of this type of licensing problem was put before the committee:

> A motor omnibus requires at least two licences . . . registration as a motor car with a revenue licence and an omnibus licence which entitles it to ply for hire. I say 'at least two' because if it plies for hire in more than one urban district (or rural district having urban powers) it requires an extra licence for every such extra district. Thus, to take a simple case of a short route within my own knowledge, a motor omnibus running on a regular service, Birmingham–Stourbridge–Wolverhampton, has to have a licence to ply for hire in Birmingham, Halesowen, Lye and Wollescote, Stourbridge, Amblecote, Kinswinford, Seisdon and Wolverhampton. If it is running on a circular route and returns to Birmingham through Dudley, it also requires licences in Sedgley, Dudley, Tipton, Oldbury and Smethwick.[17]

The committee discussed various arguments for control but decided that a more thorough examination should be undertaken by a smaller group. A sub-committee was therefore set up in late October 1922, to examine possible forms of regulation under four headings: constructional requirements; regulations relating to the carriage and conduct of passengers (analogous to the bye-laws of railways and tramways); regulations relating to the condition of the omnibus (cleanliness, soundness and efficiency); and, lastly, regulations governing the use and operation of omnibuses (routes, services to be operated, and fares). The sub-committee consisted of six members, representing the vested interests involved, in addition to the chairman, Frank Pick (then joint assistant managing director of Underground Electric Railways Company of London (UERL) which owned the London General Omnibus Company (LGOC)).[18] It soon became clear that a full exploration of their remit would require consideration of the nature of the proposed licensing authorities: the terms of reference on the sub-committee were consequently extended to include the choice of licensing body.

The sub-committee examined evidence on the important question of who should exercise licensing powers. The following extracts illustrate the divergence of views presented:

Note of an interview with Sir Robert Fox, Town Clerk of Leeds, 4 December 1922:

> In the first place, he considered that it was desirable to reduce the number of licensing authorities and not to increase them, and he took strong objection to County Councils being given any licensing powers. . . . His suggestion was that the Licensing Authorities should be confined to the larger urban areas with a population limit for which there are precedents, such as the Education Act . . .

Resolution passed by the National Conference of the Commercial Users Association, and submitted to the Ministry of Transport in January 1923:

> That where a local authority is itself interested financially as the owner or lessee for a passenger transport undertaking, it shall not be the licensing authority for road transport service, but such licensing functions shall be exercised by an independent officer appointed by the Minister of Transport.

Extract from a draft scheme of 14 January 1923 submitted to the Ministry of Transport by United Automobile Services Ltd (operators in northern and eastern England):

> The Regulations made [for the use and operation of omnibuses] to be placed under the executive control of a Central Public Service Commission who shall delegate powers to four Area Commissions as follows:
>
> 1. England – north of Humber and Mersey.
> 2. England – Thames to Humber.
> 3. England – south of the Thames.
> 4. Scotland . . .[19]

The interesting aspect of this last extract is its similarity to the licensing authority provisions of the 1930 Road Traffic Act: yet, on the decision of a civil servant, the scheme was not brought before the sub-committee. This was probably because the whole scheme was considered inoperable, but there is no record of any other evidence being withheld from either the sub-committee or the main committee.

In April 1923 the sub-committee tentatively agreed to recommend that powers for the issue of hackney vehicle licences should be vested in county and county borough councils, together with those non-county borough, urban district and rural district councils with existing licensing powers and a population exceeding 10,000. These proposals would have reduced the number of licensing authorities from 1,175 to 880. However, by the time the first draft report was circulated to the main committee, the population limit had been revised upwards to 20,000, thus reducing the number of licensing authorities even further to 302. In a memorandum circulated with the draft report to the main committee in December, Frank Pick indicated that the choice of population limit had been something of a compromise:

> . . . the fewer the number of licensing authorities, the more effective in some important aspects will be the discharge of duties with regard to licensing because the concentration of work will enable much more efficient staffs to be employed. Yet, with regard to other of the duties of the licensing authorities, it may equally be said that the more widespread the licensing powers, the more effective will the control be for purely local purposes. Purely local purposes

should, however, be subservient to the broad interests of considerable districts and, therefore, not too much weight should be attached to local consideration. In choosing the 20,000 population standard for licensing, the sub-committee endeavoured to balance fairly the conflicting interests. While a compromise situation is always a weak one from the point of view of criticism, I think it will be admitted that in this country at least a genius for compromise has characterised political action.[20]

Having resolved the issue of who should act as the licensing authority, the sub-committee turned its attention to the type of licensing to be enforced. Safety legislation inevitably involved technical matters, and so the advice of the motor bus manufacturers was sought and examined. This involved a critical evaluation of dimensions of vehicles, suspensions, turning circles, and so on. And, as with the railways, the possible pressures on safety standards – cutting costs in response to the strain of competition – inevitably led to a consideration of the whole question of competition itself. Here the sub-committee and main committee were undoubtedly influenced by evidence submitted by both operators and licensing authorities. These argued that regulation to promote safety should be accompanied by benefits to the operators in compensation for the costs of compliance. In contrast to the evidence heard by the Royal Commission on Transport at the end of the decade, these submissions on the state of competition were neither uniform nor based on the predominant fallacy of the era – that 'unfair' and 'free' competition were synonymous. The Ministry of Transport's view was given by Pool Godsell (secretary to the committee):

> Then there is the question of competition and it is for consideration how far this question comes within the terms of reference to the Committee. The question is a very serious problem because in many cases there are big companies running passenger services to timetables and they run these vehicles throughout the day. A great many of the services which are in the public interest during certain hours of the day are not paying propositions, and the companies complain of unfair competition during the busy times from smaller vehicles by people who don't desire to serve the interests of the public at all. These people don't publish or run to any timetable – but they have the advantage of seeing the responsible Company's timetable and they run their vehicles five minutes ahead of the Company's service when to do so would be remunerative . . . . On the other hand fair competition is doubtless to some extent in the interests of the public as tending to avoid monopolies but on the other hand undue competition may tend to cause the competing services to become unremunerative with the result that all are withdrawn.[21]

He later extended his personal view:

> This question [regularity of service and fares] raises the further one of competition. It is contended with some justification on behalf of the undertakers that if they are required to run to a timetable they should be protected from unfair competition, in particular from persons running buses immediately in front of the undertakers' timetable times at peak hours and taking their passengers.
>
> It seems to me reasonable that they should be protected from such competition so long as they provide an adequate service, putting on additional buses when required, and that accord-

ingly persons should only be licensed in competition who also run to a suitable published timetable.[22]

The discussions led to the incorporation of route licensing regulations in the Hackney Vehicle Committee's report. These particular regulations were designed to limit competition on omnibus routes, to provide unremunerative routes by means of cross-subsidy and to give protection to existing operators from new entrants. They would have been consistent with economic rationale if there had been evidence of increasing returns to scale in the industry. Contemporary evidence, however, seems to suggest that the road passenger transport industry was characterised more by constant returns to scale, since both large and small operators coexisted.[23] It is with this background that the evidence before the Hackney Vehicle Committee on the subject of competition should be reviewed. The incorporation of the restrictive aspects of control on the omnibus and motor charabanc industry was motivated entirely by political influences.

It is worth considering in this context the evidence to the Hackney Vehicle Committee of the only two bodies which dissented from the view that the restriction of competition was desirable. Rickards (a motor coach company) presented the evidence for the Motor Trade Association (the motor charabanc trade association). They accepted that some form of fare regulation might be necessary because, in the absence of sufficient competition, fares might be 'unnecessarily' high. However, they felt that, in general, on most routes – London to Brighton was given as an example – competition ensured that fares were not unreasonable and restrictions on competition, other than on fares, would be undesirable.[24]

The other dissentient was a member of the sub-committee, Sidney Straker, who, during Rees Jeffrey's absence, was the substitute representative of the Society of Motor Manufacturers and Traders (SMMT). He was not only involved in the motor manufacturing industry but was also active in the bus world – in partnership with E. H. Bayley he had started the first petrol bus service in 1899, with his own engine design. On receipt of the first draft of the sub-committee's report, he reflected the manufacturers' viewpoint by insisting that the road passenger industry should remain competitive for both operators and manufacturers. His position merits quotation at length:

> The inevitable consequences of granting specifically to any licensing authority powers which will confer upon any Company or group of Companies a virtual public road passenger franchise must be in the nature of a monopoly, which, in my view, cannot be carried on in the public interest. That there are very strong and cogent reasons for the development of public service road vehicles on the lines suggested in the Report, one cannot deny. At the same time such a policy, if sanctioned by the legislature, cannot but end, sooner or later, in the operation of all passenger road services throughout the country by a limited number of Companies working together under territorial arrangements, each of them exercising on the respective licensing authorities an influence indirect, but no less real, which must make it virtually impossible for

any competitor to operate anywhere within such territory. The powers of such Companies will affect directly or indirectly the manufacture of the vehicles and their parts and the retail motor trade and the tendency undoubtedly must be to create ultimately groups of Companies controlling not only road services but the whole service of supplies necessary for the operation of the services . . .

Although the safety of the public and the conditions of the road must involve public control as regards structural requirements of public service vehicles, the speed and arrangements for vehicles and other similar considerations, I would venture to suggest that the powers given to licensing authorities should be governed by no more than these two considerations . . .

Competition between manufacturers is no less important from the point of view of progress in efficiency and design than the element of competition is in the services which are given to the public, and from this point of view alone it would be undesirable to pursue a policy which would tend to confine the manufacture of public service vehicles to one or two concerns . . .

It is true that the enterprise of manufacturers and the ambition of private individuals is placing upon the streets of London so-called 'pirates' whose advent is naturally welcomed neither by the Underground Railways nor by the LGOC. It is stated, with truth no doubt, that the operations of these rival concerns cater particularly for the cream and rob existing undertakings of part of the rewards of their past enterprise and place them temporarily or permanently less able to fill the requirements of the public on less remunerative routes. Such a condition of affairs may seem inequitable and sometimes anomalous but it is surely not open to question that the public in the long run is the gainer and not the loser and that the commercial struggle always present or prospective leads to efficiency, economy and progress in the best sense of the words . . . . The pioneer, often anticipating a demand, creates the supply, trusting to the revenue of the future.[25]

This extract illustrates how strongly Straker felt about the proposed restrictions on competition, as well as representing a challenge to the interests of Frank Pick. It could be argued that the granting of a quasi-monopoly for operators would not be in the interests of the motor manufacturers, since the total demand for vehicles would be reduced thereby. This is certainly one possible interpretation of Straker's strong reaction. Rees Jeffreys held the same view.[26] In addition, it should be noted that Straker was arguing strongly for a competitive motor industry, his concern being that a limited number of operators might lead to monopoly behaviour in the manufacturing sector. On the sub-committee he was alone in this view, and, after consideration of the memorandum, the majority decision was to follow the original path and recommend some form of quantity licensing. Straker dissociated himself from the restrictive sections of the sub-committee's draft report and awaited further discussion in the main committee. This, however, subsequently endorsed the majority decision of its sub-committee.

Straker's memorandum is interesting for three further reasons. First, it illustrates the influence of selling tactics and the persuasive role of the manufacturers in the emergence of the 'pirates' on the streets of London at the time. Second, his support for the construction and maintenance sections explains the willingness of vehicle manufacturers (whom he represented through the SMMT) to work to the new specifications without complaint. Lastly the memorandum predicted accurately the actual outcome of quantity licensing as implemented by the 1930 Road Traffic Act in terms of the reduction in the numbers of operators and the scope of their operations.

By the end of 1923 the departmental committee was under pressure from both central government and the local authorities to publish its report. By then, the sub-committee had tentatively agreed who should exercise licensing powers, and the various technical matters had been discussed, so that specific constructional and maintenance requirements could be issued. An interim report of the sub-committee (dated 15 November 1923) was circulated to the main committee for consideration. Shortly afterwards, the general election of 6 December 1923 returned a minority Labour government. As a consequence, different political priorities caused the committee's work to be delayed for six months. Its meetings were not resumed until the late summer of 1924. The main committee's report was eventually completed and signed on 25 May 1925. It was based on the sub-committee's report, and there were further recommendations dealing with Scotland, London, and the effect of omnibus competition on tramways. Although this too was called an interim report, it was the principal report of the Hackney Vehicle Committee. The recommendations regarding omnibus and tramway competition deserve special mention because, although tramway interests gave evidence at an early stage, the potential harm to trams from the growth of bus services was not recognised at the end of 1923 when the sub-committee first examined witnesses. However, the number of submissions to the sub-committee from tramway interests increased from the beginning of 1924, and led the sub-committee to pay more attention to the problem. Its discussion led to the inclusion of a passage in the main committee's report which is particularly interesting when compared with the view of the Royal Commission four years later:

> . . . There would seem to be occasions on which some form of control of motor omnibus fares to protect tramway interest would be justified. For instance, such a step would appear permissible where the total traffic to be carried locally along the tramway route is justified not so much by the volume of local traffic along that route as by the fact that the omnibus service provides for traffic originating or terminating beyond the tramway route. It is desirable that passengers starting their journey outside the tramway area should not have to change vehicles when they reach the tramway route and it is hoped that, if some measure of protection is given to the tramway undertakings in borough and urban districts, objection will not be raised to the provision of adequate omnibus services to and from such built-up centres and the surrounding rural area which are in need of facilities for traffic movement.
>
> The Sub-Committee therefore suggest that there can be no objection to the practice which is already being followed in certain instances, of fixing a minimum fare to be charged for any journeys on that part of the omnibus route which coincides with the tramway route, provided that it is applied in a reasonable manner. The minimum fare to be charged locally upon the omnibuses for journeys along the tramway route should not be less than the throughout fare

on the trams for that portion of the tramway route along which the omnibus runs; at the same time reasonable fares should be provided for traffic which overlaps the tramway route and which travels partly on what is purely an omnibus and tramway route.[27]

Although tramway competition was discussed at some length by the committee, the question of coach and railway competition was not raised. Likewise, the complaint voiced frequently in the latter part of the 1920s, that omnibuses and coaches did not contribute sufficiently to road costs, was not mentioned.

The evidence (II): the Royal Commission on Transport

No further action was taken on the regulation of the road passenger industry until February 1927, when the Conservative Cabinet agreed to circulate a draft Traffic Bill (based on the interim report of 1925). The intention was 'to negotiate with those authorities and interests; and in due course to report the outcome of the negotiations to the Home Affairs Committee with a view to a decision being reached later in the year as to the introduction of the Bill'.[28] While this was in progress a Royal Commission on Transport was established in response to the dual pressures of strong public opinion and the railways' decision to seek powers to convey passengers by road. Under the chairmanship of Sir Arthur Griffith Boscawen, it was given the following terms of reference:

> To take into consideration the problems arising out of the growth of road traffic and, with a view to securing the employment of the available means of transport in Great Britain (including transport by sea coastwise and by ferries) to the greatest public advantage, to consider and report what measures, if any, should be adopted for their better regulation and control, and, so far as is desirable in the public interest, to promote their co-ordinated working and development.[29]

Later in 1928 Viscount Cecil of Chelwood introduced a Road Vehicle Regulation Bill in the House of Lords. The Minister of Transport, Colonel Ashley, reported to the Cabinet:

> I subsequently referred the question of an interim report on the subjects dealt with in Viscount Cecil's Bill to the Chairman of the Royal Commission on Transport, who has replied, 'The Commission proposes . . . an interim report dealing more particularly with the matters covered by the Regulation of Road Vehicles Bill and by part (1) of the draft Road Traffic Bill before Parliament adjourns in the summer.'[30]

The Conservative government promised to promote legislation dealing with road traffic after the submission of the Royal Commission's report if it were returned to power after the general election planned for 30 May 1929. In the event a Labour government was returned. However, Herbert Morrison, the new Minister of Transport, persuaded the Cabinet to give a Traffic Bill priority, and the second report of the Royal Commission, published in October 1929, formed the basis of the legislative treatment of public service vehicles.

In its second report the Royal Commission considered the two most contentious issues in the regulation of public service vehicles: first, the problem of who would administer any proposed legislation, and, second, the problem of competition within the industry and the best means of regulating it in order to achieve the aim of co-ordination.

In considering who should exercise the licensing powers, the Royal Commission was concerned that the contemporary licensing system allowed the local authorities to favour their own public service vehicles. Its dilemma was the same as that of the departmental committee – how to exercise a uniform system of control coupled with sufficient flexibility to reflect purely local requirements. Initially it was decided that the licensing regulations would be administered by a Traffic Board appointed in each of the new Traffic Areas which would be created. Each Traffic Board was to consist of an independent chairman, nominated by the Minister of Transport, and representatives of all the local authorities in the area which, under the scheme of the previous draft Traffic Bill, would have been licensing authorities.

However, in September 1929 the chairman, Sir Arthur Boscawen, circulated the following note to the members of the Royal Commission, with a revised version of the recommendations for licensing authorities:

> *Note by Chairman.* In forwarding the enclosed alternative scheme in lieu of our present recommendation, I am fully aware that we all (including myself) agreed to the recommendation which appears in the printed draft Report, but in thinking matters over during the holidays I have not felt happy about it for the following reasons:
>
> We propose to set up a number of new and very cumbrous local authorities. These bodies will either be unwieldy in size or else can only be reduced to proper proportions by grouping several local authorities together for the purpose of representation, a plan to which many local authorities will have grave objections. Our idea was to preserve a certain amount of local control of licensing, but this is inadequately done, and moreover does not entirely remove the objection to bodies themselves interested in transport being licensing authorities. I have reason to believe that the Government will not accept this recommendation, and I am afraid it will be criticised in a hostile spirit, which will be unfortunate after the splendid reception which has been given to our first Report. I am proposing therefore, in this alternative scheme, the plan of a single Commissioner in each area, which was suggested to us by several witnesses. At the same time I leave great powers of control as to routes, streets, etc., to the local authorities. Though I do not know that the Government will accept this scheme, I think they are far more likely to do so than they are to accept our present proposal, since I know they have a strong objection to setting up new *ad hoc* local authorities.
>
> I put this forward, however, merely for consideration and do not propose to press it if my colleagues are not in favour of it, but I wish the Commission to have an opportunity of reconsidering the whole plan.[31]

Although the exact wording suggested by Boscawen was not adhered to, the principle of Traffic Commissioners rather than Traffic Boards was accepted.

The witnesses who proposed the idea of area commissioners were John Cliff, Assistant General Secretary of the Transport and General Workers' Union, and

Richard Howley, who represented the London and Provincial Omnibus Owners' Association. The proposals, as the chairman's note indicates, found support in the Ministry of Transport. H. H. Piggot, Principal Assistant Secretary in the Roads Department, agreed that better control would be achieved if there were 'area commissions for the granting of licences . . . and in such matters as the grant or refusal of a licence on the ground of sufficiency of traffic or that it was not in the public interest to increase traffic'.[32] Sir Henry Maybury, Director General of the Roads Department, who had chaired the departmental committee, confirmed in his evidence to the Royal Commission that he thought the appointment of area commissioners could be the solution. Obviously enough, the local authorities all pleaded against their licensing powers being withdrawn. However, the Royal Commission was swayed by Cliff's suggestion, particularly as he represented one of the largest unions in the industry, in addition to its having the potential support of the government.

The issue of 'unfair' or 'unjust' competition was examined in two parts: first, the practice of 'creaming off' traffic, and, second, the effect of competing modes of transport. So far as the former was concerned, the commission thought that the existence of unlicensed vehicles, even in those regions where the licensing provisions had been enacted, often allowed unlicensed operators to make a profit by 'creaming off' the traffic. It was inferred that the practice of 'creaming off' traffic inhibited the regular operators from covering the less remunerative routes, thus decreasing the source of revenue available for cross-subsidisation. The 'creaming off' of traffic was essentially a short-stage phenomenon: the term was applied to buses that operated only on profitable routes at profitable times and were withdrawn when the service was likely to be unremunerative. The 'pirates' – the contemporary term for such operators – competed both with other buses and with tramways. This aspect of competition had been given a full hearing before the departmental committee, and not much was added in the evidence tendered to the Royal Commission. The commission appears to have been influenced on this matter by the evidence of Earl Russell, who believed the solution lay in balancing the elimination of wasteful competition against protecting the public from a potentially oppressive monopoly. Another factor was the way in which policy was being developed in other parts of the world. This was illustrated retrospectively by Sir Arthur Boscawen in a memorandum written in the preparation of the commission's final report:

> . . . we have already adopted [the policy of controlled monopoly] in the case of public service passenger traffic on roads . . . . This policy of controlled monopoly is gradually being adopted all over the world and particularly in America; for example, the Supreme Court of the State of Pennsylvania recently laid it down as follows:
>
> 'unrestricted competition in such utilities has been, by experience, definitely shown to be ultimately unwholesome for the community. The invariable rule in such cases, in companies of this character, is that in addition to the cutting and destruction of rates and other practices entirely outside the range of sound business, one company is absorbed, and the surviving

company recoups its loss through excessive charges, at the expense of an unprotected public . . . . If the power to regulate does not include the power to prevent unrestricted competition then much of the beneficial effect . . . is lost. Unrestricted competition and regulation are inconsistent . . . .'[33]

The general agreement with this memorandum suggests that the commission felt that the situation in Pennsylvania corresponded closely with that in Great Britain.

The separate issue of competition between the different modes of transport was examined in depth by the commission, and much wider evidence was sought than that dealt with by the departmental committee. The principal objection expressed by the railways and trams to road transport competition was that the industry's charges were set artificially low. Thus 'unfair' competition was created because road transport did not contribute sufficient tax to pay for its use of the public highway. In their evidence to the Royal Commission the railways maintained that 'The economic costs of rail transport are entirely borne by rail users, whereas, in the case of road transport, the users bear only a portion of the corresponding costs'.[34] The railways' claim of unfair treatment was not new. Indeed, even before the appointment of the Royal Commission it was a familiar argument on which earlier literature had commented, often adversely.[35] The view was sharply contested by Howley, who wrote in his evidence:

> Sir Josiah Stamp in his evidence referred more than once to the disability under which the railways lay in having to bear the cost of the maintenance of their way and works. For the year 1927 the cost of maintaining the way and works of the railways of Great Britain amounted to £22,700,000, and the total traffic receipts to some £200,000,000. There is, therefore, but little difference between the percentage of the revenue contributed by omnibus owners in the form of taxation, which is available for the repair and maintenance of the roads, and the percentage of the railway revenue utilised in the maintenance of their way and works. In the case of the railways they have the advantage of working their traffic over a private right of way on which they can do as they please without interference, while omnibuses are only one type of many vehicles using the roads.[36]

The motor coach section of road transport was briefly considered by the Royal Commission. The discussion was instigated by the railway companies, who commented:

> The running of motor coaches over long distances is the most recent development in passenger transport, both for regular services and for special trips. The competition set up by this type of service with the railway service is evident from the official timetable issued by the Motor Transport and Hirers' Association, but this does not contain by any means particulars of the whole of the services known to be operated. Within the period of about two years within which this section of transport has sought to establish itself, a large number of regular daily motor coach services have come into existence, some operating over routes as long as 260 miles (Newcastle and London), while efforts are being made to establish night services between important industrial centres.

> Owing to their favourable economic position, the fares charged are generally much less than the standard railway fares between the same points, and it would appear from the amount of capital which is being attracted to this section of road transport, that a substantial profit is being made on this level of fares.[37]

However, on cross-examination the railways had nothing more to add. Hence either they were not yet feeling this form of competition seriously (although significant numbers of coaches must have been running parallel to the railways) or they had decided that more was to be gained from making a fuss about the competition on local routes.

After the Royal Commission had presented its second interim report, which dealt with the regulation of public service vehicles, it concentrated on the question of co-ordination. The private Acts of 1928, enabling the railway companies to take up to a 50 per cent interest in motor bus companies, received the royal assent before the submission of the second report. The Royal Commission regarded these powers as promoting considerable co-ordination between road and rail through the acquisition by railways of substantial interests in road service organisations. Only one piece of evidence, given by Sir Josiah Stamp in December 1929 on behalf of the railway companies, suggested that the railways' motive in promoting the private Acts was co-ordination and a better return for shareholders. The cross-examination of this witness did not reveal any awareness that the railways might have been 'cutting their own throats'. The railway companies' position was more likely to have been influenced by knowledge of the great profits which had accrued to the Underground group in London when it had merged with the LGOC in 1912. All the subsequent evidence suggested that the railways companies' main interest was to maximise the bus companies' profits and so increase their income from this source rather than to enhance co-ordination as such.

The Royal Commission thus made one important recommendation that differed from those of the Hackney Vehicles Committee: the division of the country into thirteen (later extended to fourteen) Traffic Areas administered by an independent Traffic Commissioner appointed by the Minister of Transport. Apart from this concept of area commissioners, the Royal Commission did not add much to the regulatory recommendations of the departmental committee. This was partly due to its terms of reference but was occasioned more by its preoccupation, revealed in the final report, with co-ordination.

Conclusion

Whereas railway and tram pressure, as demonstrated in evidence before the Royal Commission, is popularly taken to have been the reason for the original regulation of road passenger vehicles, the historical evidence is clearly to the contrary. The 1930 Act stemmed from concern in the early 1920s for public safety only. As it had done with the railways in the previous century, government intervened to reduce accident levels; but intervention on these grounds led on to further examination and eventual control of other aspects of the industry.

The Hackney Vehicle Committee, convened in 1922, played a crucial role in the development of the omnibus industry. The London Traffic Act of 1924 relied heavily on the content of the committee's draft report, and the final form of the Hackney Vehicle Committee's report laid the foundations of the Ministry of Transport's evidence before the Royal Commission. The interesting aspect of this committee's performance was the considerable contribution made by the sub-committee. Chaired by Frank Pick, then joint assistant managing director of UERL, which had a controlling interest in the London buses, the sub-committee primarily represented parties which would benefit substantially from the implementation of quantity licensing. Indeed, it was during one of the sub-committee's meetings that quantity licensing was first raised. It was suggested then that if additional safety standards were to be sought from operators, then in all 'fairness' they should be compensated with some sort of protection on their routes. The point was taken up with alacrity. This is not to suggest that members of the sub-committee had to be persuaded to concur with the view of their chairman. Nevertheless, the organisation Frank Pick represented stood to gain considerably from the proposal. In fairness to the traditional, impartial role of the official investigator, interest of this kind should always be made clear. In addition it should be remembered that all the members of the committee were initially committed to control of the industry: the purpose of their inquiry was to decide the scope and form of such regulation, and they would, of course, have been particularly open to suggestions in this sphere. The way in which the sub-committee recommended regulation which favoured the existing operators directly may not have been entirely its fault: the composition of the main committee necessarily excluded representatives of the small independent operators (who were not organised) and the general public. The public, although sometimes suffering irregular services, would undoubtedly have benefited from the wider choice of services under the unregulated system at lower fares than might otherwise have been offered. Nevertheless the fact that regulation was accepted, in principle, as early as 1922 should not make it surprising that eight years later the Road Traffic Act was a measure that substantially protected the omnibus operator. More surprising was the way in which this was claimed to be 'in the public interest'!

So far as omnibus licensing was concerned, the Royal Commission on Transport added very little in its bird's eye view of the transport sector. It is from the Royal Commission that the popular view of the origin of regulation derives. The evidence before the commission suggests that both the railways and the trams were beginning to feel the pressure from road competition in 1927 and that it was becoming more intense. The commission provided a forum for many spurious arguments to be aired. The most interesting from the quantity licensing point of view were the way in which regulation, sought to protect railways and trams, was justified, first, by the claim that vehicles did not 'pay their way' and, second, by the enormous fuss made about 'unfair' competition. Since the Royal Commission heard witnesses from all parts of the transport sector, the subject of competition had a much wider hearing than before the departmental committee, although not much change resulted. As with the departmental committee, only the views of organised pressure groups were heard. Dyos and Aldcroft[38] suggest this could mean that the unanimity of opinion in favour of the restriction of competition was overstated. No real evidence was put before the Royal Commission, as with the departmental committee, to justify the quantity licensing subsequently incorporated in its second report and which formed the basis of the Road Traffic Act. Of course, railway and tram pressure had an influence, and their evidence before the Royal Commission probably led to the inclusion in the Act of their right to object to new routes proposed before the Traffic Commissioners. Indeed, increasing rail and tram pressure, together with the concern about safety, may have been the reason which persuaded the government to give priority to a Traffic Bill in 1929.[39] It is worthy of note that the chairman of the Royal Commission – as with Frank Pick on the sub-committee of the Hackney Vehicle Committee – made a personal contribution that has left its mark on legislation by his proposal for the particular Traffic Commissioner system.

Hence, the early 1920s' discussions on the safety aspects of road passenger industry were crucial to the development of the regulation incorporated in the 1930 Road Traffic Act. This investigation antedated the strong railway and tram pressure which is popularly taken as the *original* reason for the government's intervention in the industry. The most remarkable aspect of the 1930 quantity licensing legislation is the way in which it lasted, despite the faulty premises underpinning it, almost without change for fifty years.

Notes

1 D. L. Munby (ed.), *Inland Transport Statistics, Great Britain, 1900–1970*, I (1978), table B8.1.

2 D. N. Chester, *The Public Control of the Passenger Transport Industry* (1936), p. 66.

3

1920	*Local authorities*	*Private companies*
Capital expenditure (£ '000)	2,448	260
Passenger receipts (£ '000)	25,542	6,064
Passenger journeys ('000)	3,848,494	821,423
Vehicles	10,802	3,020
Vehicle miles ('000)	277,892	67,262

Source. Munby, *op. cit.*, tables B3.1, B8.1, B6.1, B11.1, B12.1.

4 K. G. Fenelon, *The Economics of Road Transport* (1925), chapter XVI.

5 C. T. Brunner, *The Problem of Motor Transport* (1928), p. 171.

6 C. E. R. Sherrington, *A Hundred Years of Inland Transport* (1934), chapter XI.

7 Chester, *op. cit.*, chapter VI. See also G. Walker, *Road and Rail* (1942).

8 P. S. Bagwell, *The Transport Revolution since 1770* (1974), p. 261.

9 T. C. Barker and C. I. Savage, *An Economic History of Transport in Britain* (1974), p. 192.

10 H. J. Dyos and D. H. Aldcroft *British Transport: an Economic Survey from the Seventeenth Century to the Twentieth* (1969), Pelican edition, p. 382.

11

	1918	*1919*	*1920*
Accidents caused by the motor omnibus in the metropolitan area:			

Fatal	121	136	80
Non-fatal	1,644	1,953	1,583
Motor omnibuses licensed in the metropolitan area	2,277	3,314	3,365

Source. London and Home Counties Traffic Advisory Committee, *Report on Street Accidents* (1927); Munby, *op. cit.*, table C10.1.

12 Writing about the establishment of the Ministry, Rees Jeffreys said, 'Many of the principal officials were men of railway experience, training and mentality. The chief exception was the head of the Roads Department – Sir Henry Maybury – who was appointed Director-General of Roads. For a few years he was given opportunities and used them constructively to reshape road policy and to make road history.' *The King's Highway* (1949), p. 32.

13 The official representatives were Sir Henry Maybury (chairman) and F. L. D. Elliot, Scotland Yard (police authorities). Motoring organisations were represented by Sir Thomas Berridge (RAC), who died in October 1924 and was not replaced; Sir Stenson Cook (AA and Motor Club); W. Rees Jeffreys (SMMT), who was abroad in 1922 and was deputised for by Sidney Straker until his resignation in October 1924, when A. Hacking became the SMMT representative; Frank Pick (London and Provincial Omnibus Owners' Association); E. S. Shrapnell-Smith (Commercial Motor Users' Association); and R. J. Howley (provincial charabanc interests). Local interests were represented by F. H. Berrymans (County Councils' Association); Sir Robert Fox, town clerk of Leeds (County Boroughs' Association), succeeded by H. A. Pritchard, town clerk of Leicester; Sir Walter Nicholas (Urban District Councils' Association); Seymour Williams (Rural District Councils' Association); A. J. Asher (Association of County Councils of Scotland); A. Grierson, town clerk of Edinburgh (Convention of Royal Boroughs); and G. W. Tindall (Royal Agricultural Society). There was also a representative from the Ministry of Health.

14 'To consider existing legislation and practice in connection with the use, construction and regulation of road vehicles (other than tramcars and trolley vehicles) employed for the purpose of carrying passengers for reward and to report thereon.'

15 The regulation of the railways was justified, at length, before Parliament in 1919 by an embarrassed Sir Eric Geddes, who conceded that it was a 'necessary evil'. Rees Jeffreys, *op. cit.*, p. 86.

16 Ministry of Transport Departmental Committee on the Licensing and Regulation of Hackney Carriages, MT 33/29, Pt 1, P.R.O.

17 Internal Ministry of Transport minute, 1 August 1922, MT 33/29, Pt 1, P.R.O.

18 The members of the sub-committee were Pick, Elliot, Rees Jeffreys (Straker), Howley, Berrimans and Nicholas. In addition J. H. Watson, Chief Constable's Office, Bristol, was appointed on 21 November 1922.

19 MT 33/29, Pt 2, P.R.O.

20 Memorandum, 7 December 1923, MT 33/29, Pt 4, P.R.O.

21 Godsell's evidence, 26 May 1922, MT 33/29 RV/HV/3, P.R.O.

22 Evidence, 7 July 1922, MT 33/29 RV/HV/5. P.R.O.

23 There were no formal returns of fleet ownership before the 1930 Act was implemented. The first reports of the Traffic Commissioners, however, indicated the nature of the industry just before the Act was implemented. The Northern Area Commissioner gave the following breakdown in the *First Annual Report of the Traffic Commissioners* (1 January 1931–31 March 1932):

No of vehicle licences held	*No. of operators*
1	174
1–5	216
6–10	36
11–20	19
20–100	13
100+	4
	462

In addition it was noted that 84 per cent of operators owned fewer than five vehicles and the four largest operators accounted for 40 per cent of valid licences.

24 Submitted evidence MT 33/29 RV/HV/23, P.R.O.

25 Memorandum, June 1923, MT 33/29, Pt 3, P.R.O.

26 Rees Jeffreys, *op. cit.*, p. 211.

27 *First Interim Report of the Departmental Committee on Hackney Vehicles*, 1925, para. 15.

28 Cabinet Conclusions, 13 (27), 23 February 1927, P.R.O.

29 Terms of Reference, Royal Commission on Transport, 1928, in P.P. 1929–30, XVII, Cmd 3416.

30 Cabinet memorandum, 17 January 1929, CAB 24/201, P.R.O.

31 Boscawen–Commissioners, 17 September 1929, Ministry of Transport: Royal Commission on Transport, Second Interim Report: the Licensing of Public Service Vehicles, MT 42/77, P.R.O.

32 *Minutes of Evidence taken before the Royal Commission on Transport* (3 vols, 1928–30), I, q. 377.

33 Memorandum, 10 October 1930, Ministry of Transport: Royal Commission on Transport: Third Report, MT 42/78, P.R.O.

34 *Minutes of Evidence taken before the Royal Commission on Transport*, I, Memorandum No. 4 (Sir Josiah Stamp), para. 29. Stamp was President of the Executive of the LMS from 1926 (also chairman from 1927) until his death in an air raid in 1941.

35 E.g. Brunner, *op. cit.*, p. 172.

36 *Minutes of Evidence taken before the Royal Commission on Transport*, II, Memorandum No. 17 (Howley), para. 12.

37 Stamp's Memorandum, *cit.*, para. 39.

38 Dyos and Aldcroft, *op. cit.*, p. 382.

39 Bagwell, *op. cit.*, p. 261.

8 Steaming through New England with Locomobile

L. J. ANDREW VILLALON AND JAMES M. LAUX

COMMENTS about mechanized mass production as a unique American contribution to industrial development are as commonplace as they are misleading. Misleading because they ignore earlier European examples such as printing from movable type, shipbuilding in seventeenth-century Holland, the mechanization of textile manufacturing in Britain in the late eighteenth century, musket production in France about the same time, quantity output of pulley blocks for the Royal Navy during the Napoleonic Wars, and efforts in various nineteenth-century European cities at mechanized bread baking. The common feature in all these cases is that the manufacturer perceived a very large market for identical copies of the same product.

On the heels of these precedents, Americans seem to have done more than others with mechanized mass production in the nineteenth and twentieth centuries, especially with metal articles such as firearms, sewing machines, typewriters, and automobiles. To typify these achievements Henry Ford and the Model T, introduced in October 1908, are usually cited. One cannot deny the accomplishments of Ford, his associate James Couzens, and their engineers, but several other firms in the American automobile industry perceived a mass market and made thousands of cars for it before Ford did. The Buick 10, a small and cheap four-cylinder car offered first in 1907, found a big market before Ford's T. Olds from 1902 and Cadillac from 1903 produced thousands of cars annually while Ford was having problems starting his firm. Even earlier, the Electric Vehicle Company had proposed to have 1,600 of its heavy and expensive electric cars built by the Pope bicycle and automobile factory in Hartford in 1899–1900. This scheme failed because the machines were faulty and the market wilted. But a demand for lightweight and inexpensive cars did exist. Neither Olds nor Buick nor Ford first demonstrated this in the United States; the Locomobile

Company of America did, with a small steam car of which it sold some 5,200 from 1899 to 1903. By this performance Locomobile illuminated the possibilities and made it easier for the rest. Sprouted in the Boston region but rooted in Bridgeport, Locomobile also reminds us of the New England beginnings of the American automobile industry.

EARLY STEAMERS IN BOSTON

The Locomobile story begins in the late 1890s in the Boston region with three Yankee tinkerers: George E. Whitney and the twins F. O. and F. E. Stanley. George Eli Whitney was born about 1862, attended the Massachusetts Institute of Technology for a time, and then worked in machine shops and engaged in the manufacture of small marine engines in the 1880s and 1890s. He began building steam-powered carriages in East Boston in 1895–6.[1] His first weighed only about 700lb fully loaded and although later Whitney steamers were heavier this prototype set the standard for other New England steam cars – light in weight and simple in mechanism – in contrast to most European steamers which tended toward massiveness. Whitney made some half dozen more steamers in 1897–8 and organized the Whitney Motor Wagon Company in 1897 to manufacture them in quantity. This enterprise did not succeed. It appears that Whitney lacked both capital and production experience. A grand nephew of Eli Whitney of cotton gin fame, he cast himself in the role of inventor, not businessman. In 1899 he travelled to England and France with one of his cars, aiming to sell a licence to a manufacturer there. Many years later Whitney claimed he met an American car manufacturer in Paris and made a sale,[2] but before pursuing this we must examine some other elements in the steam car story.

The Stanley brothers came from Maine where they were born in 1849. Perfectly fitting the stereotype of the eccentric Yankee inventor, F. E. Stanley in 1875 began to produce photographic dry plates in Lewiston. As this enterprise prospered F. O. Stanley joined the business and in 1888 they moved it closer to the market, locating it in the Boston suburb of Watertown, with a Newton post office address. (Many writers have mistakenly assumed that the factory itself was sited in Newton.) In 1896 F. E. Stanley saw an early automobile – it is not clear whether it was steam- or petrol-powered – and challenged himself to make a better one. He aimed at a weight of some 600lb so as to achieve rapid speeds and to use the flimsy bicycle-type pneumatic tyres of the day. But the Stanleys were not equipped to make many of the parts themselves and they had to buy most of them from specialist shops in the region. Their first steamer may have operated late in 1897. It raised little stir and the brothers went on to develop a new model. It used an engine manufactured by the Penny Machine Shop of Mechanic Falls, Maine, weighing just 32½lb. The steam boiler, frame, suspension, chain transmission, and general lines of the Stanley closely resembled the Whitney car but it weighed less, somewhat under 600lb loaded.[3]

When the Mechanics Fair in Boston opened in October 1898 it exhibited four automobiles. Two were electric, one offered by the Pope Company of Hartford, soon to become a major producer under the name of Electric Vehicle Company, and the other by Andrew L. Riker of New York City, ultimately a key figure in the present narrative. Another was a petrol-powered tricycle of which the French manufacturer, De Dion-Bouton, had sold thousands in Europe, and finally one operated by steam, but it was neither a Whitney nor a Stanley. Some days after the opening a Whitney carriage appeared. Then, for the parade on 9 November from the Mechanics Building to Charles River Park for races and other activities, F. E. Stanley showed up in his machine. He did not take part in the races but did demonstrate his car in an exhibition spin. His time for two miles, 5 minutes 19 seconds, was comparable to the 1,200lb Whitney and the French tricycle. The Stanley vehicle did win the hill climbing event, going up a 36½ per cent gradient without trouble.[4]

The Stanley brothers decided to take advantage of public enthusiasm aroused by the exhibition and prepared to manufacture a batch of their steamers, perhaps 100 of them. The Mason Regulator Co. of Boston reported in December 1898 that it was making the engines for these cars and two months later the Stanleys said they had received orders for 85 cars.[5] To undertake this new activity the Stanleys moved into a former bicycle factory adjacent to their photographic business in Watertown. The financial means and reputation as serious businessmen they had gained from the photographic enterprise appear as crucial elements in their success when contrasted with Whitney's failure to begin quantity production. They could order 100 sets of parts for a new and untried contraption and be taken seriously.

The Stanley steamer at this point employed a two-cylinder, 3½hp. engine with steam generated by a 14-inch boiler in which the heat rose through 298 small copper tubes. A petrol burner raised steam in this boiler. A delicate device, its fuel was kept under about 20lb pressure with a hand pump. The water tank held some 12–14 gallons, enough for a 15-mile trip. A chain transmitted power from the engine to a differential on the split rear axle. The frame was of bicycle tubing with a pair of elliptical springs in the rear and one transversely across the front. A tiller controlled the steering and the wire spoke bicycle-type wheels had two-inch tyres.[6]

That the Stanleys late in 1898 undertook to manufacture up to 100 cars was almost unprecedented in the United States. There were only a few other widely scattered automobile makers at this point – in the mid-west Alexander Winton was the largest with an output of 22 in 1898 – but only the Pope Company made more than a few dozen (electric) cars in this year. Another basic decision of the Stanleys, to make small, lightweight, and inexpensive cars, also set an important pattern for the earliest period of American motor car manufacturing.

George Whitney also tried again to get into production, in 1899 licensing a firm located in Portland, Maine, and Lawrence, Mass., that made shoe manufacturing equipment to construct steamers on his designs. This move brought some confusion, however, because his licensee was the Stanley Manufacturing Company, operated by Frank F. Stanley. Although this concern did not make many cars and later they received the name McKay, two Stanley firms making similar steam cars at almost the same time in almost the same place do muddy the waters for the historian, not to mention contemporaries.[7]

WALKER AND BARBER

For a time, nevertheless, one of the Stanley companies left the automobile business and gave birth to two new firms, Locomobile and Mobile. This development of 1899 came largely through the efforts of two intriguing figures from America's great age of industrialization, the magazine magnate John Brisben Walker, publisher of the *Cosmopolitan*, and the asphalt paving king Amzi Lorenzo Barber. In F. O. Stanley's reminiscences he tells how the connection began one morning in February 1899 when he arrived at the steam car works in Watertown to find the New York magazine publisher waiting on the doorstep with an offer to buy into the company.[8]

John B. Walker, then 52 years old, had enjoyed a career fascinatingly varied and productive. Born near Pittsburgh in 1847, he attended a preparatory school in Washington, D.C., and when he was 16 at the height of the Civil War in 1863 he entered Georgetown University. Two years later, the war over, he went to West Point, a not unexpected move for a young man with military forebears on both sides of his family. In 1868 Walker withdrew from the Military Academy so as to accompany J. Ross Browne, the new U.S. Minister to China, where he remained for two years.

Returning to the United States in 1870, Walker entered iron manufacturing and other business ventures in West Virginia and quickly made the first of several fortunes, but the panic of 1873 wiped him out and ended this phase of Walker's business life. He then became a journalist, accepting an offer from the *Cincinnati Commercial* to write on economic issues. This led to a job as managing editor of the *Pittsburgh Telegraph*, and in a few weeks Walker went on to fill the same position with the *Washington Chronicle*. He remained with it for a few years until the paper folded in 1877.

Once again out of a job, John Brisben Walker took Horace Greeley's advice and headed west. He determined to apply irrigation to arid western lands. Eventually he bought up hundreds of acres near Denver and successfully raised alfalfa. More profitable were his speculations in Denver real estate and soon he amassed his second fortune. In 1889 Walker moved to New York and bought the ailing *Cosmopolitan Magazine*, a monthly begun three years earlier and owned for a short time by U. S. Grant, Jr. A 'great editor', Walker made the *Cosmopolitan* profitable and achieved a circulation of 300,000 by 1898. In 1895 he moved the entire publishing operation from downtown New York City to Irvington, a suburban community a few miles up the Hudson. The new *Cosmopolitan* buildings were designed by Stanford White, a socially prominent architect who later became the victim in the notorious Harry Thaw murder case. Walker loved to promote himself but he also engaged in a variety of public endeavours including a free correspondence school called the Cosmopolitan University.[9]

Alert to new opportunities, Walker took the motor car seriously from the beginning.

Cosmopolitan publicized early automobiles and in 1896 he offered $3,000 to the car that would perform most creditably in a run of over 26 miles from New York's City Hall Park to Irvington. Although badly mismanaged, this affair, won by a Duryea petrol car, did generate the publicity that Walker wanted.[10] Nearly three years later Walker decided to enter the automobile business himself. Apparently not interested in petrol power nor in the electric cars that did attract the interest and money of some New York capitalists, Walker opted for steam. In February 1899 he went up to the Boston area to see the Stanleys. When he offered to buy a half-interest in the fledgling enterprise they were astonished.

> Had he said he had come to buy a half-interest in our wives, I doubt if we would have been more surprised. We told him we didn't know as we had what might be called an automobile business, and we certainly did not want a partner; that we had difficulty enough in getting along with each other, and we did not want to increase our trouble by taking in a third party.[11]

Walker pressed his case, emphasizing his ability to publicize the steam car, but the twins could not be budged. He left, 'greatly disappointed'.

The more Walker thought about the idea the more he liked it and after two months he returned to Watertown, reappearing at the factory in mid-April with an offer to buy out the entire business. The Stanleys were not eager to sell so they set a figure they thought would send Walker away again, $250,000. 'Exactly the figure I had in mind, a quarter of a million', smoothly replied the publisher. The Stanleys signed, foreseeing an enormous profit, for they had invested less than $20,000 so far. Further negotiations provided that for $10,000 Walker received a ten-day option to buy the firm. F. O. Stanley quickly brought a steamer to Irvington, driving it from Watertown to Providence and taking ship from there to the metropolis, where he and Walker could demonstrate it in an effort to attract capitalists to supply the $250,000. Prospects included George and Edward Gould, sons of the famous Jay Gould, and William Rockefeller. But the financiers kept saying no. The option was about to expire when a man whom Walker had known in Washington over 20 years earlier and who now was a wealthy neighbour living just a mile down the river at Ardsley, Mr Amzi Lorenzo Barber, entered the picture.[12]

A Vermonter, born in Saxton's River in 1843, Barber was the son of a forceful Congregational minister and spent most of his early years in Ohio. He entered Oberlin College at the age of 19 in 1862 and graduated five years later. After only a few months' post-graduate study at Oberlin's theological seminary, Barber encountered General O. O. Howard, head of the Freedmen's Bureau and currently developing the new university in Washington, D.C., named after himself and designed to provide higher educational opportunities for blacks. Barber joined Howard's new university and taught there for four years. His youthful idealism seems to have faded and shortly after his second marriage Barber left Howard in 1872 and entered the real estate business with some of his wife's relatives. Soon prosperous, in 1876 he witnessed an experiment that sharply changed his career. In Washington, the city authorities put down an asphalt pavement on Pennsylvania Avenue as a test venture. Grasping the possibilities of this innovation, Barber plunged into asphalt paving. The Barber Asphalt Paving Company enjoyed gratifying success. By 1892 it had paved streets in some 30 cities and dominated the industry. A master stroke was Barber's conquest of the world's major source of natural asphalt, the Pitch Lake on the island of Trinidad. In 1888 he negotiated a lease with the British government to exploit the 114-acre lake for 42 years. In 1894 he tightened his grip on the supply side of the industry when he purchased the company controlling the Venezuelan supply of asphalt.[13]

Now, in May 1899, Amzi Barber was Walker's last chance for financial support in his steam car venture. According to Stanley, who was driving, the asphalt king took his test ride and did not hesitate; he immediately decided to invest. He paid Walker $250,000 for a half-interest in the business, which made it possible for Walker to fulfil his commitment to the Stanley brothers. The new partners purchased from the brothers all steam car patents pending, the Watertown factory, and all automobiles in the course of manufacture. The Stanleys agreed to refrain from the independent production of steam cars before 1 May 1900, and furthermore signed on as general managers of the new company.[14] Walker and Barber launched their firm on 17 June 1899, forming a West Virginia corporation named the Automobile Company of America, capitalized at $2½ million, with its office in New York City. Less than a month later the firm changed its name to Locomobile Company of America when it found that another concern had already pre-empted its original name. In October 1899 it raised its capital to $5 million. Public announcements indicated that Barber would serve as president, Walker as vice-president. In addition, a key figure entered the story, Samuel Todd Davis, Jr, Barber's son-in-law, who would function officially as treasurer.[15]

Born in Washington, D.C., in February 1873, Davis attended the Columbian College Preparatory School there and in 1891 matriculated at Rensselaer Polytechnic Institute in Troy, New York, the oldest engineering school in the country after West Point. He graduated with a civil engineer's degree in 1895 and entered Barber's asphalt business. For a year Davis lived in Port-of-Spain as an executive of the Trinidad Asphalt Co. In 1897 he married Amzi Barber's daughter, Lorena. When Barber entered the infant automobile industry in 1899 his son-in-law came along enthusiastically.[16]

MOBILE

The first major steps the new automobile men took were away from each other. Barber and Walker split. Walker's plan had been to move the factory from Watertown to his own neighbourhood where he could watch affairs closely. In the spring of 1899 he negotiated to purchase a site at Kingsland Point in Tarrytown, a few miles north of Irvington. Walker, a self-made man who ran the *Cosmopolitan* as an absolute autocrat, had several sons whom he may have wanted to place somewhere in the management of the company. To Barber, another self-made man but less flamboyant, with a son and a son-in-law interested in the new venture, it may have looked like trouble to remain hitched to Walker and his large family with the factory in Walker's backyard. The issue came to a head shortly after 6 July 1899 when Walker closed the deal on the Kingsland Point property of 600 acres for $165,000. On 19 July the *Horseless Age* announced a Barber–Walker split with Barber keeping the Watertown factory and the Locomobile name while Walker retained the Kingsland Point estate with a new name, Mobile Company of America. Both companies had equal rights to use the Stanley patents and designs and the services of the Stanley brothers.[17]

Walker moved at breakneck speed to catch up with Locomobile, already in production at Watertown. On 14 July 1899 he broke ground for his new 'model' factory, designed by Stanford White to be 300ft by 50ft, and three stories high. Although the local builders Dinkel and Jewell rushed construction to finish in November, it took longer to find equipment, supplies, and to train labour. Only in March 1900 did Mobile turn out a completed automobile. Engines and wooden bodies had to be bought but most of the rest of the car was manufactured in this plant.[18] Walker promoted his car vigorously and sold it at $650 through nearly 70 sales outlets.

LOCOMOBILE

Barber, like Walker, and several months ahead of him, moved quickly in 1899 to increase output of Locomobile's small steam cars, weighing only 400lb empty and priced at $600. As a first step he expanded operations in the Boston area. Manufacture of boilers and final assembly remained at the Watertown factory and Mason continued to supply the engines, but already in July he had obtained the Humber bicycle factory in Westborough (east of Worcester) to make the running gear. Then early in 1900 Locomobile leased the facilities of the Speirs Manufacturing Company in East Worcester and appointed its head, J. C. Speirs, superintendent of all Locomobile manufacturing operations. Speirs' company had once made bicycles. It now specialized in forgings and engines (replacing Mason) for Locomobile cars, although it is not clear if it had its own foundry.[19]

Speirs took over his managerial post from the Stanley brothers, originally general managers but who faded quickly from the picture, for by September 1899 they had ended their connection with Locomobile.[20] One can assume that they found it intolerable to work for other people. On specific issues they may have objected to the company's redesign of their car that was going to make it heavier, and they probably opposed Barber's fundamental decision to move the firm away from the Boston area.

Sometime in 1899 or 1900 George E. Whitney began to work for the Locomobile Company as a design engineer. Several decades later Whitney declared that he and Barber had met in Paris in 1898 and made some sort of financial arrangement.[21]

Whitney's date of 1898 could not have been correct but such a meeting may have occurred in August 1899 when both men were in Paris promoting their steam cars. Whitney did soon join the Locomobile staff although after the company left the Boston area he remained there until late in 1902. If Whitney did join Locomobile in the late summer of 1899 this appearance of a rival may have been another reason for the Stanleys to cut their ties with the firm.

Barber and his son-in-law Samuel Davis sought to concentrate production of Locomobiles in one place, and that place was not Boston but much closer to Barber's and the company's headquarters in New York City. They found the new location in Bridgeport, Connecticut, through the good offices of Dr I. D. Warner, of the Warner Brothers Corset Co. of that city. They acquired 40 acres on Long Island Sound next to Seaside Park (most of whose land had come to the city from local hero P. T. Barnum), with railway and water transportation immediately available. Bridgeport, a city of 71,000 people, had several favourable features: metalworking and carriage-building shops to supply materials as well as skilled labour, and it was a convenient distance – 50 miles – from Manhattan by rail or water. The latter may have had a particular significance, for Barber was an ardent yachtsman. He could not wait for the new factory to be built before getting away from Boston so he found still another disused bicycle factory in Bridgeport and leased it as a temporary site for assembly of Locomobiles previously carried on at Watertown.[22] Such assembly began in March 1900, after an estimated 600 of the machines had been built at the earlier location.

The new Bridgeport factory began to rise in November 1900, allowing some production activities to be transferred there from the Westborough and Worcester facilities in the following March. It was soon finished and Locomobile centralized all manufacturing in the new plant by June 1901, by which point nearly 3,000 of the cars had been sold. The company may have been turning out about 150 cars a month in its makeshift quarters. The main factory building, constructed of brick and steel, comprised two wings, 208 and 300ft long, making an L-shape, each wing 54ft wide.[23] It had four floors and a basement, supplying 127,250ft^2 of floor space. Smaller one-floor buildings housed a power plant, forge, testing shed and (water) pump house. Among early automobile factories the extent of Locomobile's floor space was second only to the De Dion-Bouton works in suburban Paris. Contemporaries considered the new factory a modern facility but we can see it as old-fashioned, reminiscent of New England textile mills with its long and narrow wings of four floors. Originally the steam engines in the power house drove machines in the other buildings by shafting but this outdated system was quickly abandoned in favour of generators to supply electric current for large motors to drive shafts and belts in each section of the factory. Presumably a separate motor for each machine was thought too large an investment. The company generated its own electric power because at this period the electric utility in Bridgeport supplied electricity to its customers for lighting only, and then only during the hours of darkness.[24]

Descriptions of the factory reiterate that the company carried on most of the manufacturing processes in the plant. It did not have a foundry so it probably bought its engine castings from outside. Its wooden bodies and wire spoke wheels also came from outside suppliers. The tubular steel frames for Locomobiles were welded together in the forge shop and then whisked all the way to the fourth floor of the main building for painting, as were the wooden bodies. Boilers and burners were made on the first floor, water and fuel tanks on the third. Machine shops occupied parts of the first and second floors. Engine assembly and testing occurred on the third floor and final assembly on the second. This kind of factory arrangement was traditional, with different parts made in separate shops and moved from floor to floor on three lifts, ultimately to the final assembly operation where each car was put together by a group of men at a fixed station. One finds no attempt at continuous flow assembly, nor was this needed, it seems, for an output of 15 cars was considered a very good day's work and most days it fell far short of this figure.[25] All engines were thoroughly tested in the factory and after assembly the cars also received long test runs along the paths of Seaside Park. Such extensive testing suggests some difficulties in manufacturing and a lack of completely interchangeable parts.

LARGE-SCALE PRODUCTION

The Locomobile company from 1899 to 1901 was outstanding among all the the other firms in the young industry for its large-scale production of low priced cars.

Estimated Production of Locomobile Steam Cars

Year	Authors' estimates	Serial numbers
1899	600	1–1,200
1900	1,600	1,200–2,800
1901	1,400	2,800–4,200
1902	1,100	4,200–5,300
1903	500	5,300–5,800
Total	5,200	

Sources: Authors' figures are derived from the company's claims made in advertisements, copies of which are found in the Locomobile Collection, Bridgeport, and from *Cycle and Automobile Trade Journal* (August 1901), 14; *Horseless Age*, x (21 May 1902), 612; and *Automobile Topics* (12 July 1902), 354, (13 Sept. 1902), 1007. Serial numbers of the cars, compiled by Herb Ottaway and Hayden Taliaferro, are reported in *Horseless Carriage Gazette* (May–June 1977), 28. Company claims would be expected to magnify rather than minimize production; serial numbers assigned to a given year are not necessarily the same as actual production in that year.

Its production far outpaced the results of other domestic companies. The Electric Vehicle Company may have made as many as 1,500 of its Columbia electric cabs and passenger cars from 1899 to 1901 in Hartford but this effort with heavy and expensive machines had little success. This company's problems contrasted with the sales success of the light steam cars were instructive. Another object lesson, the small, French one-cylinder De Dion-Bouton petrol car introduced late in 1899, sold about 3,000 units up to 1902. Some of these (200?) were exported to the United States in these years, called Motorettes, and sold at $850 and up. The next large American producer, Ransom E. Olds, began making his successful Curved Dash one-cylinder petrol runabout in Detroit only in 1901, turning out some 425 in that year and some 2,500 in 1902. Its price began at $600, then rose to $650. In Kenosha Thomas B. Jeffery made 1,500 Rambler cars – also one-cylinder petrol runabouts – in 1902 at $750, and after these came Cadillac and Ford in Detroit in 1903 with production of 1,895 at $750–900 and up to 500 at $850, respectively.[26] These four large mid-western producers quickly followed the trail blazed primarily by Locomobile and Mobile which by 1901 had clearly demonstrated the reality of a large market for small, cheap cars.

Where did Locomobile find buyers for some 5,200 motor vehicles? The firm sought out clients with a vigorous marketing effort headed by J. A. Kingman, a college classmate of Samuel Davis, who emphasized the car's simplicity, reliability, and low price. Some buyers found that it was neither simple nor reliable, but with its low price it took advantage of the considerable publicity that had spread along with horseless vehicles since 1895. In comparison with petrol cars in 1900, when about 1,000 were manufactured in the United States, the Locomobile moved without apparent effort, with none of the vibration and little of the noise associated with that alternative. It had none of the problems of changing gears or worn out clutches. It could do wonders on short hills. Locomobile advertised heavily in a wide variety of publications, from *The Black Cat* and the programme of an international yacht race to the *North American Journal of Homeopathy*, the *Montreal Star*, *Savannah Morning News*, and *San Francisco Call*.[27] It publicized its machines in auto shows, races, and stunts such as climbing Mount Washington in New Hampshire and Pike's Peak in Colorado. It established several branch sales agencies and recruited many dealers not just in its own region but from coast to coast. Late in 1899 it superseded its standard model no. 1 with an improved no. 2, which weighed 640lb empty and cost $750. This car replaced the lightweight Mason-built engine with a much sturdier one of its own (Whitney's?) design made in Speirs' factory in Worcester. Its water capacity was raised to 21 gallons, the steering tiller was moved to the side, and comfort and safety were increased by many other improvements.[28] Other models soon accompanied this new standard type for a total of six by March 1900, including a Locosurry weighing 800lb empty, seating four, and priced at $1,200, and a racing motorcycle with two saddles.[29] Although the company continued to sell its cheapest car for $750 for as long as it made the steam type (except for a few months in 1901–2 when it sold at $850), most of its other models betrayed a tendency toward more substantial and higher priced cars.

Locomobile eagerly sought foreign markets. A few Canadians imported Locomobiles in 1899 and in October of that year some American bicycle interests formed the National Cycle and Automobile Company Ltd to make Locomobiles in Hamilton, Ontario. It began to assemble these cars and presumably made some of the components but in the summer of 1900 the Canada Cycle and Motor Company, owned by Canadians, bought out the National concern. It continued to make and sell Locomobiles until 1902.[30] Already in the summer of 1899 A. L. Barber and F. E. Stanley had visited Europe, arranging for Locomobile agents in London and Paris. While these steamers never caught on in France or the rest of the Continent, in Britain they found a receptive market. In the spring of 1900 one took part in the 1,000 Miles Trial, a reliability demonstration run by dozens of cars from London to Edinburgh and back. Several months later another Locomobile was driven from one end of Britain to the other, 981 miles, a journey that almost wore the machine out, and certainly tired the driver who had to pour a reported five tons of water into the water tank during the trip.[31] Nevertheless, a strong advertising campaign and the avid British demand for imported cars led to the sale of some 400 Locomobiles by 1903.[32]

Locomobile's sales of thousands of cars while other American firms had trouble making and selling dozens or hundreds actually disguised serious flaws and problems.[33] The 1899 models were flimsy, with frequent failures of bearings, sprockets and chains. Sturdier construction added weight which reduced the car's already low fuel economy. To heat its boiler it burned more petrol per mile than the typical petrol car of the period. To start the car when cold one had to warm up separately a petrol vaporizer or 'firing iron' to get the burner to operate, and then get up steam in the boiler. Ordinarily it took about half an hour to manage the entire process, and then there was always the chance that the wind might blow out the burner. While driving one had to watch the water gauge on the boiler and alter the rate of water feeding into the boiler when necessary. Miscalculations were common and burned out boilers occurred frequently. One also had to pump air into the petrol tank to keep its pressure up. Despite rumours, Locomobile boilers never blew up but some of the cars burned when the burners back-fired and set the car on fire. This particular feature made insurance companies reluctant to cover these cars. Boilers might fill up with scale and the cars could not be operated reliably in temperatures below freezing. One of the most glaring faults was high water consumption, about one gallon per mile. The water supply even for a 20-mile trip would weigh about 160lb. A possible solution was a closed system, sending the exhaust steam back to the water tank after running it through a condenser. The French steam cars made by Léon Serpollet and the American White steamers from 1902 employed condensers. But the engines used on the Stanley, Mobile, and Locomobile cars required copious lubrication and in a closed system this oil would foul the condenser and boiler. Locomobile did increase the size of its water tanks, a 1902 touring car carried 47 gallons, but the greater weight reduced the car's efficiency. Without redesigning the engine so as to adopt a condenser the only way to solve the water consumption problem would be to change the motive power itself, to shift to petrol engines.

NEW POLICIES

Although we do not have complete sales figures for the Locomobile Company, these may have become somewhat discouraging late in 1901, after the opening of the new factory. Total production in 1901 probably failed to reach that of 1900, although the automobile industry nationally continued its rapid expansion. In this situation the company took three steps to protect itself. It prepared a new gamut of models for introduction in the spring of 1902, it filed suit against another steam car producer for patent infringement, and it decided to investigate the possibility of adding a petrol car to its line. These steps all accompanied the rise of Samuel Davis in the company, for he became president of Locomobile as 1902 opened, Amzi Barber becoming chairman of the board.

To investigate the petrol engine option Davis and Barber turned to a prominent electrical and automotive engineer, not a mid-westerner but a New Yorker, Andrew L. Riker. Now 33 years old, Riker was largely self-taught, although he had spent a year at Columbia College. In 1888 he had established the Riker Electric Motor Company and in the mid-1890s began making a few electric cars. In June 1899 he formed the Riker Electric Vehicle Company operating from Elizabethport, N.J. Riker sold this concern to the Electric Vehicle Company of Hartford in December 1900, becoming vice-president and superintendent of the larger firm.[34] Already the Hartford company was in serious technical and financial trouble and Riker, apparently persuaded by his own long experience that electrical power was not the answer, began experimenting with petrol cars. In August 1901 Electric Vehicle alerted its agents that it had in preparation some two- and four-cylinder petrol machines for delivery in October.[35] These announcements were premature and may have been issued by Riker without the assent of President George Day, ill and away from his office during much of 1901. In any event Riker did drive a new two-cylinder petrol model in the September 1901 New York to Buffalo Endurance Run. Designed not as a horseless buggy but on the French style developed by Emile Levassor, it had its engine with two vertical cylinders in front. This car had difficulties in the Run and Riker withdrew from the competition north of Albany. In December 1901 he also withdrew from the Electric Vehicle Co. which did not pursue development of his petrol machines.

No matter, Riker had known Amzi Barber and Samuel Davis for several years through participation in races and on automobile committee work. When he was 27 years old Davis had been elected the first president of the National Association of Automobile Manufacturers in December 1900 and Riker sat on its board of directors. They got together quickly and Andrew Riker joined Locomobile in January 1902 as the company agreed to finance his further development of a two-cylinder petrol car;

a decision to manufacture such a machine might come later.[36] To protect current sales of its steam cars Locomobile tried to keep Riker's activities quiet and he carried them on at the Overman Automobile Company in Chicopee, Mass. This firm had earlier made some experimental petrol cars and were currently producing the Victor steam car in small numbers. Locomobile made an unpublicized alliance with Overman in January 1902.

The interest in petrol cars and in Andrew Riker did not at all mean that Locomobile had chosen to abandon steam. At the very time that Riker was beginning his duties with Locomobile the firm acted vigorously to protect its steam car business by bringing suit against the Stanley brothers for patent infringement. The Stanleys had left Locomobile in September 1899 but they continued their experiments with steam cars. By early 1901 they bought back their property and equipment in Watertown from Locomobile for just $20,000 and they offered a new and improved steam car for sale in the winter of 1901–2. They hit a snag, however, for Locomobile now controlled George Whitney's patents and it claimed that the new Stanley infringed on one of them, granted to Whitney on 3 July 1900, for which he had made application as early as 30 April 1897. When an amicable agreement between Locomobile and the Stanleys could not be reached, Locomobile filed suit in January 1902. Later in the year it brought similar suits against the White Company of Cleveland and other steam car manufacturers. As it turned out, this affair did not grow into another Selden case which had so exercised the petrol car makers. The Stanleys solved their problem by thoroughly redesigning their car – most notably they adopted transmission by gears rather than chain – and eventually they bought all the steam car patents owned by Locomobile.[37] The Stanleys made steam cars for many years thereafter, usually about 500 or 600 per year, gradually improving the design and adding weight, finally adopting a condenser in 1915. The company went out of business in 1924 after having produced some 14,000 steam cars since 1901.[38]

To appeal to the market Locomobile had to do more than enforce its patent rights. In the early spring of 1902 it began introducing new model steam cars to replace the types it had manufactured for about two years. In its most striking innovation it almost completely abandoned the earlier buggy design and on all but one of the seven 1902 models placed some of the mechanism under a box on the front end of the car, in this way imitating the best European petrol car designs. Artillery wheels with 3½-inch tyres were mounted on most of the new models and on some of them buyers could specify a steering wheel rather than a tiller. Water tanks held from 30 to 47 gallons and prices ranged from $750 to $2,400.[39] Locomobile offered 'a car for every pocketbook'. It also offered steam car components, including engines, to other manufacturers.

By August 1902 the company also found Riker's petrol car worthy of adoption, decided to manufacture it, and made Riker a vice-president with 1,000 shares of Locomobile stock.[40] Within weeks the public learned the news. *Automobile Topics* reported in late September that Locomobile soon would offer two- and four-cylinder petrol cars designed especially for touring (where the steamers' thirst for water often proved an embarrassment). Riker had designed heavy and expensive cars, about 2,000lb in weight with a $5,000 price tag on the four-cylinder model.[41] Deliveries began in November.

STEAM IN TROUBLE

By the end of the summer of 1902 the petrol car may have become not only another product for Locomobile but a possible way out of financial difficulties. The market for steam cars, at least those made by Mobile and Locomobile, was evaporating. Looking back some 13 years later, J. B. Walker of Mobile summed up the two major problems of this type of car as the 'necessity of filling its water tanks every so many miles – fifteen or twenty – with the regularity that one must water a horse. The other was the constant danger to the careless driver of having his boiler burnt out, through neglect in turning on his pumps at the proper time.'[42] As these negative features became known to prospective buyers many turned to other makes. Those still interested in steam cars could buy a better one in the Cleveland-built White (introduced in 1901) with a semi-flash boiler and condenser, or one of the new cars made by the Stanley brothers. Those considering petrol could now choose from the low-priced models offered by Olds (from late 1901), Rambler (1902) and soon a variety of others. One of Olds' first advertising slogans alluded to the complexity of the steamers: 'Nothing to watch but the road.' A correspondent to the *Horseless Age* revealed the disaffection from Locomobile and Mobile cars by 1903 when he remarked that 1900 or 1901 models of these types could be acquired for $100 or $200.[43]

After some consideration of a possible shift to petrol cars the Mobile Company gave up, closing its doors early in 1903 after selling up to 600 steam cars altogether from 1900.[44] Within a year Maxwell-Briscoe bought the Tarrytown plant to make petrol cars, in turn selling it to Chevrolet in 1915. John B. Walker also sold the *Cosmopolitan*, to Hearst in 1905, and a few years later retired to alfalfa farming in Colorado where he lived on until 1931. Walker lost a sizeable sum of money with his gamble on steam, but Barber apparently sustained an even greater loss.

The Locomobile Company operated in the red for the year ending 31 August 1902 and the situation grew worse.[45] In March 1903 Amzi Barber's money and credit ran out. Locomobile earnings did not appear to have offset his large outlays for designs and patents to the Stanleys and to Whitney and for the new Bridgeport factory. Other personal expenditures may have aggravated his position. In sum, he needed financial relief. He appealed to his brother-in-law J. J. Albright of Buffalo, with whom he had once been associated in Washington, D.C., real estate development. In March 1903 Albright agreed to endorse some Locomobile commercial loans in return for collateral comprising various of Barber's securities and properties.[46] From this point Barber seems to have dropped out of active Locomobile management and in 1904 he returned to the asphalt business until his death in 1909. As Barber gave up the moneyman's role Albright took it on and became the leading stockholder in 1910.

Actual management of Locomobile devolved upon S. T. Davis, Jr and Andrew Riker, with the latter in charge of engineering and production. In 1903 the company disposed of an estimated 500 steam cars and just 77 of the new petrol type. It lost money again, but in 1904 production of petrol models rose to 199 with steamers down to a handful; the company declared a profit.[47] The steam era had ended for Locomobile.

LOCOMOBILE'S LATER HISTORY

To gain publicity and sales for its petrol cars Locomobile raced them, following the line of many European makers of powerful and expensive machines. In 1908 it gained a lustrous triumph when one of its racers won the Vanderbilt Cup Race on Long Island, the first domestic winner of the premier American auto race. This victory and healthy sales in these years repaired the company's finances. In 1912 it entered the truck market with a large 5-ton model. This branch of production grew to major proportions once the European war broke out. Britain, France, and Russia bought Locomobile trucks and in 1916 the United States Army began using them on the Mexican expedition. In this year the company gave the name Riker to its trucks (Davis had died suddenly in 1915, a serious blow) so as to preserve the Locomobile name for its fashionable and non-commercial passenger cars. Output of cars had to be cut in 1917 and 1918 to concentrate on trucks, as well as to prepare for manufacture of Liberty aircraft engines and to work on a heavy tank.

The success and profits Locomobile enjoyed during the war did not continue long into the post-war period. In 1920 the company joined the Mercer and Simplex automobile companies in a new group organized by Emlen S. Hare, a former Packard executive, and called Hare's Motors. Hare's vision was to manufacture quality cars in quantity and sell them at substantially lower prices than hitherto. Whatever the merits of this approach, it had little chance of success, for the post-war recession of 1920–1 set in and the market for Hare's Locomobiles and Mercers faded away. The industrial group collapsed and a grievously weakened Locomobile regained its independence in August 1921. As its business did not improve Locomobile went into bankruptcy in 1922. William Crapo Durant, now building a new automobile empire after being ousted from General Motors for the second time, bought Locomobile for only $1,750,000. This sum allowed about 35 cents on the dollar for the company's creditors.

The Bridgeport factory resumed production but never did well. Durant directed it to make some medium-priced cars as well as expensive models but used the Locomobile name on both. The factory also turned out parts for other Durant cars. Death throes began early in 1929. By March Locomobile production had stopped. The management struggled fitfully, engaging to overhaul Paramount taxicabs during the summer of 1929 while preparing a new Locomobile model for the fall, but the Crash then erased this dream and put a final end to Locomobile.

CONCLUSION

However impressive Locomobile's elegant petrol cars may have been, in the sweep of automobile history in the United States its little steam cars of 1899–1903 had a much greater impact. The thousands of these models that buyers snapped up showed the reality of a large market for cars despite the wretched roads that inhibited inter-city driving. Their low price, in the $600–$850 range, put them within the means of ordinary professional men and the middle class generally. Other manufacturers soon moved into this market on the heels of Locomobile with thousands of small petrol cars and the American automobile boom was under way. We have found no evidence that the Locomobile added anything significant to production methods despite its relatively high output. Its production was not large enough to require innovations in methods so as to avoid heavy investment in new plant or to overcome shortages of skilled labour.

Walker and Barber chose a steam-driven car when they entered the business. This seemed wise enough in 1899, when American petrol cars appeared crude and unreliable. In France, the leading area of automobile development at this time, steam already had lost out to internal combustion but most Americans did not know this and those who did may have considered the French precedent irrelevant. In a few years Americans did find that steam propulsion, given the current state of technology, could not do as much and caused more difficulties than petrol engines. A more careful design of the early Locomobile to make it sturdier, simpler, and safer to operate might have enabled it to survive longer but Walker and Barber at first kept the original Stanley design on the market. The new Locomobile models that began to appear at the end of 1899 corrected or mitigated some of the earlier faults but improvement seemed to come faster in the competing petrol cars. By 1902–3 this type's advantages even converted Locomobile's management.

When Locomobile turned on to the same road as its mid-western rivals and switched to petrol it completely abandoned the low-priced field where it had disposed of so many cars through an extensive dealer network. It chose to appeal to the wealthy with elegance, quality, and high price. It seems as if Davis and Riker, young engineers, preferred a strategy emphasizing technical excellence as against the policy of Walker and Barber, older and experienced businessmen, who had tried to appeal to a mass market. It is possible that if Locomobile had continued in the low-priced market with its petrol cars it might have competed successfully with the mid-western companies and kept New England as a centre of this industry. However, its decisions and the earlier one of the Pope Company of Hartford to go to electric cars, a dead end at this time, meant that the industry would shift westward.

NOTES

The authors acknowledge with pleasure the valuable assistance provided by David Palmquist, Barbara Strong, A. Lawrence Riker, Langdon R. Stevenson, Walter F. Robinson, Jr, Harlan Appelquist, and Gary Levine.

1. Deborah Cozort (Asst Archivist at M.I.T.) to authors, 14 July and 11 August 1978; *Horseless Age*, I (March 1896), 17–18; II (Dec. 1896), 5; and II (April 1897), 13. A recent survey of steam car history can be found in G. Levine, *The Car Solution: The Steam Engine Comes of Age* (New York, 1974).

2. *Bridgeport Post*, 18 Jan. 1925; *Bridgeport Life*, 17 Dec. 1932.

3. *Horseless Age*, III (Oct. 1898), 44; *American Machinist*, XXI (1 Dec. 1898), 897–8; F. O. Stanley quoted in T. Derr, *The Modern Steam Car* (Newton, Mass., 1932), 45–6.

4. *Horseless Age*, III (Nov. 1898), 12–16.

5. *Horseless Age*, III (Dec. 1898), 22, and (Feb. 1899), 18.

6. H. L. Arnold, 'Some American steam-driven motor vehicles', *Industries and Iron*, XXVII (2 July 1899), 2.

7. Stanley Manufacturing Co. records in the Baker Library, Harvard University. *Horseless Age*, IV (19 April 1899), 24, and later issues in 1899.

8. Derr, *op. cit.*, 48.

9. F. L. Mott, *History of American Magazines*, 4 vols. (Cambridge, Mass., 1930–57), IV: 35, 480–91.

10. *Horseless Age*, I (June 1896), 5–6, 12–13.

11. F. O. Stanley quoted in Derr, *op. cit.*, 48.

12. *Ibid.*, 48–53; J. B. Walker in *Motor* (Feb. 1916), 52.

13. J. B. Severance, 'Amzi Lorenzo Barber', *Oberlin Alumni Magazine*, V (June 1909), 341–3.

14. F. O. Stanley quoted in Derr, *op. cit.*, 53.

15. State of West Virginia, 'Certificate of incorporation of the Locomobile Co. of America', copy made 17 November 1976; *Horseless Age*, IV (21 June 1899), 10.

16. *Bridgeport Post*, 1 Sept. 1915.

17. *Horseless Age*, IV (19 July 1899), 12.

18. *Horseless Age*, VI (4 April 1900), 18–19; J. Canning and W. C. Gross, *History of the Tarrytowns* (Harrison, N.Y., 1975), 139.

19. *Worcester Magazine*, XI (May 1908), 91–2; *Horseless Age*, IV (19 July 1899), 12, and V (14 Feb. 1900), 13; *Bridgeport Post*, 26 Jan. 1900.

20. *Horseless Age*, IV (20 Sept. 1899), 20.

21. *Bridgeport Life*, 17 Dec. 1932.

22. *Bridgeport Post*, 25 Jan. 1900; *Horseless Age*, V (14 Feb. 1900), 13.

23. This description is drawn from City of Bridgeport, Building Permits 6094, 6161, 6162, 6163, 6234; *Automotor Journal* (Oct. 1901), 21; *Cycle and Automobile Trade Journal* (August 1901), 14–16; and *Automobile Topics* (August 1901), 563–70.

24. E. Danenberg, *The Story of Bridgeport* (Bridgeport, 1936), 67–8.

25. Annual production in 1901 is estimated at 1,400, or an average of under five per day.

26. The figures are stated or suggested by W. Greenleaf, *Monopoly on Wheels* (Detroit, 1961), 65–74; J. B. Rae, *American Automobile Manufacturers* (Philadelphia, 1959), 68–70; J. M. Laux, *In First Gear* (Montreal, 1976), 30, 212; G. S. May, *R. E. Olds* (Grand Rapids, 1977), 136, 187; T. Mahoney, *The Story of George Romney* (New York, 1960), 255; G. Brigham, *Serial Numbers of the First Fifty Years*, 5th ed (Marietta, Ga, 1974), 93; W. C. Leland and M. D. Millbrook, *Master of Precision* (Detroit, 1966), 69, 72; A. Nevins, *Ford*, 3 vols (New York, 1954–63), I, 231, 240–1, 246, 288.

27. Locomobile Collection, Bridgeport Public Library.

28. C. Figge, in *Horseless Carriage Gazette* (May–June 1977), 29–31.

29. Automobile Collection, Connecticut State Library, Hartford; Locomobile Collection, Bridgeport Public Library.

30. H. Durnford and G. Baechler, *Cars of Canada* (Toronto, 1973), 52, 84, 230–1.

31. Lord Montagu of Beaulieu and A. Bird, *Steam Cars: 1770–1970* (New York, 1971), 95.

32. M. Sedgwick in G. N. Georgano (ed.), *Complete Encyclopedia of Motor Cars* (1968), 349.

33. An excellent account of the technical aspects of the Locomobile is in Montagu and Bird, *op. cit.*, 96–107; issues of the *Horseless Age* in 1901 and 1902 frequently carry letters and articles on steam car problems and advantages.

34. A. L. Riker papers, Manchester, Conn.

35. Electric Vehicle Company, Bulletins 46 and 47, in A. L. Riker papers.

36. The contract is in the A. L. Riker papers.

37. *Horseless Age*, VII (13 Feb. 1901), 32, IX (29 Jan. 1902), 151–3, X (24 Sept. 1902), 327–8; and *Motor Age* (3 Jan. 1907), 27.

38. See C. C. McLaughlin, 'The Stanley steamer: a study in unsuccessful innovation', *Explorations in Entrepreneurial History*, VII (1954), 37–47; and R. C. Sprague, Jr, 'The Stanley steam cars', *Antique Automobile* (Jan.–Feb. 1977), 30–41.

39. Automobile Collection, Connecticut State Library, Hartford; Locomobile Collection, Bridgeport Public Library.

40. Letter from Amzi Barber to Andrew Riker, 28 August 1902, A. L. Riker papers.

41. *Automobile Topics* (27 Sept. 1902), 1078–9; *Horseless Age*, X (1 and 15 Oct. 1902), 368–9, 434.

42. *Motor* (Jan. 1916), 73.

43. *Horseless Age*, XII (8 July 1903), 46.

44. Canning and Gross, *op. cit.*, 140.

45. Locomobile Collection, Bridgeport Public Library.

46. Samuel T. Davis papers, Ardsley on Hudson, New York.

47. Brigham, *op. cit.*, 59; Locomobile Collection, Bridgeport Public Library.

9 *Improved earth: travel on the Canadian prairies, 1920–50*

ROD BANTJES

This article is about means of travel used in the Canadian province of Saskatchewan before 1950; equally, it is about a social system which minimised travel by keeping important destinations near at hand and making many kinds of travel unnecessary. The Saskatchewan case challenges existing assumptions about the history of automobile use and the role of automobile transport in shaping travel behaviour. Saskatchewan is part of the North American midwest, which, during the period between 1920 and 1950, was a rural region characterised by enormous physical distances between households and between households and market services.[1] In the United States, midwestern farmers were quick to adopt the automobile. By 1930 in 'west north central' states,[2] over 80 per cent of farm households owned cars, proportionally more than in most other North American regions (see table 1). Rural sociologists have assumed that the automobile was readily accepted because it fulfilled a pre-existing need, one defined by geographic dispersal and the supposed isolation experienced by midwestern farmers. Radical increases in the speed of travel were thought to have eased the travel burden on farmers and led to changes in the travel behaviour involved in social interaction and economic exchanges. New travel patterns in turn affected the spatial dimensions of communities and associations, as well as the locations of businesses and even of whole towns.[3] Rural sociologists assumed that these changes took place early in the century with the rise of automobile ownership, and that they were brought about by the combined power of technology and consumer demand:

> roads and automobiles gave farmers new freedom in the realm of trade and markets as in other things, and despite slogans designed to build loyalty to the home town, farmers, given the automobile and the open road, began to exercise choice. . . . Between 1900 and 1920 thousands of general stores closed, many hamlets losing every business enterprise they possessed. In place of the old general store in surviving hamlets came the gasoline filling station. In all towns came a growth in

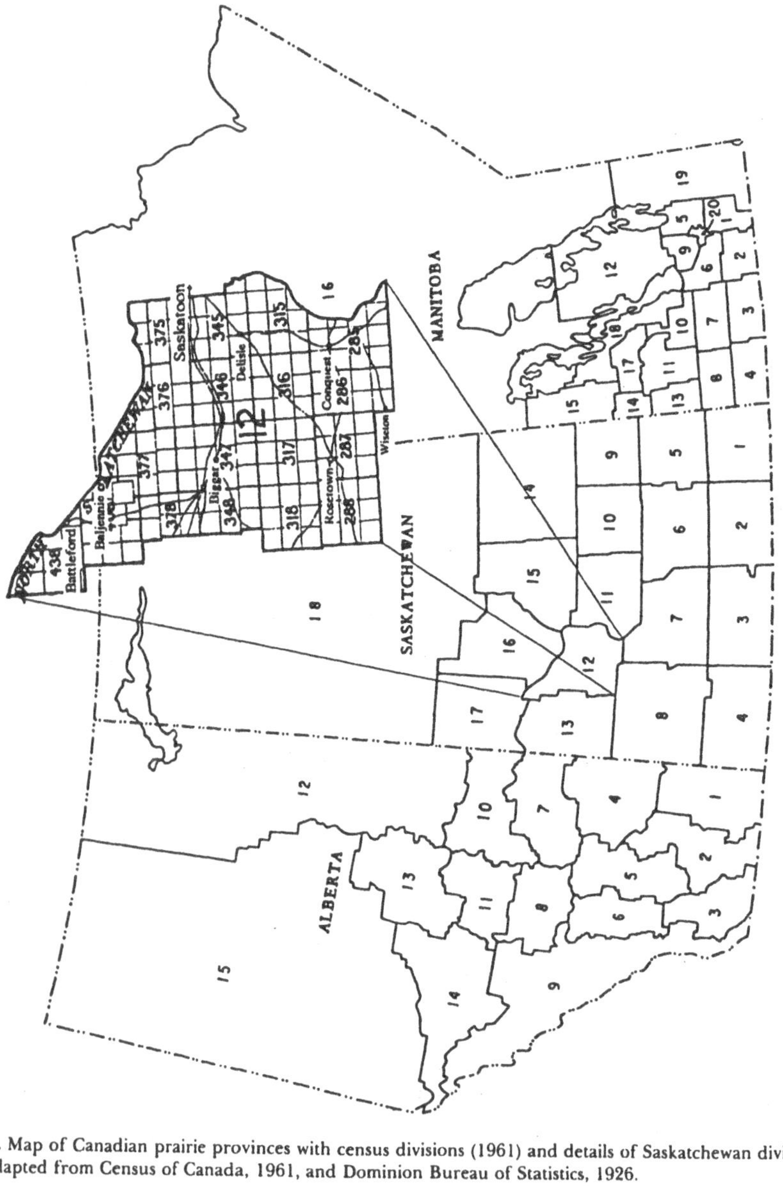

Fig. 1. Map of Canadian prairie provinces with census divisions (1961) and details of Saskatchewan division 12. Adapted from Census of Canada, 1961, and Dominion Bureau of Statistics, 1926.

Table 1. *Vehicles on farms, Canada and the United States, 1921–51*

		1921		*1931*		*1941*		*1946*		*1951*	
Region	*State/Province*	*Autos/*	*Trucks*	*Autos/*	*Trucks*	*Autos/*	*Trucks*	*Autos/*	*Trucks*	*Autos/*	*Trucks*
Canada	Manitoba	–	–	45	6	46	12	51	18	59	38
Canada	Saskatchewan	–	–	46	8	40	15	46	21	54	44
Canada	Alberta	–	–	42	7	43	14	46	19	53	42
East N Cent.	Ohio	47	3	78	17	81	14	84	18	82	29
East N Cent.	Indiana	46	2	78	16	81	15	83	20	80	32
East N Cent.	Illinois	53	2	80	18	83	19	84	26	82	40
East N Cent.	Michigan	40	2	79	21	82	16	85	21	84	32
East N Cent.	Wisconsin	50	2	84	28	84	25	86	32	86	40
East N Cent.	Total	47	2	80	20	82	18	84	23	83	35
W N Cent.	Minnesota	57	2	86	19	88	18	88	23	87	35
W N Cent.	Iowa	73	4	90	15	90	12	91	17	89	29
W N Cent.	Missouri	31	2	64	8	64	12	64	18	63	31
W N Cent.	North Dakota	57	1	87	21	83	27	86	47	86	68
W N Cent.	South Dakota	69	6	87	17	86	19	87	30	88	48
W N Cent.	Nebraska	76	5	92	19	89	19	90	28	88	43
W N Cent.	Kansas	62	2	87	19	83	25	85	38	83	55
W N Cent.	Total	57	3	83	16	82	17	83	25	81	39
W South C	Oklahoma	26	1	58	11	57	15	58	25	59	42
W South C	Arkansas	7	0	26	4	21	9	26	15	32	31
Pacific	Washington	42	5	72	25	75	30	80	41	78	50
Pacific	Oregon	41	3	75	17	79	24	81	37	79	50
Pacific	California	53	5	77	26	80	35	83	45	81	52

Note. Figures are percentages of farms reporting at least one of the indicated vehicles. The years listed are Canadian census years; American data are always recorded a year earlier.

Source. Census of the United States; Census of Canada.

specialization. The smaller town and village stores turned to providing necessary articles in which the farm populace demanded little choice, whereas enterprises supplying specialized items like furniture, jewelry and ready-to-wear garments left the small town for the large town or city where they could carry a better stock of goods and thus meet the newly created needs which the growing standard of living in the farm community demanded.[4]

Recent scholars tend to adopt these assumptions.[5] Case-studies in the history of rural automobile use in the states of Illinois and Iowa also affirm the early timing of changes wrought by the automobile.[6]

My own research, by contrast, suggests that the 'age of the automobile' brought few changes in travel behaviour in the Canadian west, where severe winters and lack of state support for road building limited the usefulness of automobiles.[7] While Bloomfield has recently claimed of Saskatchewan that 'due to the automobile . . . [p]rofound changes did take place in the 1920s', he is merely generalising from the American model.[8] I challenge the validity of this generalisation. I also question the voluntarism and technological determinism of existing studies, finding more support for Interrante's claim that demand for automobiles was less a cause than a result of what he calls the 'reconstitution of transport needs', brought about by 'the reorganization of the physical and social environment which the car facilitated but did not require'.[9] In Saskatchewan, local institutions and travel needs were adapted to more reliable but slower technologies than the car. Here the 'physical and social environment' supported conservative travel behaviour until the end of the Second World War, despite the availability of the automobile.

Environmental and technical limits to automobile usefulness

In the summer of 1920 Miss Eva Hasell made an arduous tour across the Canadian prairies in a small covered truck 'on behalf of religious education'. Conscious of pioneering a new missionary technique, she made careful observations of the performance of her machine and of the natural and man-made obstacles to its progress. Of Saskatchewan's roads she concluded that 'the best trail is much like the worst cart road in England', a condition she attributed to the scarcity of stone and gravel for paving.[10] There is no record of gravel being used for paving until seven years later. In 1927 64 miles, or 0·06 per cent of Saskatchewan's total of approximately 100,000 miles of road, had been gravel surfaced.[11] The remainder were dirt — 'earth' and 'improved earth' in the Department of Highways' lexicon.

Dirt roads were generally constructed by farmers working as payment-in-kind towards municipal taxes. The Department of Highways encouraged these efforts by publishing in its annual reports techniques of 'improving' earth roadbeds, and by sponsoring 'road dragging' competitions.[12] Despite the initial effects, proudly displayed in photographs of competition winners, improvements generally did not last long. One good rain and a sprinkling of traffic could turn a provincial highway into meandering furrows of axle-deep muck, or else wash it out altogether.[13]

Surveyors moving camp on a provincial highway about 4 miles north of Parry, Saskatchewan, 1923. G. C. Cowper/National Archives of Canada/PA-19367

Eva Hasell records one journey of 89 miles between Rosetown and Kerrobert which took her and her companion three days because of the damage that 'one tremendous thunderstorm' had done to the roads.[14] Even into the 1940s it was not uncommon for people to leave their cars enmired in the highway and walk home, their feet large as dinner plates with clinging mud, to get the team or to wait until the roads dried out.[15] Even newly graded surfaces were often too soft or had large clumps of turf left sticking up high enough to obstruct a car. The official width of the grade,[16] 16 ft, was not overly generous for passing vehicles:

> Meeting another car was an awkward matter as it meant climbing out of the ruts and running with one wheel in the gutter. Sometimes, in trying to avoid a mud hole or something we ran at such an angle that I only kept my seat by clinging to the steering wheel, and how Winifred kept hers is a mystery.[17]

Deep ruts, common on prairie roads, did as Hasell implies have their virtues. As Saskatchewan's chief field engineer pointed out in 1927:

> A road should be smooth for motor traffic . . . We usually object to deep ruts on any road, but ruts on a high crowned grade across a slough are a real necessity on

> a rainy day — they offer the only hope of being able to pilot a car across the grade without skidding into the slough.[18]

To be fair to the Department of Highways and the rural municipalities (responsible for the bulk of the road system), the scale of their task for decades exceeded the available resources. In 1920 Saskatchewan's sparse, overwhelmingly rural, population provided a slender tax base to support its vast cartesian grid of roads. The problem was only partly one of overcoming physical space; equally troublesome was the way in which the Dominion Land Survey had structured the use of this space. The mathematical grid plan, which must have looked so rational on surveyors' drafting tables, forced people to zig-zag absurdly across dead flat terrain or travel in unerringly straight lines towards sloughs, ravines and other natural obstacles en route to most destinations.[19] Surveyed road allowances[20] typically went the long way around. In addition, the way in which squares of land were apportioned to settlers maximised the space between farmsteads, and likewise maximised the mileage of road needed to connect them. Before 1909 road allowances had been ignored in favour of a more efficient network of direct cross-country trails. Fences, first required by law in that year, began to force travellers and road-builders to conform to the perverse logic of the grid.[21] Fencing progressed unevenly, depending on local availability of resources and the amount of nuisance caused by wandering cattle, until the mid-1920s, when it had formed a nearly complete net constraining prairie space.[22]

For years this extravagant system of road allowances remained unimproved and unpaved. By 1946 only 11 per cent of Saskatchewan's roads had been gravel surfaced, and less than 0·5 per cent had some form of bituminous surfacing (see table 2). The province consistently had more miles of road per person than any other in Canada and three times as many as the average for the country.[23] The effects that this over-extension had on road standards were evident to the first cross-Canada motor tourist who, in an article solicited by Regina's *Morning Leader* (1920), pronounced them to be the worst in the country:

> The All-Red route across Saskatchewan — let us face the matter frankly — is one of the hazards and impediments of a Canadian highway today. The stretch from Wapella to Whitewood is in shocking condition, from Mortlatch to Chaplin is another thirty miles of trouble, but one of the gravest indications of road policy is the main thoroughfare to the east of Swift Current. Here the original trail was fenced off by a farmer who doubtless had a patent on the land, but instead of building another road into this splendid and hospitable town, the vehicles have been left merely to beat down a fresh part of the hillside.[24]

The earth roads which carried most motorised traffic until the early 1950s, even when dry and reasonably maintained, by no means assured motorists a clear speed advantage over competing means of travel. For instance, when in

Table 2. *Rural road construction, Canada and the United States, 1925–60 (% with paved, surfaced)*

		1925		*1930*		*1940*		*1950*		*1960*
Region	*State/Province*	*Paved*	*Surf.*	*Paved*	*Surf.*	*Paved*	*Surf.*	*Paved*	*Surf.*	*Surf.*
Canada	Manitoba	–	–	1	16	–	43	–	55	62
Canada	Saskatchewan	–	–	0	3	–	4	–	15	33
Canada	Alberta	–	–	0	3	–	3	–	33	74
East N Cent.	Ohio	10	37	35	71	42	85	58	91	–
East N Cent.	Indiana	18	24	18	77	27	88	40	90	–
East N Cent.	Illinois	7	22	11	32	16	69	27	84	–
East N Cent.	Michigan	8	45	10	58	21	74	32	76	–
East N Cent.	Wisconsin	7	39	9	57	23	76	41	83	–
East N Cent.	Total	10	33	17	59	26	78	40	85	
W N Cent.	Minnesota	1	30	2	44	10	66	16	80	–
W N Cent.	Iowa	1	11	4	27	9	57	13	76	–
W N Cent.	Missouri	3	14	4	20	9	44	17	65	–
W N Cent.	North Dakota	0	2	0	7	3	31	5	48	–
W N Cent.	South Dakota	0	5	0	14	5	42	10	67	–
W N Cent.	Nebraska	0	2	1	13	5	37	8	51	–
W N Cent.	Kansas	2	4	3	13	9	43	16	62	–
W N Cent.	Total	1	12	3	22	8	49	14	67	–
W South C	Oklahoma	1	3	2	8	7	18	14	38	–
W South C	Arkansas	3	12	3	18	6	27	14	54	–
Pacific	Washington	10	53	11	65	26	74	45	82	–
Pacific	Oregon	15	52	19	65	26	74	38	82	–
Pacific	California	20	40	32	50	60	68	79	84	

Notes. (1) The American figures represent the percentage of farms located on each road type; similarly for the 1931 data for Canada. The Dominion Bureau of Statistics henceforth collected only figures on the number of miles of various types of road surfaces. Listed are percentages of total road miles in each category. Canadian figures are taken primarily from Statistics Canada Bulletin 53-201 (1963), supplemented by DBS 23-201, 23-203 and DBS 53-201 (annual).
(2) 'Paved' includes the following surfaces: concrete, asphalt, macadam, bituminous mulch; 'surfaced' ('surf.') includes 'paved' and gravel surfaces.

Source. Census of the United States; Census of Canada.

1909 Tom Clayton of the Eagle Creek district bought a brand-new International car, he kept it only long enough to have a photograph taken with him at the wheel. It went back to the dealer as soon as Clayton realised that a pony going overland could outrun his car toiling along 'on the square'.[25] In 1920 the only 'good run' clocked by Eva Hasell was on a provincial highway running straight between Kindersley and Rosetown. She left at 4 p.m. and arrived at 9 p.m. Even according to her inflated estimate of the distance (70 as opposed to 56 miles measured on the map) she averaged only 14 miles per hour.[26] On another fine day early in the summer of 1914 a party of Regina men motored north from the Queen City to survey the crops and report on the business scene in Saskatoon. Their detailed log of travel times and distances was newsworthy enough to be published in the *Regina Leader* and shows an average speed of about 17 miles per hour.[27] These cars were not performing much better than a good team of driving horses, which reportedly could pace at about 15 miles per hour and could more easily be taken overland.[28] Some people recall that well into the 1930s a Model T would have to give way on most roads to a spirited team.[29]

Mechanical problems also slowed the progress of early machines. Eva Hasell was constantly fidgeting with her carburetter, replacing spark plugs, fussing with her tyres (covering them when she stopped in the heat to prevent them from exploding) and dealing with mishaps like broken steering rods, all on a vehicle which had been fresh off the Ford assembly line that spring. Even the normal operation of a vehicle could prove tiresome. One man recalls driving his new truck home from the dealer's in Regina on a hot day and being forced to stop at every slough along the way to refill the radiator, which had burnt dry.[30]

Car travel remained at average speeds below 21 miles per hour until after the Depression, during which time most people still drove cars built in the late 1920s.[31] Even in 1939 a sociologist, in an effort to impress his readers with the convenience of modern travel on all-weather gravel highways (4 per cent of all roads at the time) cited an average speed of only 35 miles per hour.[32] Generally, though, automobiles provided a considerable advantage over horses. For, while a good team of drivers might be capable of a sustained 15 miles per hour, few farmers could actually keep such horses in addition to their work teams. The cost of fast horses would typically be much higher than that of a second-hand car. A farmer's primary means of transport, the all-purpose horse or 'farm chunk', ambled along at between 4 and 7 miles per hour, depending on what it was hauling.[33] The main competition for high-speed travel, and for years the most practical and convenient means for long journeys, was the passenger train. Eva Hasell tried racing one where the highway ran parallel with the railway to Regina. She lost: not surprisingly, since the train, even stopping at every request stop along the way, averaged around 30 miles per hour, which was twice the maximum of Hasell's little Ford.[34]

The meager advantages of early automobile travel were further diminished by Saskatchewan's extreme winters, where temperatures of –20°C are expected and –40°C not uncommon.[35] Bitter cold tried the endurance of passengers and vehicles alike, and drifting snow on the poorly maintained roads normally blocked all wheeled traffic. Speed, an obvious rationale for motoring in summer, could become a cruel liability in winter. Before the 1940s, heaters were not standard equipment in most cars and many were open or not fully sealed. Winter driving, recalled one woman, shivering at the thought, 'was desperately cold, just terrific . . .'.[36] Early inventions such as the 'Perfection Exhaust Heater' (a detachable heat exchanger), 'never proved out', according to another informant. People used the same technologies for keeping warm in their cars that they used in sleighs. These included a carpeted metal box designed to hold coals or a hot brick and hot water bottles (which would freeze by the end of most trips).[37] The heavy sleighs, converted from wagons, could be filled with straw for children to nestle in and travelled slowly enough that someone with cold feet could jump out and walk or run behind until sufficiently warm to climb back in. The warmest means of transport was the 'caboose'. This was a prairie invention consisting of a shed, of varying design, mounted on runners, furnished with a wood stove and drawn by one or more horses. As late as 1950 a photograph shows them congregating in the village of Arelee on train day, where only a single automobile made its appearance.[38]

A major problem for those who did drive in the cold was preventing the automobile's engine coolant from freezing and damaging the radiator or perhaps cracking the engine block. Ethylene glycol (the basis of modern

Caboose used by schoolchildren near Montmartre, Saskatchewan. Saskatchewan Archives Board/R-A 10368(2)

antifreeze), became available in 1928 under the brand name of 'Prestone',[39] but at $4 a gallon it represented a major expense which most people considered a luxury. A variety of cheaper solutions was generally employed until well after the Depression. Coal oil (kerosene) or diesel fuel could be substituted at some risk and expense. Usually people filled the radiator with water heated on the stove, then wrapped the engine casing in thick blankets in an effort to retain heat. When a trip was finished the water was simply drained onto the ground. However, if the car stood for any length of time, for example at a dance or outside the billiards hall in Rosetown, it would have to be restarted periodically.

Drifting snow was a further deterrent to winter driving. The wind concentrates Saskatchewan's meager snow cover, stripping all but a thin crust off open fields and depositing deep powder or brittle streamlined drifts wherever it encounters the slightest resistance. A line of wolfwillow or uncut weeds along a ditch or even the profile of a road embankment could (particularly before the late 1950s, when roads began to be built well above the surface of the fields)

Liyer's home-made snow-plane, Gravelbourg, Saskatchewan, 1946–47. Saskatchewan Archives Board/R-A16611

provide just enough obstruction to start cycles of drifting. At times, drifts were deep enough all but to bury trains, sometimes stopping them for days.[40] Recalling winters before 1950 people repeatedly use the phrase 'there were no roads then . . .'. They mean literally that a day of blowing would obliterate all trace of the grid pattern under snow. The Department of Highways might (after 1936) clear a few main roads, then, over the top and with little regard for the underlying grid, people traced a network of sleigh trails organised according to a more pragmatic logic. These winter trails were used for most country travel.

The caboose was one example of an 'appropriate technology' adapted to the sleigh trail. Another was a propeller-driven sled called a 'snow-plane'. Hundreds of design variations emerged from machine shops and idle garages around the province. The sleeker versions consisted of a light cockpit suspended upon three skis set wide enough apart to follow sleigh trails. The propeller was mounted on the back; often directly on the drive shaft of a Model-A engine. These machines were reportedly difficult to control because of imperfect braking systems and the tendency to be overbalanced by the torque of the propeller, but must have been thrilling for their drivers since they could travel faster than the cars from which they were made.[41] Owners of snow-planes typically put them at the disposal of doctors for making emergency calls or hired them out for other delivery services such as mail. Enormous inventiveness went into means for conveying doctors and travelling ministers. Dr Mainprize of Midale, Saskatchewan travelled in a home-made half-track (a vehicle equipped with rear caterpillar treads and front wheels) in winter, and during spring thaw or any major rain he was driven in a vehicle with enormous tyres which he called a 'mudmobile'.[42] Ministers near Loverna, Saskatchewan were flown in a light aircraft fitted with skis and capable, presumably, of landing on open prairie fields.[43] Another was able to perform God's work in winter by driving a motor-bike fitted with an outrigger along the railway. 'Jiggers' (rail cars) of various descriptions were frequently used in emergencies as the rails could generally be relied upon to remain clear of snow.[44]

Efforts were made to adapt the automobile to winter conditions. These included modifications to the vehicles themselves to make them more resistant to the cold,[45] or reliance on mutual aid to ensure the success of winter driving. If located near a main road, neighbours might 'club together' for a rare automobile expedition. Two or three couples converged at one of their farmsteads on foot or by horse and together ploughed a road out to the highway, perhaps with a tractor. They then piled into the most reliable car, equipped with tyre chains and shovels, and ventured into town for shopping, to collect mail or perhaps to pick up some orders for snowed-in neighbours.

Notwithstanding variations due to snowfall, terrain and road access, with the arrival of the first permanent snowfall in most areas the majority of farmers drained their radiators and jacked their cars up onto blocks, where they remained undisturbed until summer. A minority of farmers sold all of their horses and converted to tractors before either the Department of Highways or municipalities had begun making any significant effort to clear winter roads. Twenty per cent of farmers were without horses by 1941.[46] In most of these cases the sale of horses was necessary in order to move to town for the winter months to find wage work or to be nearer to the school once country schools began to close. The small remainder who stayed on the farm without horses had to use their tractors, hitched perhaps to the sleigh (usually a wagon box fitted with four runners) for the deepest snow. The newer '1-ton' trucks had enough power and weight to provide traction in less-severe conditions. In fact, these trucks, purchased in the 1940s and 1950s (see table 1), probably provided most people with their first taste of all-winter driving. The experience was not yet a comfortable one since even these vehicles were rarely heated. Occupants bundled into layers of outdoor clothing, yet it was hard to keep the driver's fingers from going numb gripping an icy steering wheel.

The winter of 1935–36 was the first in which the Department of Highways made any effort to remove snow from its roads. During the previous winter the maintenance crew had erected 34 miles of snowfence. Discreetly overlooking the 99,000 unprotected miles, the maintenance engineer optimistically reported that the measure 'made it possible for traffic to use a considerable mileage of road the greater portion of the winter'.[47] Ten years later, the province, using forty-five V-ploughs and two rotary ploughs on loan from the airforce, was able to provide snow removal for 3,849 miles of highway. Still, snowstorms defeated even these limited efforts for two weeks in March.

By 1956 the Department was gaining sufficient control of its own roads to be able to provide limited assistance to rural municipalities (RMs) for snow removal on municipal roads.[48] The province was still clearing less than 3 per cent of the total road miles and few RMs had assumed responsibility for their part of the network.[49] However, by this time most farmers, mostly through their own efforts, found it possible, if not terribly easy, to drive all winter. The RM of Milden, on a clear level plain with the lowest mean annual snowfall and the highest rate of automobile ownership,[50] was one of the first areas where, in the late 1940s, driving all winter became common practice. In the hilly, wooded country to the north near Baljennie people did not customarily drive all winter until the early 1960s. Len Worthington, who ran the mail service out of Biggar north to Baljennie and south to Marriott, described what it was like in the 1950s as winter travel habits began to change:

> In the course of these last years times were changing in such a way that all farmers were mechanized and the horse was definitely out. Also winters were mild with the advent of grid roads on all the main drags, farmers were using cars and trucks all through the winter. The municipality bought a snow plow and farmers formed snow plow clubs to plow their own driveways.

> It became increasingly difficult for me to use teams in the winter on the main roads and yet I needed them on the side roads. In 1954 everyone plowed the snow and I had an extremely hard time getting around. I vowed I would not do another winter, but would sell my horses and buy a four wheel-drive, and be like everyone else. Everyone had confidence in the truck and the snow plow.[51]

Federal statistics confirm the accuracy of Mr Worthington's observations. In 1951 the percentage of farms reporting horses began its precipitous decline just as the ownership of cars and trucks exceeded 50 per cent and continued climbing for another decade (see table 1 and figure 2). The war was over, gas rationing had ended and farm incomes had started to rise. More people had tractors and could afford more modern cars, which were beginning to be weatherproofed and heated. Mutual aid in winter driving frequently became formalised and

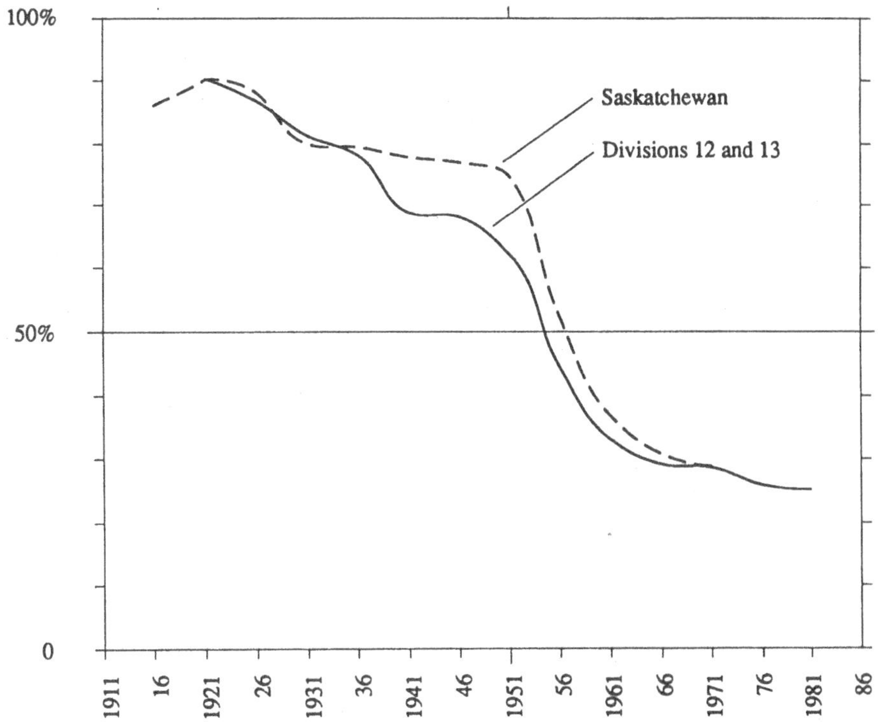

Fig. 2. Horses on Saskatchewan farms

Source: Canada, *Census of Agriculture*.

regularised, with families taking turns at being responsible for snow clearing or else collectively hiring a neighbour who owned a V-plough and a good tractor to do the work. For a brief period in the 1950s many of these 'clubs' were incorporated as co-ops, and thus became eligible for provincial grants.[52]

Perhaps more important than an increase in personal resources in explaining people's willingness to plough their driveways and access roads was the fact that, increasingly, they could connect with minor roads now being kept open for the new school bus routes. School consolidation and improved farm road access were two interdependent elements in the CCF[53] government's rural development programme. However, it was consolidation, beginning in the 1940s, which forced the municipalities to start maintaining more road mileage through the winter. The grid road programme mentioned by Len Worthington was not begun until 1956. It was jointly funded by the provincial and municipal governments but represented a shift of responsibility for municipal road construction away from the municipalities as well as a step towards 'professionalisation' of municipal road engineering. The idea was to produce more durable roads with a grade and surface easier to keep clear of snow.[54]

Slow travel systems

So far I have considered only the environmental and technical limits to the use of automobiles in Saskatchewan. In this section I argue that, despite the slowness of travel, most purposes were adequately served, and that rejection of the automobile as a means of winter travel need not be interpreted as a 'failure to dominate nature'. Rather, the car was replaced by more appropriate winter technologies such as the caboose and direct cross-country trails (which needed no maintenance). The problem of achieving travel convenience was partly technical but also largely social. On the prairies a set of social institutions was maintained which made life in winter tolerable without extensive travel. Most of these were restricted to the 'open-country'. Prairie farmers built their homes on their land rather than in villages. Farm communities were defined by social networks among neighbours in the open-country[55] and these, at least initially, excluded residents of villages and small towns. Farmers' contacts with the local village or 'service centre' could be very infrequent, particularly before the Second World War.

The most tangible means by which the travel needs of farm households were reduced were by a variety of institutions which brought services to the farm. Pedlars were particularly active until the 1920s. Agents for Neil Brothers of Winnipeg provided bulk quantities of staples and fancy items such as dried fruit until the mid-1920s[56] and in some areas as late as 1942.[57] Occasionally a gypsy pedlar might arrive by caravan or on foot loaded down with 'telescope suitcases' on his back, filled with hard-to-get items like scissors, coloured threads, cloth, beads, buttons, kitchen utensils, patent medicines, dolls and other toys.[58] Butchers were known to canvass the open-country with their goods.[59] Independent pedlars also sold clothing, fish and crockery.[60] During this early period, it was even possible to order farm machinery from itinerant salesmen.[61] Raleigh and Watkins's representatives travelled door-to-door first by caravan and later by car until the mid-1940s.[62] Unlike many of the pedlars of the 1920s these were usually local people who brought news and gossip along with their wares. Watkins specialised in spices, baking products and cosmetics,[63] but was occasionally known to carry such things as fresh vegetables.[64] Mail order was used extensively by farm people. Clothing, in particular, if it was not made at home, was likely to be bought through the mail order catalogue. This practice continued until quite recently; it was possible to recognise mail order dresses at country dances into the 1960s.[65]

Health care was dealt with mostly without visits to town. Few farm families could afford the services of a physician,[66] but in extreme instances or when money was available the doctor was expected to travel to the patient. House-calls were taken for granted as part of a physician's work until the end of the 1940s.[67] The practice continued until very recently but became increasingly rare and would depend upon the illness and the physician's committment to the selfless ethic of the traditional country doctor.[68] Some physicians attempted to extend the reach of their services by travelling to smaller hamlets for consulting on certain designated days.[69] It was not unknown for dentists to tour the countryside rather like pedlars with a motor-caravan fitted with a dentist's chair and manual drill. Pharmacists also carried their services to rural areas in this way.[70] Many children received professional health care only through the visits of public health nurses who toured the open-country schools. A large proportion of health care, midwifery for example,[71] was non-professional. Such services were provided either within the household or by local experts who generally paid house-calls. Ministers travelled to visit parishioners and to hold services at open-country schoolhouses.[72] Touring Sunday School vans brought moral education to the countryside in the 1920s and 1930s,[73] no doubt inspired by the pioneering efforts of Eva Hasell.

Of these various services which 'travelled' to the open-country, professional services and mail order were the only which were depended upon. Pedlars reduced travel needs, but their services were neither reliable nor complete enough to eliminate the need to travel to town. Mutual aid was used extensively to reduce the amount of travel necessary. Anyone travelling to town expected to give rides to neighbours or to carry in produce and deliver groceries for the families of the 'district' (usually a school district). One woman describes how her family, located at 'the tail end of the line' took one of four routes home depending on 'who wanted what'.[74] Those with cars were particularly depended upon to 'haul stuff out' for neighbours. Travellers were either intercepted as they passed by a farmstead and given cans of cream to sell and asked perhaps to pick up an order of groceries which had been telephoned to the local merchant, or they phoned around the neighbourhood offering to pick up anything that might be needed. Where mail delivery did not exist, neighbours' mail was picked up for them as a matter of course. Where rural mail delivery was provided, the local mail carrier 'never hesitated to make that special effort to bring anything from medicine to machinery parts that were required by farmers in an emergency'.[75] Mutual aid in travel was extensive until the late 1940s, particularly during the winter. Shopkeepers took telephone orders until the 1950s, at which time most of them began to operate on a 'self-serve' basis, thus making it less convenient for people to pick up orders for others.[76] In some areas the practice of delivering for neighbours was common until the 1970s.[77] However, by 1987, rather than neighbourhoods collaborating on trips to town individual family members were making independent trips: 'You see them come in now: one family with two or three cars. Nobody drives together anymore.'[78]

Travel needs of prairie farmers were also affected by their need to purchase or sell commodities. This need varied according to the degree of self-sufficiency of the farm household, or the degree to which exchanges were limited to social networks within open-country. In Saskatchewan, as elsewhere, the shift has been from domestic self-provisioning to greater dependence on commodities. However, the change became sufficiently pronounced to affect travel behaviour far later than standard texts in rural sociology would have us believe. Prairie farm families produced their own dairy and poultry products, meat and garden produce. In addition, many supplemented their production by hunting, trapping, and collecting wild fruits.[79] With the exception of milling grain, most of the primary processing was done domestically. Up to half of the food requirements of the family was produced on the farm before 1930.[80] Food supplies which had to be bought were purchased in bulk both to save money and reduce shopping trips. An efficient farm household could in theory get by with two major trips to town for food supplies in one year. However, in practice enough other purposes took household members or neighbours to town that this was not necessary.

A 1947 study of Saskatchewan farm families offers some telling clues to the importance of self-provisioning in the production of clothing and bedding. While only 9 per cent of farm families could afford running water, 93 per cent of them owned sewing machines; indeed, there was no more ubiquitous household machine. Even automobiles were owned by only 64 per cent of families.[81] Clothing for children and women was more likely to be home-made; men's clothing would be extensively mended.

Self-provisioning also helped to reduce costs in the production of agricultural goods for sale. Before 1940 many of the resources required for wheat growing were provided on the farm. Two changes increased the dependence on commodities which had to be purchased off the farm: the shift from animal-based to petroleum-based power in the 1940s; and the increasing use of chemical fertilisers after the Second World War. Work horses were 'fuelled' by resources grown on the farm; the few fertilisers which were used were also produced on the farm. The increasingly automated machinery associated with petroleum-based power became harder to repair with the basic blacksmithing and woodworking skills available on the farm.

The economic pressures to increase the productivity of their farms were the first to influence farmers' travel needs. They bought tractors before they bought cars. As they mechanised in response to competitive pressures they found that they increasingly needed to travel to service the growing fleet of farm machines, equipment and, after the war, stocks of chemicals. The need to be in contact with the service centre for oil and gas, fertiliser, parts and repairs, increased markedly. The need for frequent, unscheduled trips, particularly during periods of peak activity, produced the new activity of 'running', that is, running to town by car to pick something up or to deliver it. This was generally women's work. As one woman recalled:

> I can remember out on the farm . . . I started to make a boiled icing one time, and I had it on the stove the third time before I got it made. I had been to Conquest for repairs [29 miles] and I was in Rosetown for repairs [29 miles in the other direction]. They'd just come in and make a holler and I'd pull it off and go.[82]

Running also involved increasing distances as implement dealers began to centralise operations. Driving on the farm itself, to deliver meals to those operating the combine harvesters for instance, could consume an enormous amount of time. Farms were rapidly expanding and new sections[83] could not always be purchased adjacent to one another.

Aside from the forces put into motion by mechanisation, there were few inducements for prairie farmers to change their travel habits. The slightly greater speed afforded by the car did not in itself influence the distance farmers were willing to travel to shop or to sell their products, nor did it increase the number of destinations which farmers habitually visited. Part of the reason for this reluctance to change lay in the fact that, on the prairies at least, existing destinations were widely dispersed from the outset. The trip to town by horse-drawn means was a hardship, but even by car it remained a full day's undertaking. The initial use of cars was to make traditional travel patterns more convenient. If anything, people might frequent the same destinations more often; but rarely would they make a regular habit of visiting further destinations.[84] Most families preferred the pleasures of town to the pleasures of being on the road. Travelling further afield in search of better prices and more attractive amusements meant forgoing a hard-won convenience and risking the vagaries of rain and bad roads. Driving could be an ordeal in an early model car full of six or seven people, equipped with springs but no shock absorbers and open to the clouds of dust it threw up on unpaved roads.[85]

Because of the excessive travel burden for dispersed farmers at some distance from service centres, a constant effort was made to combine trip purposes. A trip to town might involve hauling wheat and perhaps a neighbour's cream cans one way; socialising with more distant neighbours in town; hauling a load of coal, a few groceries and mail for the family and neighbours along the route on the return trip. People invariably used a team and wagon or sleigh for a trip like this since wheat was not commonly hauled by truck until well into the 1950s. Ownership of trucks was almost nil until 1936 for a number of reasons.[86] Hauling by truck was about three times faster, but the box would hold only about half the wheat of which a wagon was capable. Also, a truck could not be relied upon because of the weather in late fall and winter, when most hauling was done. Few farmers could justify the expense of having both a wagon box and an automobile to do the same job.[87] The combining of trip purposes meant that for much of the year travel destinations were defined by the 'slowest' trip purpose, the hauling of wheat.

Perhaps the main reason, though, that automobiles had little influence on travel destinations was that travel behaviour was not narrowly instrumental. People's loyalty to particular destinations was not reducible to reasons of economic utility. Throughout the province 'train-day', or in some towns Saturday night, was a festive social institution.[88] Train-day was defined by the arrival of the mail train, which briefly transformed the station platform into a spectacle of jostling human activity. Saturday night, a traditional time to converge on a small town or hamlet, was more likely to focus on the main street. Stores were often furnished with benches or chairs in front of the counter which allowed customers to relax and chat with each other or the storekeeper while an assistant, usually a son or daughter, filled customers' orders from the aisles located behind the counter. Stores stayed open and visiting continued often late into the evening whether patrons had business to do or not. A final treat to cap the evening might be a brick of ice cream at the café or ice-cream parlour, followed by the long journey home ending as late as midnight.[89] Particularly in winter, when trips were made once every three weeks rather than weekly, people looked forward to seeing the town. Work was arranged during the week to leave Saturday or train-day free. The events and even some of the facilities in the town were constructed as much for the purposes of fraternising as shopping. For sociability a familiar location served better than a more distant one. The logistics of spending a day in a larger centre might also be more difficult. Stores were less likely to provide benches or card tables. Women rarely found adequate places to sit down with their groceries, feed the children their packed lunches or change a baby's diapers.[90]

The traditional day in town remained intact as an institution until the early

1950s, but was rapidly eroded over the next decade and a half. On an immediate level, people saw the store shift to a 'self-serve' basis and the benches and card tables disappear. Customers were kept moving and their attention directed towards the activity of consumption. Fixed closing hours were adhered to, signalling the end of lingering informal gatherings. In the early 1960s first passenger services then, in many hamlets and villages, freight services were discontinued, putting an end to train-days. By the mid-1960s it was rare to see a team in town at any time of the year, and in most places the hitching rails had been removed, if only recently. Going to town was no longer a full day's event combining many purposes which people were able to draw out for long hours before the reluctant expedition home; nor did it concentrate activity on a single day of the week.[91]

While the town was an important meeting place on Saturday night, the country schools provided the main focus of rural social life. The closeness of these was of tremendous importance in reducing isolation and the travel required to maintain social contacts. People often volunteer that their parents, who were original homesteaders, might have felt isolated. Certainly before about 1915–19 when, in many places, the railway, towns and schools were still in the process of being built, and settlement was still sparse, the experience of prolonged isolation was more common. The children of pioneers consistently deny having experienced isolation themselves, and are quick to elaborate: 'Of course, people visited so well in those days';[92] 'there was always someone going by the door';[93] 'we just never thought of anything else'.[94] By 1920 those who were prevented from getting out to see neighbours or taking part in community life appear to have been hindered more by work than distance or even access to transport.

Certain types of work, such as hauling wheat and supplies, threshing, school or municipal administration or 'building bees', did have a collective, social element, but were typically male-dominated. Various types of 'hauling', for instance, became part of women's work only after the Second World War. House- and yard-work, which absorbed most women's time was solitary or shared only with children. The kind of work, particularly for women, and the amount, particularly at peak seasons (spring and fall) could prevent people from visiting. When the work was reasonably well under control, people commonly walked or took one of the horses to drop in on a neighbour for part of the day. Work schedules were somewhat more flexible since unannounced visits were universally tolerated.[95] Work rhythms before the widespread use of the tractor (beginning in the 1940s) were defined by the need to rest horses. In many districts all field-work halted at six and the community converged on the schoolyard for a ball game or other evening recreation. From the perimeter of the district, the walk to school took only about 20 minutes, yet the area was large enough at the peak of settlement to produce gatherings of twenty to thirty families.

The school district was most active as a community centre in winter. No field-work could be done and, depending on the number of livestock a farm possessed, farm work was considerably reduced, leaving time which could be devoted to politics, card playing, dancing and socialising. Visits could last for two or three days, particularly if cards were being played. The school building was used on different nights for political study groups (such as the CCF clubs), quilting bees or the inevitable country dances. Usually two, and in some cases three, school districts scheduled their dances on alternate weeks so that throughout the winter it was possible to attend a dance at least once a week. These were well-attended and high spirited affairs. They offered a varied social milieu: local musicians supporting instruments ranging from pianos to saxophones to fiddles; unattached farmers vying for the attention of the schoolteacher; grandparents; married couples accompanied by their progeny of all ages.[96] In addition to its closeness, the country dance had other advantages over competing entertainments in town. People felt there was more 'mixing' at country dances than at town events. Also, attending a movie or the local tavern created problems of child-care which were easily accommodated at a school dance.

A frequent claim made for the automobile is that it reduced isolation. The assumption being made is that people experienced isolation and sought to overcome it by changing their travel habits. My interviews with Saskatchewan residents suggest that if they experienced isolation between 1920 and 1940 this was more likely to have been a result of the nature of their work than of their means of transport. Any improvement in travel resulted, work permitting, in more frequent trips, largely confined to familiar open-country spaces.[97] Travelling beyond the tightly knit community of the school district or beyond the familiar trade centre could as easily result in an experience of greater isolation.

With the exception of many domestic tasks the intensity of work on the prairies followed quite extreme seasonal variations. During winter and midsummer, time simply lost much of its value. Eva Hasell describes a very generous attitude towards deadlines, necessitated in part by the unpredictability of travel, as well as the rural resistance to shifting onto railway and city time in summer.[98] Even a man who describes himself as the first, and for many years one of the only, to haul wheat by gasoline in the Dinsmore area, and who gleefully recalls passing his horse-drawn neighbours on the road to the elevators in the fall of 1921, could in the winter pass up the sleigh in favour of walking or skiing 15 miles into town for groceries.[99] Walking, and in some districts cycling, was an accepted means of covering the shorter distances, to the school building and nearest town, well into the 1930s.[100]

With few exceptions social exchanges were largely confined to the open-country before the clearing of winter roads in the 1950s. As late as 1960, according to Willmott's study, farmers in the Biggar area were resistant to taking part in town organisations and social activities. The most frequent explanation given by respondents concerned travel-related difficulties.[101] By 1966 school consolidation, which was intended to improve the quality of rural life by providing larger, modernised schooling facilities, had destroyed 80 per cent of the institutions which had supported rural Saskatchewan's decentralised community life.[102] No 'country' schools remained and few schools were left in the smaller hamlets. It had become impossible to live on the farm during the winter without considerable travel to the towns, which now provided the primary focus of social life.

Having children attend school in town created the previously unknown need

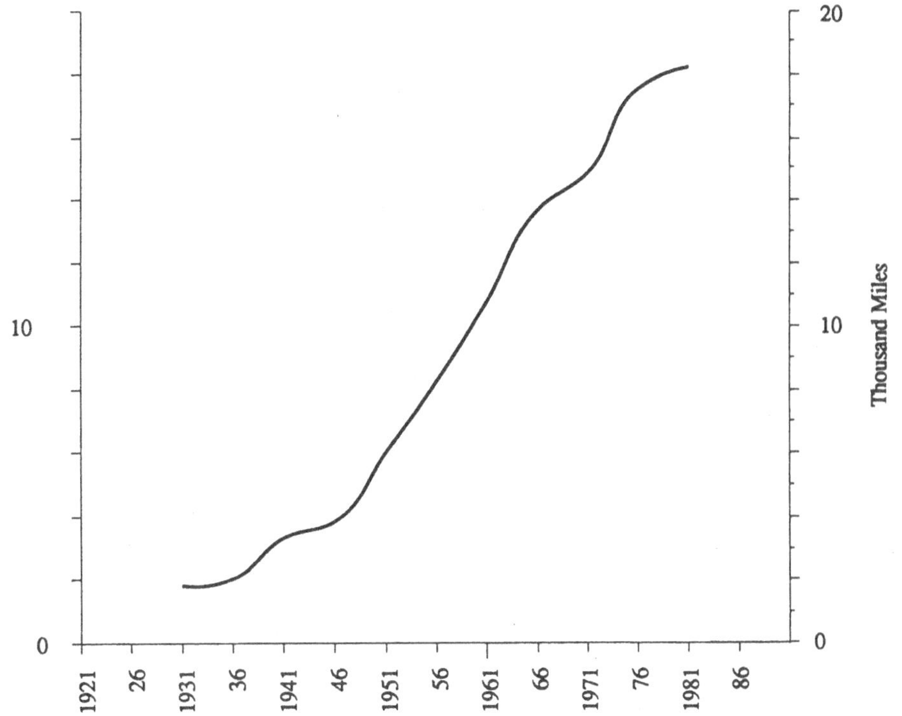

Fig. 3. Travel in Saskatchewan (miles per household)

Source: The figures for miles travelled per household were derived simply by dividing total travel by number of households (only between 3 and 7 per cent of highway travel is by commercial as opposed to private vehicles). A detailed study of actual travel behaviour (Stats Can 21-501, 1958) contains figures very close to these cruder estimates for 1958.

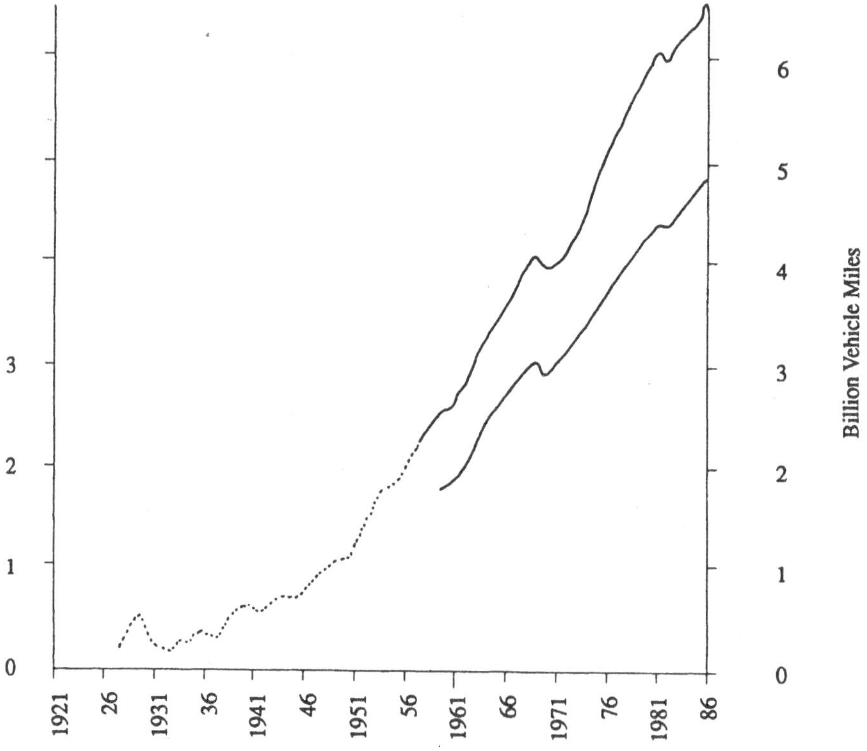

Fig. 4. Travel in Saskatchewan (all vehicles)

Source: Total travel (total miles travelled by any and all motor vehicles in the province in a given year) figures were obtained from Saskatchewan Department of Highways and Transportation, *Travel on Saskatchewan Highways*, for census and intercensal years after 1958. A historic table giving total travel from 1928 onwards is republished in a number of these reports, but present staff members at the department do not know how these figures were derived. Al Schaan, Director of Rural Development (Department of Municipal Affairs) advises that before 1966 information on travel on municipal roads (as opposed to provincial highways) was arrived at by using a small sample of rural municipalities (10 per cent) and that some years are estimates only (personal communications, 1987). (Municipal roads make up the bulk of the road mileage but receive only a quarter of total travel.)

to convey them to extra-curricular activities — ice hockey, band, figure skating and so on — now centred on the town. Children's circles of friends drew from a much broader radius, and maintaining contact with them required considerable travel. The weekly expedition into town for train-day or Saturday night began to be replaced by numerous, and in some cases incessant, trips back and forth. One older woman, appalled at the demands on young mothers, explained: 'Now women just about go crazy. Every kid they've got is in a different hockey team, ball team . . . and they're just going continually. . . . Some south of here make four or five trips to Wiseton in a day.'[103]

The average number of miles travelled in the province per household was increasing yearly at an extraordinary rate over this period (see figures 3 and 4) and many of these miles were taken up in 'running' by members of rural households in pursuit of children, machine parts and generally the material blandishments of a 'better life'. Increased use of the automobile to pursue further and more-varied destinations was a response to previously unheard of needs which had emerged with the mechanisation of the farm enterprise and the spatial reorganisation of farm implement dealers and rural schools.

Established needs, market exchanges and social contacts had, until this time, been adequately served by slower travel technologies. The ownership of automobiles had provided little inducement for farmers to travel faster and further afield. In striking contrast to rural regions in the United States, travel behaviour in Saskatchewan did not change markedly until the 1950s. Although spatial restructuring had already begun for some services, others remained highly decentralised, putting off for another two decades that more decisive geographic change, the abandonment of small towns. In the 1970s grain elevator closures, rail line abandonment and the 'death' of small towns became political issues for the first time.[104]

Travel patterns changed in the 1950s and again in the 1970s. Still, for Saskatchewan there was no 'automobile age' in the sense of an era which saw the introduction of a new technology accompanied by marked changes in travel behaviour and in the institutional geography which framed this behaviour. The social context defining travel needs changed by degrees according to its own logic. The introduction of automobiles had little effect on the timing of these developments. Patterns of automobile use conformed to, and later changed with, the changing institutional context.

Notes

1 At the peak of settlement (1936) rural population density in Saskatchewan was 6·5 farm residents per square mile of farmed land ('total area in farms' from the 1936 census rather than 'total land area' which would include the non-arable precambrian shield which covers the northern half of the province). Comparable population densities for Manitoba and Alberta in 1936 were 10·7 and 6·3 persons per square mile, respectively.

2 With the exception of Missouri, see table 1.

3 This approach was pioneered by the American rural sociologist C. Galpin, 'The social anatomy of an agricultural community', *University of Wisconsin Agricultural Experimental Station Bulletin* XXXIV (1915), *passim*. Galpin anticipates many of the principles of 'central place theory' developed by Walter Christaller in the late 1950s. For a critical discussion of the American tradition see J. Hodge, 'The Prediction of Trade Centre Viability in the Great Plains', unpublished Ph.D. thesis, MIT, 1965; C. Zimmerman and G. W. Moneo, *The Prairie Community Systems* (Ottawa, 1971); R. Bantjes, 'Improved Earth: Land Settlement, Community and Class in Rural North America, 1900–1960', Ph.D. thesis, University of Lancaster, 1991.

4 P. Landis, *Rural Life in Process* (New York, 1940), pp. 82–3.

5 See, for example, J. Flink, *America Adopts the*

Automobile 1895–1910 (Cambridge, Mass., 1970); J. Rae, *The Road and the Car in America* (Cambridge, Mass., 1971).

6 N. Moline, *Mobility and the Small Town, 1900–1930: Transportation Change in Oregon, Illinois* (Chicago, 1971); T. Morain, *Prairie Grass Roots, an Iowa Small Town in the Early Twentieth Century* (Ames, 1988); see also M. Berger, 'The Social Impact of the Automobile on Rural America, 1893–1929', Ph.D. Columbia University, 1972.

7 Saskatchewan data were collected with increasing comprehensiveness at each of the following levels: census divisions 2, 6, 10, 12 and 13 (see attached map); census divisions 12 and 13; and rural municipalities ('RMs', also census subdivisions) 286 and 377. Conditions are fairly uniform throughout the province, and I think it is safe to generalise from these regions to the entire settled part of the province. Quantitative data describing the institutional context for travel behaviour (market services, state services, roads, community institutions) come from a variety of official sources; for instance, Dun and Bradstreet records (divisions 12 and 13), reports of government departments (for the whole province), special census reports (the province and special sample areas). Data on actual travel behaviour come from travelogues, local histories (one or two of these have been published by local history societies in each RM; I looked at all of those from divisions 12 and 13) and a series of taped interviews with residents of RMs 286 and 377 which I conducted between April and December 1987. The interviews are largely illustrative; most information, concerning dates and so on, is corroborated with other published material.

8 G. T. Bloomfield, '"I can see a car in that crop": motorization in Saskatchewan, 1906–1934', *Saskatchewan History*, XXXVII (1) (1984), p. 13. Given the scarcity of hard evidence for this claim, Bloomfield is forced to admit that 'the details are now obscure'. See also G. T. Bloomfield, 'Motorization on the New Frontier: the Case of Saskatchewan, Canada, 1906–1934', in T. Barker (ed.), *The Economic and Social Effects of the Spread of Motor Vehicles* (1986).

9 J. Interrante, 'The road to autopia: the automobile and the spatial transformation of American culture', in D. L. Lewis and L. Goldstein (eds), *The Automobile in American Culture* (Ann Arbor, 1983); see also J. Interrante, 'You can't go to town in a bathtub: automobile movement and the reorganization of American space, 1900–1903', *Radical History Review*, XXI (1979), p. 153.

10 F. H. Eva Hasell, *Across the Prairie in a Motor Caravan* (Toronto, 1922).

11 Canada, Department of Railways and Canals. Total miles are from Statistics Canada, *Road and Street Mileage and Expenditure*, 53–201 (1963); other sources, such as the Department of Railways and Canals, and Bloomfield, '"I can see a car in that crop"', p. 20, appear to overestimate unsurfaced miles. I have taken the most conservative figures. Bloomfield's source also gives slightly larger figures for surfaced miles — 1,000 in 1927 — still only 1 per cent of the *Road and Street Mileage and Expenditure* total or 0·07 per cent of Bloomfield's Canadian Tax Foundation total.

12 'Dragging' was a technique for levelling and sloping the crown of a road.

13 The highway maintenance division expected as a matter of course to redrag all 'improved' roads after a heavy rain. Saskatchewan Department of Highways, *Annual Report* (1924–25), p. 79.

14 Hasell, *Across the Prairies*, pp. 64–71.

15 Saskatchewan Local History, *Preserving the Past*, p. 639.

16 The levelled crown.

17 Hasell, *Across the Prairie*, pp. 35–6.

18 R. H. Mackenzie, Department of Highways, at the 22nd Annual Convention of the Saskatchewan Association of Rural Municipalities, 1927; cited in Bloomfield, '"I can see a car in that crop"', p. 24.

19 For an English readership Eva Hasell admirably describes what a slough is: 'These sloughs are like great ponds, their bottoms are covered with deep mud, and if one gets in, a car sinks deeper and deeper and cannot be got out.' (Hasell, *Across the Prairie*, p. 33).

20 Road allowances are strips of crown land set aside for the construction of roads. These bordered surveyed 'sections' of land (each 1 mile square) and allowed for the construction of a road travelling north–south every 1 mile and one travelling east–west every 2 miles.

21 Statutes of Saskatchewan, 1909.

22 Interview, Willis Clarke, Dinsmore, Saskatchewan, 10 December 1987.

23 Based on calculations for 1921, 1931 and 1941 from *Road and Street Mileage and Expenditure* (1963) and Census of Canada.

24 Cited in J. Archer, 'Pathfinders of the Trans-Canada Highway', *Saskatchewan History*, VII (1950) p. 25 n. 15. The 'All-Red' route referred to one which remained within British (i.e. red on the map) territory particularly north of the Great Lakes where a detour south through the United States would be infinitely easier.

25 Interview, Sam Clayton, Saskatoon, September 1987; Saskatchewan Local History, 'North Biggar History' (n.p.).

26 Hasell, *Across the Prairies*, p. 85.

27 The *Leader* (Regina) 18 June 1914. cited in 'The newspaper scrapbook', *Saskatchewan History*, VII (3) (1954), p. 110.

28 Interviews, Willis Clarke; Bill and Margaret Goldie, Wiseton, Saskatchewan, 26 October 1987.

29 Interviews, Willis Clarke; Vie Hall, Wiseton, Saskatchewan, 26 October 1987.

30 Interview, Willis Clarke; Hasell, *Across the*

Prarie, passim.; Saskatchewan Local History 'Prairie Tapestry — A Superb Story' (n.p.), p. 134; 'The newspaper scrapbook; auto trip — Regina to Strassburg, 1908', *Saskatchewan History*, VI (1953), p. 69.

31 Interviews: informants' estimates of speed in miles per hour are usually greater than calculations based on their estimate of the time it took to travel between two familiar locations. The latter are being used here. Written sources not already mentioned include P. Gombrey, *A Motor Scamper Across Canada* (Toronto, 1922), p. 121.

32 C. Dawson and E. Younge, *Pioneering in the Prairie Provinces: the Social Side of the Settlement Process*, Canadian Frontiers of Settlement, VIII (Toronto: 1940).

33 Interviews, Willis Clarke; Bill and Margaret Goldie, Wiseton, 26 October 1987.

34 Hasell, *Across the Prairie*, p. 95. Train times were taken from *Waghorn's Guide* for 1921 and 1946. Average speeds were calculated from track distances as measured on the map.

35 The average temperature in January in one of Saskatchewan's major cities (Saskatoon) is −19°C. This is the lowest for western Canada and the northern United States.

36 Interview, Fay Beattie, Dinsmore, 10 December 1987.

37 Interviews; H. Durnford and G. Baechler, *Cars of Canada* (Toronto, 1973).

38 Saskatchewan Local History, 'Reflections: a History of Arelee' (n.p.).

39 Durnford and Baechler, *Cars of Canada*, p. 203.

40 *Atlas of Saskatchewan*; interviews.

41 Durnford and Baechler, *Cars of Canada*; interview, Lloyd and Joyce Ross, Spinney Hill, Saskatchewan, 18 October 1987; Saskatchewan local histories: most contain at least one photograph of a local snow-plane.

42 H. Chatenay, *Echoes of Silence* (Red Deer, 1978); H. Chatenay, *The Country Doctors* (Red Deer, 1980).

43 Saskatchewan Local History, 'Borderline Memories', p. 124.

44 Saskatchewan Local History, 'Preserving the Past' (n.p.), p. 41.

45 Durnford and Baechler, *Cars of Canada*, p. 204.

46 Census of Canada.

47 Saskatchewan Department of Highways, *Annual Report*, 1934–35.

48 *Ibid.*, 1945–46; 1951–52; 1956–57.

49 As late as 1961 only 7 per cent of rural municipalities operated their own snow removal equipment (Saskatchewan Local Government Continuing Committee, *The Rural Road Function* [Regina, 1961], p. 106).

50 In census divisions 12 and 13: see note 7.

51 Saskatchewan Local History, 'North Biggar History' (n.p.).

52 Saskatchewan Department of Co-operatives and Co-operative Development, *Annual Report*, 1956.

53 'Co-operative Commonwealth Federation': a left-wing agrarian based party.

54 Government of Saskatchewan, Task Force, *Strategy for the Development of Rural Saskatchewan* (Regina, 1985); Government of Saskatchewan, Royal Commission, Municipal Road Surfacing Commission, *Report* (Regina, 1974). Department of Highways reports begin in the 1950s to discuss how grade 'profiles' can be designed in such a way as to use the prevailing winds to clear rather than bury roads (Saskatchewan Local Government Continuing Committee, *The Rural Road Function*, [Regina, 1961]).

55 These generally coincided with the boundaries of school attendance districts. The country schoolhouse, an isolated building on an unpaved road, was the only public building serving most open-country communities.

56 Interview, Willis Clarke, 1987.

57 Interview, Bill and Margaret Goldie, Wiseton, 26 October 1987. Bill Goldie gives the 1942 figure, Deloris McDonald says that they persisted 'through 1932'; interview, Deloris McDonald, Wiseton, 24 October 1987.

58 Interviews, Faye Beattie, 1987; Linda Custer, Baljennie, Saskatchewan, 18 November 1987.

59 Saskatchewan Local History, 'Through the Years' (n.p.).

60 Saskatchewan Local History, 'Preserving the Past' (n.p.), p. 41.

61 Interview, Willis Clarke. Binders, ploughs and so on would be sold 'out of an order book'; presumably the purchase would be delivered on a separate trip.

62 Interviews, Deloris McDonald; Lloyd and Joyce Ross, 1987.

63 Advertisements, the *Nor-West Farmer*, 5 June 1922, p. 579; the *Nor-West Farmer*, 5 August 1922, p. 761.

64 Interview, Bill and Margaret Goldie, 1987.

65 Interviews, Bill and Margaret Goldie, 'Pretty well all clothing' was bought this way until the 1940s; Faye Beattie, 1987; Ken and Margaret Hodges, Wiseton, Saskatchewan, 26 October 1987; Lloyd and Joyce Ross, 1987: mail order was extensively used into the 1960s.

66 Interviews, Faye Beattie: '... you didn't call the doctor much in those days'; Lloyd and Joyce Ross: 'Couldn't afford to get sick ...'.

67 Interview, Vie Hall, Wiseton, Saskatchewan, 26 October 1987: 'As the roads got better people started to come in usually ... but when Dr Blakely [1931–39] was there people couldn't get in; people expected him to come out'; see also Joyce Ross, Spinney Hill, Saskatchewan, 18 October

1987; interview, John Sarvas, Biggar, Saskatchewan, 4 September 1987.

68 Often the death or retirement of a traditional practitioner would mark the end of house-calls.

69 Interview, Deloris McDonald, 1987.

70 Saskatchewan Local History, 'Memoirs of Hillsburgh' (n.p.), p. 222.

71 Interviews, Lloyd and Joyce Ross, 1987; Deloris McDonald, 1987.

72 Travelling ministers performed services in open-country schools even after 1949; interview, Bill and Margaret Goldie, 1987.

73 Saskatchewan Local History, 'Borderline Memories' (n.p.), p. 123; Saskatchewan Local History, 'North Biggar History' (n.p.), p. 463.

74 Interview, Faye Beattie, 1987.

75 Saskatchewan Local History, 'Wilkie' (n.p.).

76 Interview, Deloris McDonald (a store-owner), Dinsmore, Saskatchewan, 10 December 1987.

77 Interview, Lloyd and Joyce Ross, 1987.

78 Interview, Vie Hall, 1987.

79 Interview, John Sarvas, 1987.

80 Saskatchewan Royal Commission on Agriculture and Rural Life, 'The Home and Family', Report no. 10, *Royal Commission on Agriculture and Rural Life* (Regina, 1955), p. 28.

81 M. MacNaughton, 'Changes in Farm Family Living in Three Areas of the Prairie Provinces from 1942–3 to 1947', Publication 815, Technical Bulletin 69, Economics Division, Department of Agriculture (Ottawa, 1949), p. 74.

82 Interview, Vie Hall, 1987.

83 A 'section' is a unit of the land survey, 1 mile square. Land is typically bought in sections or quarter sections ('quarters').

84 Even shortly after the Depression, the overwhelming majority of farm families supplied most of their needs from one centre (Dawson and Younge, *Pioneering in the Prairie Provinces*, p. 57).

85 Few people could afford the elaborate accessories designed to make driving more comfortable (for some examples of these, see Durnford and Baechler, *Cars of Canada*, pp. 206–7.

86 See table 1. Economic comparisons were discussed in farm journals and government reports of the 1920s (cf. Canada, Department of Railways and Canals (Highways Branch), *The Canadian Highway and its Development*, Bulletin no. 7 (Ottawa, 1925), pp. 12 ff.; also the *Nor-West Farmer*, 20 June 1916, p. 679; 6 March 1916, p. 240). In addition to the fact that they assume summer conditions these calculations miss the point that many of the costs of operating a horse could be supplied on a non-cash basis.

87 The same wagon box was generally used all year; wheels were removed and four heavy runners attached in winter.

88 The towns referred to in the following section were typically very small. In Saskatchewan in 1930, 49 per cent of all 'trade centres' had populations of fifty or less; 95 per cent had populations under 501. Calculated from C. A. Dawson, and E. R. Younge, *Pioneering in the Prairie Provinces: the Social Side of the Settlement Process*, p. 49.

89 Interviews (Sachko, Clarke, Mcdonald — see above). Saskatchewan Local History, 'Grassland to Grainland' (n.p.).

90 Barry Potyondi, 'Country Town: the History of Minnedosa, Manitoba 1879–1922', M.A. thesis, University of Manitoba, 1978.

91 The dates in this paragraph are based on interviews from the rural municipality of Milden (no. 286) where all of these changes are likely to have occurred earlier than in many parts of the province.

92 Interview, Faye Beattie, 1987.

93 Interview, Bill and Margaret Goldie, 1987.

94 Interview, Deloris McDonald, 1987. She continued: 'We had neighbours, eh? A mile in each direction. And you'd walk over there; play with the kids. They'd come over in the evening and play cards. There was a community.'

95 Interviews; Saskatchewan Local History, 'North Biggar History' (n.p.), p. 20.

96 John Charyk, *Pulse of the Community* (Saskatoon, 1968), p. 198; interviews; Saskatchewan Local History, 'North Biggar History' (n.p.), pp. 20, 90, 166.

97 This principle was confirmed in some American studies of transport technology and travel behaviour in the 1930s; T. McCormick, *Rural Social Organization in Washington County, Arkansas*, Arkansas Agricultural Experiment Station Bulletin 285, 1933; Morgan and Howels, *Rural Population Groups*, University of Missouri Agricultural Station, Research Bulletin no. 74 (1925), p. 327.

98 Hasell, *Across the Prairie*, p. 56.

99 Interview, Willis Clarke, 1987.

100 Teachers and pupils regularly walked to school. A Wheat Pool fieldman in his report of April 1941 mentions giving two Pool committee men rides home after a meeting — one of whom had walked 8 miles to attend (Secretaries' Report, Country Organisation Division, Saskatchewan Wheat Pool, 1941). See also Saskatchewan Local History, 'Through the Years' (n.p.), p. 215; Saskatchewan Local History, 'North Biggar History' (n.p.), pp. 18, 163.

101 D. Willmott, *Organizations and Social Life of Farm Families in a Prairie Municipality* (Saskatoon, 1964), p. 56. Willmott says that 30 per cent of the fifty-nine farm leaders he spoke to on this issue mentioned 'practical difficulties'; the five examples he lists are all travel related.

102 Saskatchewan Department of Education, *Annual Report*, 1967.

103 Interview, Vie Hall, 1987.

104 See R. Bantjes, 'Improved Earth: Land Settlement, Community and Class in Rural North America, 1900–1960', Ph.D. thesis, University of Lancaster, 1991, Chapter 9.

10 'See this amazing America': the long-distance bus industry's use of advertising in its first quarter century

MARGARET WALSH

In the early years of the twentieth century new transport technologies brought both a huge increase in travel and competition between different types of passenger and freight carriers in the USA. With the advent of cars, buses, trucks and airlines alongside existing steam and electric railroads, pipelines and waterways, the different modes of transport attempted to gain, retain or increase their activities. This they did not only through greater efficiency, better vehicles and modern business practices but also through influencing consumer tastes by national advertising campaigns. The long-distance bus industry, though always a small contributor to intercity travel, quickly learnt how to market its facilities and soon came to rely on advertising for promoting both regular and special features. This article outlines the leading bus companies' advertising efforts between 1925 and 1950 and relates them to the performance of the industry during these years.[1]

The bus industry and its advertising

By the late 1920s major changes in patterns of American transport were visible in the shift from railroads to roads. Cars were well established and had become so popular during the decade that they already accounted for over 80 per cent of intercity travel (table 1). Buses emerging from their experimental stage in the second decade of the century had steadily increased their business to gain over 20 per cent of the public carrier service (table 2). In the freight sector trucks were entering the gaps left by the railroads and would soon challenge for the high-value, long-distance trade. The depression of the 1930s curbed the buoyancy of the American economy but road transport withstood the pressures. Americans might not buy new cars, but they still drove their existing vehicles or acquired used cars. Buses increased their share of public carrier service to one-third of the total while trucking became a vibrant activity. The railroad, however,

Table 1. *Intercity travel 1929–51 (percentage distribution)*

Year	*Total intercity travel*	*Private automobiles*	*Public carriers*				
			Total	*Railroads*	*Intercity buses*	*Airlines*	*Waterways*
1929	100·0	82·7	17·3	13·0	3·6	–	0·7
1930	100·0	85·0	15·0	10·7	3·7	–	0·6
1931	100·0	87·7	12·3	8·3	3·5	–	0·5
1932	100·0	89·1	10·9	6·8	3·6	–	0·5
1933	100·0	88·8	11·2	6·8	3·7	0·1	0·6
1934	100·0	88·3	11·7	7·3	3·7	0·1	0·6
1935	100·0	88·4	11·6	7·1	3·8	0·2	0·6
1936	100·0	87·1	12·9	8·0	4·1	0·2	0·6
1937	100·0	86·4	13·6	8·1	4·8	0·2	0·7
1938	100·0	88·0	12·0	7·3	3·9	0·2	0·6
1939	100·0	87·5	12·5	7·3	4·3	0·3	0·6
1940	100·0	87·5	12·5	7·4	4·2	0·4	0·5
1941	100·0	85·8	14·2	8·6	4·5	0·5	0·6
1942	100·0	72·5	27·5	18·3	8·0	0·5	0·7
1943	100·0	55·9	44·1	32·2	10·6	0·6	0·7
1944	100·0	55·0	45·0	33·6	9·8	0·8	0·8
1945	100·0	59·8	40·2	29·3	9·1	1·1	0·7
1946	100·0	72·8	27·2	17·3	7·5	1·7	0·7
1947	100·0	78·9	21·1	11·8	7·0	1·8	0·5
1948	100·0	80·8	19·2	10·1	6·9	1·7	0·5
1949	100·0	83·6	16·4	8·0	6·1	1·9	0·4
1950	100·0	85·1	14·9	6·9	5·5	2·2	0·3
1951	100·0	84·5	15·5	7·2	5·4	2·0	0·3

Source. National Association of Motor Bus Operators, *Bus Facts*, XXI (1952), p. 10.

suffered severely, recovering only during the emergency of the Second World War, when gasoline and rubber shortages impeded private travel and co-operative efforts speeded rail freight flows. With the return of peace and an increased awareness of the need for better highways, road transport resumed its popularity, but new challenges in the passenger sector emerged with the airlines.[2]

The bus industry, which was providing local and regional services in the 1920s and offered a national service in the 1930s, was born into competition.[3] The car already offered short-distance mobility to many Americans while the train had a

Table 2. *Intercity travel by public carrier 1929–51 (percentage distribution)*

		Type of carrier			
Year	*Total*	*Railroads*	*Intercity buses*	*Airlines*	*Waterways*
1929	100·0	74·9	21·1	–	4·0
1930	100·0	70·9	24·9	0·3	3·9
1931	100·0	67·1	28·3	0·4	4·2
1932	100·0	62·5	32·8	0·5	4·2
1933	100·0	60·9	32·5	1·0	5·6
1934	100·0	62·3	31·8	1·0	4·9
1935	100·0	61·3	32·3	1·3	5·1
1936	100·0	62·3	31·5	1·4	4·8
1937	100·0	59·9	35·4	1·1	3·6
1938	100·0	60·7	32·8	1·6	4·9
1939	100·0	58·7	34·7	2·1	4·5
1940	100·0	59·3	34·2	2·8	3·7
1941	100·0	60·6	32·0	3·2	4·2
1942	100·0	66·5	29·1	1·9	2·5
1943	100·0	73·0	24·0	1·4	1·6
1944	100·0	74·6	21·7	1·9	1·8
1945	100·0	72·9	22·6	2·8	1·7
1946	100·0	63·8	27·6	6·2	2·4
1947	100·0	55·7	33·5	8·3	2·5
1948	100·0	52·9	35·5	9·1	2·5
1949	100·0	49·0	37·2	11·6	2·2
1950	100·0	46·6	36·8	14·6	2·0
1951	100·0	46·2	35·0	17·0	1·8

Source. National Association of Motor Bus Operators, *Bus Facts*, XXI (1952), p. 10.

well-established short and long-distance clientele. Bus operators who emerged from running local lines to provide routes which extended over 30 miles quickly adopted the systematic administrative structures and the business techniques of managerial capitalism to improve their efficiency, but they also recognised the importance of public relations and advertising in stimulating demand.[4] Initially in the 1920s bus operators relied on informational advertisements which listed towns and cities *en route* with departure and arrival times and fares. These schedules were frequently drafted by bus company employees. In the search for more passengers, entrepreneurs turned to the advertising industry, which, by the 1920s, had developed sophisticated sales techniques and was skilled in creating emotional copy which shaped tastes and moulded opinions in the age of high mass consumption.[5]

Clearly the basic commodity which the emerging long-distance bus industry and its advertising agents had to sell was travel.[6] Either those who already travelled must be enticed to use a bus rather than a car, train or plane, or more Americans must be encouraged to gain mobility by using a bus. For regular commuters advertisements were designed to highlight the virtues of motor coaches, namely economy, convenience, comfort, safety and dependability. Whatever the condition of the times most of those who journeyed frequently for business or family reasons could be persuaded to take the bus by appealing to one of these themes which bus managers and their advertisers constantly reiterated in various guises and with catchy slogans. Tourism presented a different and highly promising market for bus operators. Advertisements appealed to the desires of an increasingly prosperous population to enjoy their leisure in distant places.[7] By taking a bus Americans could become fashionable and relax in some exotic location at any time of the year. Indeed, this romantic or perhaps even therapeutic appeal of seeing new places came to dominate bus advertising. The bus promotional literature was clear, inventive and picturesque, and its artistry compared well with that of train and plane companies,[8] but it captured the interest of only a small proportion of the travelling population. Most Americans preferred to drive their own cars. Some of those who used public services were persuaded to switch from trains to buses, but advertisers needed to be constantly alert to retain a share of the market for buses.

Advertising for regular clients

Among the practical advantages offered by bus travel, economy was a consistent selling point. Buses were cheaper than their main competitors, trains or cars.[9] In their first national advertising campaign in 1929 Greyhound informed the travelling public that they could now afford to go across the USA (figure 1). A decade later economy remained important, when Greyhound suggested that two bus passengers could travel as cheaply as one in a small car. Santa Fe Trailways supported this low-cost travel pitch by offering fares at less than 2 cents per mile. By the late 1940s Greyhound was still claiming to provide good value for money with bus fares costing one-half to two-thirds of the cost by private car. If Americans were interested in cheap travel then buses provided a sound answer.[10]

This appeal to economy could be made even more attractive when related to specific economic fluctuations. Facing a severe and lengthy depression in the early 1930s, Greyhound managers thought that they could make more inroads

Fig. 1. *Saturday Evening Post*, 14 September 1929, p. 244.

into middle- and upper-class markets. They thus appealed to those who normally travelled on Pullman trains, or who drove cars, by advertising their buses as '$20,000 autos' and as the 'Second car in a two car family' (figure 2). When prices rose in the two years before the American entry into the Second World War, Santa Fe Trailways stressed that their fares stayed low, and in the 1940s, when average living costs increased by 64 per cent, Greyhound fares remained at their 1939 levels making a bus trip an outstanding bargain (figure 3). Economy was a theme which had a strong appeal to a variety of people.[11]

Cheap fares did not mean poor standards. Bus operators argued that buses offered low-cost luxury and thus their advertisements also featured comfort and safety. Comfort came in the shape of the modern motor coach, while safety depended both on the improved technology of vehicles and the skills and good sense of drivers. Comfort was rarely mentioned in the first days of bus travel, when vehicles were basic and road conditions appalling. In the 1920s, however, when manufacturers began to design motor coaches rather than build buses on wagon chassis, operators boasted of the merits of these new vehicles. Early national advertising in magazines featured all-steel buses with individual, deep-cushioned seats, cradle springs, balloon tyres and an effective heating and ventilation system. In the mid-1930s Greyhound's new 'Supercoach' provided increased room for passengers and baggage, better visibility for driver and passengers, improved ventilation, and new lighting systems and less vibration, all conducive to a more comfortable ride (figure 4). The newly merged Trailways System offered the smooth-gliding luxury of the Nite-Coach Sleeper and was already experimenting with air-conditioning. In an effort to break into the car market, advertisements suggested that buses were more comfortable than cars in the late 1930s, and they also tried appealing to rail users by offering some of the attractive facilities of trains.[12]

The emergency of the Second World War forced many Americans into travelling in overcrowded discomfort on buses and the advertisements of the leading companies in the late 1940s made strenuous efforts to make bus travel attractive by emphasising luxury. In 1946 Greyhound's 'Silverside' featured numerous advances for passengers, like wider seats, glare- and heat-resistant window glass, night reading lights and air conditioning, while safety features included superior brakes, better driver's mirrors and more room for the driver. The company's slightly later fifty-passenger bus the 'Highway Traveler' offered many more innovations for passenger comfort, while the 'Scenicruiser', introduced in 1954, provided excellent panoramic sightseeing, smoother riding and restful seating. Trailways' 'Aerocoach' also offered high levels of comfort, and operators suggested that travelling could be a genuine pleasure for passengers.[13]

A refreshing, carefree journey was also important if more passengers were to be attracted from trains and cars, and this could be assured because drivers were

Fig. 2. *Saturday Evening Post*, 12 November 1936, p. 36.

Fig. 3. *Saturday Evening Post*, 24 April 1948, n.p.

Fig. 4. *Saturday Evening Post*, 29 August 1936, pp. 27 and 29.

well trained, skilled and courteous. Indeed, Greyhound prided itself on its driver training and safety, and encouraged high standards by a system of rewards and penalties. Early advertisements boasted that every Greyhound driver was a man of character and responsibility who had passed rigorous examinations, and they frequently pictured this strong reliable uniformed man in support of their claim (figure 5). Announcements regularly pointed to the safety record of bus travel and by 1955 Greyhound boasted that their buses were eleven times as safe as travelling by car. Not only was safety important but driver courtesy was also a major ingredient in ensuring comfort. Personnel managers stressed that politeness and passenger attention brought satisfaction and repeat business, and in the difficult post-war years, when Americans turned increasingly to cars, Greyhound made a concerted effort to identify their company name with courtesy. Bus operators wanted potential customers to know that they would be well looked after.[14]

Promotional literature also paid attention to the convenience and dependability of bus travel. Customers wanted frequent reliable service from easily accessible terminals with good connections and stopover privileges, whether they were travelling regularly or taking occasional trips. Timetables provided the simplest way of providing schedule and fare information for frequent customers. At the same time bus managers needed to reassure these clients that they were acting wisely and they wanted to encourage more Americans to take to the buses. In 1940 Jefferson Lines frequently announced their convenient Iowa services in the local and daily newspapers of that state, thereby hoping to increase their shorter distance trade and bring bus travel into the daily lives of many people, like farmers' wives doing their shopping, teachers commuting home for the weekend and local business representatives.[15]

The ease of travelling longer distances needed to be advertised nationally as well as locally and not only in newspapers but also in popular magazines. As early as 1929, when Greyhound was a new entity, the corporation looked to an audience of millions when it informed readers of the *Saturday Evening Post* that the travel habits of a nation would change rapidly thanks to the convenience of frequent and time-saving bus services between a thousand cities and towns.[16] As Greyhound's route network expanded to 50,000 miles, and more frequent and direct services were added, advertisements claimed that their buses reached more places than any other public transport system. Convenience meant swift, time-saving, prompt and dependable service. Further incentives of liberal stopovers, alternative return routes at no extra cost, one ticket only to any part of the country and central city terminals aimed to maintain business in the depths of the depression in the mid-1930s (figure 6). Greyhound was not alone in appealing to convenience. Trailways quickly put together a similar package in 1936. Within months of their formation as an integrated system, they operated a route network of 30,000 miles and glowingly reported good connections,

20 MILLION MILES
OF SAFE BUS TRAVEL
– the Record of
these Greyhound Drivers
ALERT, responsible drivers in a hundred cities today swing into the control seats of the outbound Greyhound Buses. Before them stretch smooth highways to distant cities. In their competent charge is the good name of Greyhound Lines, largest motor transportation system in America.
Greyhound buses travel daily a distance equal to three times the mileage around the world. They carry millions of passengers in safety, in comfort, at the lowest cost ever offered for dependable overland travel.
Measures of Safety
Every Greyhound driver, schooled in the standards of safety and service which have built the Greyhound system, is a man of character, reliability. Physically and mentally he has stood the most rigorous of examinations.
He has come up through operating and mechanical departments that have taught him every nut and bolt in the coach he drives. Safety, courtesy and care he has earned in countless safety meetings and experience tests on the road. Not only is he courteous to his own passengers but to the thousands of other motorists he meets on the highways.
Responsible Ownership
In every terminal city great service garages check motors, chassis, tires and brakes, before each run. Every mechanism must be fit, every safety device operating at highest efficiency, always.
Winter and summer, day and night, millions of people depend on Greyhound bus travel. For a hundred miles or a trip across the continent you save money, enjoy new travel convenience and pleasure, on these Greyhounds of the highways.
Write for Greyhound bus fares and time tables from your city. An illuminating booklet "Motor Bus Transportation" will also be sent you. Address, Department of Travel Information, Motor Transit Management Company, Chicago.
DEPENDABLE
GREYHOUND
Lines
NEW YORK • LOS ANGELES • JACKSONVILLE • CHICAGO • PHILADELPHIA • CLEVELAND • DETROIT • CINCINNATI
BALTIMORE • WASHINGTON • PITTSBURGH • INDIANAPOLIS • ST. LOUIS • KANSAS CITY • DENVER • ATLANTA • NEW ORLEANS

Fig. 6. *Saturday Evening Post*, 25 October 1935, n.p.

frequent schedules, modern terminals and stopover facilities.[17] Indeed, bus passenger miles picked up in the second half of the 1930s (see table 3).

This type of service was lost during the Second World War, but with the easing of travel restrictions and the threat of competition, Greyhound planned a promotional campaign featuring ease and speed. Improved scheduling brought express service on many runs under 200 miles and limited stops meant improved times on longer runs. Additional services enabled Greyhound to offer more

Table 3. *The intercity bus industry 1925–50 (year ending 31 December)*

Year	*Number of companies*	*Number of vehicles*	*Route miles*	*Bus miles (millions)*	*Passenger miles (billions)*
1925	3,610	21,430	218,601	na	na
1926	4,040	22,800	250,396	960	na
1927	3,950	16,750	233,829	1,030	na
1928	3,610	16,050	251,999	1,170	na
1929	3,910	16,140	229,936	1,190	7·5
1930	3,520	14,090	318,715	1,230	7·1
1931	3,140	14,220	354,745	1,020	6·7
1932	2,760	13,640	364,676	920	6·3
1933	2,370	12,230	338,018	820	6·4
1934	2,210	10,660	321,449	800	7·1
1935	2,120	11,160	330,216	960	7·6
1936	2,130	11,260	312,825	1,110	9·2
1937	1,790	11,940	315,668	910	10·0
1938	1,880	11,700	320,640	880	9·0
1939	1,990	11,600	317,298	860	9·6
1940	1,830	12,200	313,136	820	10·1
1941	1,770	14,520	330,359	840	13·6
1942	2,190	18,020	345,049	1,070	21·5
1943	2,160	20,210	391,642	1,250	27·4
1944	2,310	21,750	402,005	1,350	26·9
1945	2,320	23,210	360,856	1,400	27·0
1946	2,430	23,880	376,567	1,560	26·3
1947	2,490	25,040	405,379	1,540	23·9
1948	2,460	26,140	421,832	1,600	23·5
1949	2,460	25,380	414,086	1,500	22·4
1950	2,480	24,420	412,284	1,350	21·2

na: Not available.
Source. Burton A. Crandell, *The Growth of the Intercity Bus Industry* (Syracuse, NY, 1954), Appendix A, Table A-2, pp. 280–2.

frequent departures than any other form of transport. The corporation attempted to set the pace with the smoothly running, highly integrated network of buses which were now supported by better amenities like more, and larger, terminals and the company's own chain of restaurants. Trailways also highlighted convenience with its new slogan 'Thru-Travel'. In a campaign started in 1951 the company's new advertising agency, J. Walter Thompson, told Americans that they would have no connection worries because they did not need to change buses when they chose Trailways. They could keep the same seat straight through to their destination.[18] Convenience was an essential ingredient in making the image of bus travel attractive in a period when more Americans had access to cars and thus to greater individual flexibility.

The necessity of advertising the main advantages of bus travel was ever-present in the second quarter of this century. Whether facing prosperity, depression, wartime restrictions or modest affluence, bus managers knew that they must keep telling Americans that coach travel was economical, convenient, efficient, comfortable and safe if they were to hold, let alone increase, their operations. Regular clients who travelled for work or family reasons needed to be assured that they were taking the right decision. The self-same virtues of buses also applied to pleasure travellers. In the growing leisure market it was possible to create new business by persuading Americans that economy, convenience or comfort could equally apply to taking a vacation, to sightseeing or to going to specific events in a chartered coach. Emotional copy appealing to a better quality of life could stimulate new travel wants and new patterns of travel consumption.

Advertising in the leisure market

The vacation market was not a new phenomenon in the early twentieth century. The rich had regularly travelled to warmer, scenic or exotic parts of the USA, usually by train. The advent and mass production of the car, improved roads, the shorter working week and entitlement to vacations created greater prospects for the tourist industry. A variety of businesses, including hotels, restaurants, construction firms and transport services, started to advance recreational travel in the 1920s. Progress was slow in the Depression and came to a virtual halt during the Second World War, but it surged in the more affluent and unrestricted mid-century years. The long-distance bus industry, well aware of the growing attractions of leisure travel to millions of Americans, rapidly promoted itself as an attractive tourist facility.[19]

The merits of economy, comfort and convenience were useful assets in moving into the vacation trade, but seasonality or the viability of travel throughout the year was a feature which was attractive not only to consumers but also to bus operators. These entrepreneurs early appreciated that their annual traffic flow was irregular. Following a steady build-up in the spring, peak demand came in the summer. Trade then declined in the autumn to a low point in mid-winter. One way of evening out and increasing this traffic was to persuade people to alter their existing, or acquire new, travel habits. Such changes could be marketed positively by suggesting new levels of social mobility. It would not only be adventurous and fulfilling but also fashionable to visit distant places at any time of the year.[20]

In the mid-1920s regional bus companies like Northland Transportation approached this type of advertising by extolling the newly discovered joys of vacationing in the wooded lakelands of Northern Minnesota during the summer. Once they were part of the Greyhound system they quickly told Minnesotans that they could travel beyond the Midwest for pleasure at any time of the year. Early Greyhound advertisements, even in the depths of the Depression, offered exciting new kinds of vacations anywhere in the USA because regular bus routes reached such interesting places as national parks, mountain ranges, ocean beaches, major cities and historical sites.[21]

Furthermore, each season could be promoted as a holiday venture. In the spring, when nature was at its best, there were many picturesque places to visit (figure 7). In the summer, when most people took time off, the full variety of holidays was offered, with emphasis on better facilities and more scenic routes than other means of transport. Recreational travel usually declined in the autumn, but bus executives aimed to stimulate business by special campaigns stressing less crowding, pleasant weather and marvellous colours, in addition to bargain fares.[22] Winter, the low season for tourism, was marketed vigorously by suggesting that an escape to the southern sunbelt or even northen ski grounds was within everyone's reach (figure 8). In the more competitive and affluent post-war years travel agents made bus vacations more attractive and convenient by creating an individual package tour, making hotel reservations and planning special sightseeing trips.[23] Bus advertisements sought to capture the public's imagination and to improve trade by portraying the positive features of each season for taking a break.

Other pleasure trips could be marketed without reference to the weather. National holidays like Thanksgiving and Christmas were occasions when Americans were urged to go home to celebrate in a traditional, family style in a new fashioned way, on time, warm and relaxed in their motor coaches.[24] Special events, like sports matches, historic pageants or fairs, were excellent opportunities for day or weekend trips. The big breakthrough in this type of recreational travel came with the Chicago World's Fair in 1933 and 1934, when Greyhound successfully marketed package tours to the 'Century of Progress' (figure 9). For the rest of the 1930s Greyhound and Trailways offered cheap fares to all city and regional expositions. This advertising generated business by suggesting new areas of entertainment.[25]

Fig. 7. *Saturday Evening Post*, 28 March 1953, p. 191.

Fig. 8. *Saturday Evening Post*, 20 December 1947, p. 11.

Fig. 9. *Saturday Evening Post*, 26 May 1934, p. 121.

Part of Greyhound's success in transporting Americans to and through the Chicago World's Fair in 1933 and 1934 was due to its novel offer of planned expense-paid tours. This product was very attractive to a variety of customers and both Greyhound and Trailways quickly organised a series of set itineraries taking tourists from one attraction to another, all with accommodation and meals pre-arranged and often with a tour guide. Despite the Depression, Trailways offered seventy-five sightseeing tours in 1937. With greater demand for vacations and increased spending power in the immediate post-war years, Greyhound extended its range of all-expense tours to over 200 and their selection grew in the 1950s. Bus firms were catering to the convenience of Americans by allowing the tourist to purchase a package, and their promotional campaign stressed the friendly and carefree nature of this travel adventure.[26]

Closely allied to planned and escorted trips was the charter business, which, thanks to the flexibility of buses to reach places not served by trains, had potential for growth. By the early 1950s Greyhound offered a full range of chartered services not only for business trips and sports events but also as fun excursions for clubs, societies and groups. Furthermore, they attempted to evoke an air of luxury by suggesting that a chartered bus was akin to having a limousine and private chauffeur at one's beck and call.[27] Advertising stimulated people to think about bus services as a private operation. At the same time it conveyed a new sense of well-being by suggesting a different type of social and geographical mobility. Charter operations were certainly a bright spot for the long-distance bus industry in the growing post-war affluence.

How to get the message across

Bus managers and their advertising agents might well plan campaigns to sell bus travel, but unless their ideas were communicated to a wide audience, they were unlikely to be successful. From the variety of media outlets available in the second quarter of this century, they selected the press as the most effective.[28] The press consisted of two distinct parts. Newspapers were sold locally and regionally, while magazines circulated among a much larger, and frequently nationwide audience. As most Americans travelled shorter distances, most advertising money went to newspapers. National bus companies spent their second highest amounts in major periodicals in order to tap the growing leisure market. They then used newer means of communication — films, radio and television — judiciously, while a diverse range of support materials, including direct mail, pamphlets, billboards, calendars, window displays, printed cards and teaching aids, offered further backup.[29]

Newspapers were widely read and all bus operators were aware of the potential publicity of black and white newspaper space. Dailies were particularly good as a means of revenue promotion. Smaller companies often relied on informational copy which listed the 'nuts and bolts' aspects of travel like destinations, fares, company name, terminal location and telephone number, and was sometimes illustrated by sketches of vehicles. Larger companies also used informational advertisements, but they tended to feature more graphic descriptions and scenic illustrations. Greyhound and Trailways agencies were able to use a pool of national advertisements on which they 'piggybacked' local information.[30] They supplied dummy copy featuring tableaux, sketches, illustrations and suggested footage, and requested terminal managers or travel agents to insert specific destinations with appropriate fares and the location of terminals (figure 10). These local officials then selected the position, frequency and size of the advertisements so as to maximise its impact. The travel section was usually the best location for factual information, but the news section was more likely to attract the attention of people who used alternative means of transport. Mid-week advertisements caught the attention of the weekend traveller and avoided the congestion of department-store promotions on Thursdays and Fridays. Special advertising like a chartered or a scheduled service to a football game obviously went on a sporting page. Newspapers had, and retained, the potential of attracting the attention of different types of audiences in numerous communities. Even after twenty years of experience as a national operator, Greyhound spent over 50 per cent of its mid-century advertising budget in local newspapers. Almost every daily — some 3,000 in number — and over 2,000 weeklies regularly carried Greyhound copy.[31]

While newspaper advertisements earnt the bus companies their daily bread, the jam for the larger firms came from the full-page, brightly coloured copy which they placed in national magazines. As soon as Greyhound became a national enterprise, in 1929, its executives followed the example of other corporations and undertook a nationwide promotional campaign. They broadcast the Greyhound idea by telling the middle-class readers of the *Saturday Evening Post* and the *American Magazine* about their new and exciting transcontinental service. The former magazine, with its large-page format suitable for dramatic pictures, had already been used by leading companies like Chrysler, General Electric and Fisher Body. The latter was a family periodical with the largest paid circulation of any magazine. Before the end of the year Greyhound also took to 'narrowcasting' and targeted special interest groups reading *Liberty* and *College Humor*. Though sceptics questioned the uncertain payoff for such advertising expenditure, the bus managers thought that they had not only made readers more bus conscious but that they had also increased the number of bus users.[32] Indeed, they were sufficiently persuaded to step up national promotions despite the onset of the Depression. By the mid-1930s Greyhound advertisements were carried in other general magazines, like *Collier's* and *Cosmopolitan*, as well as in review, women's, country homes, romance and movie periodicals, and also in educational publications. The backbone of the

Fig. 10. From the files of Walter Grosvenor of Beaumont & Hohman.

national campaign remained the full-colour pages in the *Saturday Evening Post*, but careful use of specialist publications meant that different groups of customers could be regularly targeted. This was of major importance at a time when long-distance buses did not yet have the image of low-status travel.[33]

Bus companies continued to recognise the importance of reaching a middle-class audience through magazine advertising. Even during the war, when travel was restricted, the trade association, the National Association of Motor Bus Operators, decided that it should build goodwill by advertising the industry's war contribution in leading magazines like the *Saturday Evening Post*, *Collier's* and *Life*.[34] There was no change of direction after the war. In 1949 Greyhound spent 29 per cent of its promotional budget on magazines and in the following year it ran advertisements in forty-four such publications, with a possible audience of 250 million.[35] In a period when the mass media was deemed important in providing guidelines for patterns of personal behaviour, bus executives joined their business counterparts in using popular periodicals to make emotional appeals to a widespread and aspiring readership.

Success in the competitive travel market, however, was also dependent on having the enthusiastic support of producers as well as consumers. To encourage their employees to have high standards of public relations, Greyhound officials invested advertising dollars on in-house newspapers. As early as 1929 the monthly *Greyhound Limited* was distributed to employees, ticket agents and bus enthusiasts. This was soon replaced by regional house organs like Pacific Greyhound's *Pacemaker*, Southeastern Lines' *Backfire* and Northland Greyhound's *Rear View Mirror*, which offered employees more personal contact. At the same time the *Highway Traveler* aimed to arouse the enthusiasm of tourists and travel agents through travel stories, humour, editorials and information on the latest developments in the bus industry. Initially free, this bimonthly publication with a circulation of between 75,000 and 100,000 generated sufficient interest among Americans enjoying recreational travel to reach a circulation of 410,000 in 1947 and to be available by subscription. For national companies it was important to have a high profile among as many groups of readers as possible and thus spending on employee and travel gazettes was worthwhile.[36]

While bus executives favoured newspapers and magazines for the bulk of their advertising, they did not neglect other means of communication in their promotional campaigns. Oral and visual media provided the advantages of speed and panoramic scenery. The radio, like the newspaper, was primarily a local instrument of news and entertainment, and could thus stimulate local business. In the late 1920s bus advertising was heard as spot announcements sandwiched in between programmes. These fifty-word messages had a direct sales appeal and induced enquiries about regular services and special attractions. Two other radio approaches became important in gaining publicity and prestige. Fifteen-minute travelogues describing interesting places to visit and sponsored programmes gave bus companies exposure. More ambitious quiz programmes about places of historical and geographical importance in North America, backed up by listener contests, provided further information and entertainment. Despite the ease with which radio found new audiences and stirred consumer interest, it did not become the leading promotional outlet. In 1940 no major intercity bus firm spent more than 15 per cent of its budget on radio, while the average was just over 7 per cent. Even in 1949, with radios playing in 39 million of the nation's 42 million homes, Greyhound devoted only 5·6 per cent of its expenditure to broadcasting. Certainly, the radio had a recognised function with spot announcements and this role was shared by television in the early 1950s, but bus executives preferred the written message.[37]

Films offered a more enticing means of attracting attention. Bus managers were interested in both the sponsored documentary and the popular motion picture featuring buses as romantic objects. Only major companies like Greyhound could afford to produce and distribute their own films, but these were reckoned to be a good investment in generating goodwill and prestige. By 1953 Greyhound had made four films — *They Discovered America, This Amazing America, Shortest Way Home* and *America for Me* — for showing to private groups and organisations and in movie theatres. Of more widespread impact were Hollywood films featuring buses, and these fortunately hit the screen when the bus industry was at a low point in the Depression. In 1934 MGM's *Fugitive Lovers* was the first motion picture to feature a bus as a source of drama. Universal Pictures soon followed with *Cross Country Cruise*, which used Greyhound buses as a background. The most famous movie of this genre, however, was Columbia Pictures' *It Happened One Night*, starring Clark Gable, Claudette Colbert and a Greyhound bus. The popularity of this film was such that some twenty years later Greyhound officials were delighted at the 1956 remake, *You Can't Run Away With It*, starring June Allyson. Greyhound saw the advantages of co-operating with films featuring their buses or even their terminals. As movie-going was a leading recreational activity in the second quarter of this century, this was virtually free advertising.[38]

Other subsidiary advertising methods varied widely among bus companies. In the early days of highway travel, promotional folders containing schedules, pictures and descriptions of scenic routes were available in depots, hotels, restaurants, shops, bus agencies and chambers of commerce. Brochures promoting special services, like expense-paid tours, vacation packages and seasonal trips, continued to be popular and were available from agents, at terminals and by postal and phone requests. These materials were also distributed through direct mail. Posters were sufficientlv attractive to be used not only in terminal window displays but also in department stores, hotels and travel bureaux. Wall exhibits in full-colour panels were available to teachers and schools, picturesque calendars were distributed to clients, and billboards, either near the terminal or on the bus routes, remained in regular use. Occasional novel schemes, like charms in the shape of the Greyhound dog, window streamers, lapel tags, stickers, souvenir booklets of trips and round-trip sales contests, added zest to particular campaigns.[39] Recognising the function of advertising in providing information and arousing new consumer interest, bus companies used a range of secondary measures to reinforce their main campaigns.

Conclusion

Ironically the impact of all the time, money and effort spent on advertising was immeasurable. The long-distance bus industry expanded rapidly in the 1920s, weathered the major Depression of the 1930s, grew during the emergency of the Second World War and held on to this market in the late 1940s (see table 3). Throughout these years bus operators were committed to spending on promotional materials. They made regular expenditure on informational advertising in the form of schedules announcing changes in timetables, fares and routes. They also advertised each season, though with differing emphasis. In addition they allocated substantial 'one-off' amounts to underwrite specific campaigns, as, for example, in the depths of the Depression in the early 1930s, when trade was declining, or in the immediate aftermath of the Second World War, whey they needed to re-establish peacetime travel flows.[40] Executives and their advertising agencies were anxious to ascertain the effectiveness of their promotional efforts. They analysed figures before a particular drive or for a similar time-period in a different year. They also obtained some feedback from telephone enquiries, letters and questionnaires completed by travellers. Nevertheless they emerged with inexact answers. Their conclusions were generally positive but imprecise, as their review of the 1950 'Fall round up of travel bargains' suggests:

> We realise the overall income picture is not pleasing when compared with the previous periods — but who knows what our position would be had there been no campaign? Everyone who took an active part seems to agree, however, that [the campaign] was effective, and that it resulted in more sales than otherwise would have been made.[41]

Though such sentiments may seem unsatisfactory for enterprising businessmen, the bus executives were not alone either then or since. Other leading businessmen have faced similar situations and have publicly acknowledged that half of their advertising money was probably wasted — but they did not know which half.[42] Bus men joined their fellow entrepreneurs and accepted that advertising was part of a modern business enterprise even though its cost effectiveness was problematic. They thus tended to spend as much as they could afford rather than asking how much was needed to do a specific job.[43]

Increasingly in the twentieth century advertising has come to be regarded as an inevitable part of any major enterprise and of a capitalistic economy. With the growing impersonality of national markets in the USA, producers needed some means of informing consumers about which goods and services were available. Advertising as a means of communication became a permanent force in business life. This fact was readily recognised by bus entrepreneurs who also quickly learnt that advertising could create consumer demand by suggesting new patterns of social behaviour. Stimulated primarily by their desire to gain more passengers, but also by the established patterns of corporate behaviour and the presence of a dynamic advertising industry which could plan campaigns on a long-term basis, they offered their distinctive features — economy, convenience, safety, comfort and dependability — to any traveller and they promoted recreation as a new and fashionable activity for the middling classes. The consumer interest in the reception of these messages, however, depended on the alternative ways in which Americans might participate in geographical and social mobility. Increasing numbers wanted to drive their own cars to their chosen destinations, and public transport remained a low priority. Within the public sector, bus operators clearly demonstrated that they could win markets and retain them in the face of competition and in this endeavour advertising played a necessary part.

Acknowledgements

I wish to thank P. Fearon, R. Marchand and M. Pumphrey for their constructive comments on an earlier version of this paper, and the Nuffield Foundation, the British Academy and the Minnesota Historical Society for their generous financial support, without which my research could not have been undertaken.

Notes

1 This study is based on the advertising material of either the Greyhound Corporation or the National Trailways Bus System. The American intercity bus industry is composed of a large number of small operators who provided a local or regional service. The two leading long-distance companies are Greyhound and Trailways. The former emerged to national status in the late 1920s. The latter was formed in 1936 as an amalgamation of independent carriers. In 1937 Greyhound operated 16 per cent of the total bus miles in the USA while Trailways operated 12 per cent. By 1950 their shares were 20 per cent and 17 per cent respectively. (Trailways and the Continental Bus System are treated as one corporate entity.) Greyhound had 4 per cent of the passenger market in 1937 and Trailways had 1 per cent. The respective figures for 1950 were 15 per cent and 6 per cent. See B. B. Crandall, *The Growth of the Intercity Bus Industry* (Syracuse, NY, 1954), p. 288.

2 Discussions of the growth and competitive position of the main means of transport in the USA in the early twentieth century can be found in J. B. Rae. *The Road and the Car in American Life* (Cambridge, Mass., 1971); W. R. Childs, *Trucking and the Public Interest: the Emergence of Federal Regulation, 1914–1940* (Knoxville, Tenn., 1985); D. V. Harper, *Economic Regulation of the Motor Trucking Industry by the States* (Urbana, Ill., 1959); Crandall, *The Growth of the Intercity Bus Industry*; M. Walsh, 'The early growth of long-distance bus transport in the United States', in T. C. Barker (ed.), *The Economic and Social Effects of the Spread of Motor Vehicles* (London, 1987), pp. 81–96; D. M. Itzkoff, *Off the Track: the Decline of the Intercity Passenger Train in the United States* (Westport, Conn., 1985); R. M. Kane and A. D. Vose, *Air Transportation* (Dubuque, Ia, 8th edn, 1982).

3 In addition to Crandall, *The Growth of the Intercity Bus Industry* and Walsh, 'The early growth of long-distance transport in the United States', there is one general history of buses and two company studies. A. E. Meier and J. P. Hoscheck, *Over the Road: a History of Intercity Bus Transportation in the United States* (Upper Montclair, NJ, 1975) was sponsored by the Motor Bus Society, which is dedicated to the history of motor buses in the USA. C. Jackson, *Hounds of the Road: a History of the Greyhound Bus Company* (Bowling Green, Ky, 1984). is a social history of the Greyhound buses. O. Schisgall, *The Greyhound Story: from Hibbing to Everywhere* (Chicago, 1985) is a company-sponsored book. Schisgall was fortunate to have access to materials at the Greyhound Corporation which have not been accessible to other authors. Nevertheless his

book, like Jackson's, lacks the systematic analytical approach appreciated by transport and business historians.

4 The major authority on the growth of managerial capitalism is Alfred D. Chandler jr, *The Visible Hand: the Managerial Revolution in American Business* (Cambridge, Mass., 1977). See also his *Strategy and Structure: Chapters in the History of American Industrial Enterprise* (Cambridge, Mass., 1962).

5 For surveys on the growth of advertising see Daniel Pope, *The Making of Modern Advertising* (New York, 1983); Frank S. Presbrey, *The History and Development of Advertising* (Garden City, NY, 1929); Otis A. Pease, *The Responsibilities of American Advertising* (New Haven, 1958); David M. Potter, *People of Plenty* (Chicago, 1954), Ch. 8. For contrasting discussions on the role of advertising and advertisers in American society see Stuart Ewen, *Captains of Consciousness: Advertising and the Social Roots of the Consumer Culture* (New York, 1976); Vance Packard, *The Hidden Persuaders* (New York, 1957); Stephen Fox, *The Mirror Makers: a History of American Advertising and its Creators* (New York, 1984); Roland Marchand, *Advertising the American Dream: Making Way for Modernity 1920–1940* (Berkeley, Calif., 1985); Michael Schudson, *Advertising, the Uneasy Persuasion: its Dubious Impact on American Society* (New York, 1984). Advertising and cultural issues are examined in Warren I. Susman, *Culture as History: the Transformation of American Society in the Twentieth Century* (New York, 1984) and T. J. Jackson Lears, 'Some versions of Fantasy: towards a cultural history of American advertising, 1880–1930', *Prospects*, IX (1984), pp. 349–405.

6 Greyhound employed an advertising manager and an outside agency, Beaumont & Hohman of Chicago. The company remained Greyhound's agency from the late 1920s until 1956 when they were replaced by Grey Advertising. Trailways employed Ferry Hanly Co., of Chicago in 1937 and Needham Louis & Brorby of Chicago in 1939. With much stronger competition in the post-war years they looked to a leading advertising agency, J. Walter Thompson. *Advertising Age*, 20 Feb. 1939, p. 1, 10 Dec. 1956, pp. 3, 119 (hereafter abbreviated to *AA*), J. Walter Thompson, *Newsletter*, 28 May 1951, p. 5 (J. Walter Thompson Archives, Manuscript Department, William R. Perkins Library, Duke University, Durham, NC, hereafter abbreviated to JWT).

7 W. R. Fowler jr, 'The why of Greyhound advertising', *Bus Journal*, March (1929), pp. 26–7; W. R. Fowler jr, 'Advertising in the motor bus business', Greyhound Corporate Archives, University of Wyoming, File 3, No. 5, *c.* 1929, 5pp. (hereafter abbreviated to GCA). John B. Walker, 'How to sell bus rides', National Association of Motor Bus Operators, *Proceedings*, V (1931), pp. 86–91 (hereafter abbreviated as NAMBO, *Proc.*); *Rear View Mirror*, XIX, 2 (1952), p. 7, XX, 4 (1953), p. 9 (being the in-house newsheet of Northland Greyhound Lines, hereafter abbreviated to *RVM*).

8 It is possible to compare advertisements for leading companies and for the trade associations in the bus, railroad and airline industries by examining the material they published in leading magazines during the Second World War. See, for example, the *Saturday Evening Post* (hereafter abbreviated to *SEP*), and *Collier's*, 1940–45.

9 Statistics on the comparative costs of travelling by different means of transport vary. The printed evidence in the major trade journals like *Railway Age* and *Bus Transportation* (hereafter cited as *RA* and *BT*) point to lower running costs for buses in the 1920s and 1930s as did Interstate Commerce Commission, *Coordination of Motor Transportation* (Decisions of the Interstate Commerce Commission of the United States), CLXXXII (Washington, DC, 1932). However, the chief competitor of buses and trains was the private car and here the evidence on comparative costs is much more difficult to establish. Both the bus and rail industries claimed that the true cost of driving a car was higher than rail or bus fares, but motorists tended to measure costs of driving in terms of individual mobility rather than dollar expenses only.

10 *SEP*, 14 Sept. 1929, p. 244, 21 Jan. 1939, third cover, 24 Sept. 1949, p. 121. *Highway Traveler*, I, 4, (1929), p. 3, III, 5 (1931), p. 33, XXII, 1 (1950), fourth cover (being a travel magazine sponsored by Greyhound, hereafter abbreviated to *HT*). *Trailways*, IV, 11 (1938), p. 13 (hereafter abbreviated to *Tr.*). Many examples of Greyhound advertisements from the popular magazines can be conveniently found in the D'Arcy Collection of Clippings located at the Department of Communications Library of the University of Illinois at Urbana-Champaign.

11 'Report of the Committee on Advertising and Publicity', NAMBO, *Proc.*, V (1931), pp. 49–50; *RA*, 28 May 1932, pp. 913–14; *SEP*, 21 Nov. 1936, p. 66, 22 Jan. 1938, third cover, 24 Apr. 1948; *Tr.*, VII, 6 (1941), third cover.

12 *SEP*, 22 Feb. 1930, p. 151, 12 Apr. 1930, p. 300, 27 Mar. 1937, p. 131, Sept. 1937, p. 73; *HT*, IV, 2 (1932), p. 27, VIII, 4 (1936), p. 26, 46–7; *Tr.*, I, 1 (1935), fourth cover, II, 1 (1936), third cover, II, 3 (1936), p. 19, III, 4 (1937), pp. 10, 13; Northland Greyhound Lines Bus *Timetable*, 1 Feb. 1937, p. 30 (hereafter abbreviated as NGLB*TT*).

13 *RVM*, XII, 8 (1946), p. 7, XV, 3 (1948), pp. 6–7, XVI, 4 (1949), pp. 10–11; *HT*, XIX, 4 (1947), pp. 18–19, XX, 2 (1948), pp. 16–17, 46–7, XXVI, 3 (1954), fourth cover; *Tr.*, XII, 2 (1948), pp. 31, fourth cover, XIV, 3 (1950), second cover; NGLB*TT* 26 Sept. 1954, fourth cover, 27 June, 1956, fourth cover; *Look*, 15 Dec. 1954, p. 45; *Ladies Home Journal*, Sept. 1955, p. 98; Meier and Hoschek, *Over the Road*, pp. 89–91, 98, 100, 103, 118, 121.

14 *SEP*, 23 Mar. 1929, p. 180, 26 Mar. 1955, p. 163; *HT*, I, 2 (1929), p. 21, I, 4 (1929), p. 3, II, 2 (1930), p. 31, IV, 5 (1932), pp. 27–8, IX, 5 (1937), third cover, XXV, 3 (1953), fourth cover; *RVM*, XV, 1 (1948), pp. 1–2, XV, 2 (1948), p. 1, XV, 3 (1948), p. 2.

15 The Jefferson Company was a leading regional operator in the states of the Upper Mississippi Valley. See, for example, *Indianola Record*, 15 Feb. 1940; *Mason City Globe-Gazette*, 17 Feb., 30 Sept. 1940; *Iowa Falls Citizen*, 24 Sept. 1940; *Eldora Index*, 26 Sept. 1940; *Hampton Chronicle*, 3 Oct. 1940; *Sheffield Press*, 3 Oct. 1940. (All clippings gathered by the Mid-West News Syndicate and Clipping Service, Des Moines, Ia and the Commercial Clipping Service, Des Moines, Ia, in the Edgar F. Zelle Collection, the Jefferson Company, Minneapolis.)

16 *SEP*, 23 Feb. 1929, p. 135, 'Advertising budget and revenue quotas for 1929', n.p. File 1, no. 1 (GCA); Fowler, 'Advertising in the motor business', n.p.; *The Greyhound Limited*, I, 6 (1929), p. 2, II, 2 (1929), p. 2; *Saturday Evening Post* had a circulation of 2,900,868 in 1928 and 3,028,408 in 1929; JWT, *Newsletter*, 1 Oct. 1928, p. 2 and 'Advertising budget and revenue quotas . . .' n.p. It was generally assumed that an average of three persons read each magazine, JWT, *Newsletter*, 6 Sept, 1928, p. 1; 'Report of the national advertising and publicity committee', NAMBO, *Proc.*, XVI (1942), p. 134.

17 *SEP*, 12 Sept. 1931, p. 120, 11 Mar. 1933, p. 70; 15 July, 1933, p. 54, 14 Sept. 1935, p. 73, 26 Oct. 1935, p. 97; *AA*, 2 Sept. 1935, p. 15; *Tr.*, I, 5 (1936), second cover, I, 6 (1936), p. 8, II, 1 (1936), fourth cover, II, 2 (1936), p. 8, II, 4 (1937), p. 1, fourth cover, II, 5–6 (1937), p. 21.

18 *RVM*, XII, 7 (1945), pp. 1, 7; *HT*, XX, 4 (1948), pp. 14–15, 40–1; *SEP*, 24 Jan. 1948, p. 66; NGLB*TT*, 5 June 1946, p. 3, fourth cover, 12 Nov. 1947, fourth cover; JWT, *Newsletter*, 28 May 1951, p. 5; Trailways Bus System, East Coast Group, 'Advertisements, 1951–59', Microfilm AD70 (JWT Archives).

19 There has been remarkably little scholarly interest in the growth of tourism. General information on the tourist in western America is available in E. Pomeroy, *In Search of the Golden West* (New York, 1957); J. A. Jakle, *The Tourist: Travel in Twentieth Century North America* (Lincoln, Nebr., 1985) offers a broader perspective. Some useful insights can also be found in W. J. Belasco, *Americans on the Road: from Autocamp to Motel, 1910–45* (Cambridge, Mass., 1979); J. B. Rae, *The Road and the Car in American Life*, especially Ch..7; J. Weinberger, 'Economic aspects of recreation', *Harvard Business Review*, XV (1936–37), pp. 448–63. For the bus industry see D. Short, 'What can bus lines do to promote year-around vacations?', an address to the annual meeting of NAMBO in 1948. This address and the discussion which followed can be found in NAMBO, *Proc.*, XIX (1948), pp. 170–85.

20 'Advertising budget and revenue quotas . . .', n.p.; *AA*, 3 Oct. 1949, p. 18, 7 Aug. 1950, p. 24; *RVM*, XVII, 9 (1950), p. 10.

21 Minnesota Motor Bus Association, *Travel By Bus*, 25 June 1925, insert between pp. 16 and 17 (schedule and information brochure); *BT*, XVI, 12 (1927), pp. 671–3; *SEP*, 23 May 1931, pp. 134–51, 10 June, 1933, p. 52, 30 Jan. 1934, p. 68; *Tr.*, II, 1 (1936), fourth cover, II, 5–6 (1937), p. 15. For the relationship of Northland Transportation to the Greyhound Corporation see M. Walsh, 'Tracing the hound: the Minnesota roots of the Greyhound Bus Corporation', *Minnesota History*, XLIX (1985), pp. 310–21.

22 *SEP*, 27 July, 1935, p. 52, 27 Mar. 1937, p. 121, 26 Mar. 1949, p. 117, 28 Mar. 1953, p. 191; *BT*, XVI, 4 (1937), pp. 9–11; *Tr.*, II, 2 (1936), second cover, fourth cover, IV, 10 (1928), third cover, VII, 5 (1941), p. 17, XI, 1 (1946), p. 31; *Ladies Home Journal*, Oct. 1939, p. 107, May 1949, p. 244; *Collier's*, 6 Sept. 1947, p. 58, 28 May 1949, p. 244; *RVM*, XIV, 7 (1947), p. 3, XVI, 4 (1949), p. 2, XVII, 9 (1950), p. 10, XVIII, 10 (1951), p. 4, XX, 1 (1953), p. 17.

23 *SEP*, 9 Nov. 1929, p. 208, 18 Nov. 1933, p. 64, 17 Nov. 1934, p. 71, 11 Jan. 1936, second cover, 21 Dec. 1946, p. 88, 18 Dec. 1948, p. 77; *HT*, IV, 1 (1932), p. 29; *Tr.*, II, 7–8 (1937), fourth cover, VI, 1 (1940), fourth cover; NGLB*TT*, 1 Feb. 1937, third cover; *BT*, XIX, 2 (1940), pp. 79–80.

24 *SEP*, 21 Dec. 1935, p. 48; *HT*, VI, 6 (1934–35), second cover, XI, 6 (1939–40), pp. 4, XII, 6 (1940–41), fourth cover; *Tr.*, I, 3 (1935), third cover, II, 3 (1936), p. 17, VI, 4 and 5 (1940), third cover.

25 *HT*, V, 1 (1933), p. 4, VI, 3 (1934), pp. 7, 45, XII, 2 (1940), p. 2, XX, 2 (1948), fourth cover; *SEP*, 13 May 1933, p. 83, 26 May 1934, p. 121; *Ladies Home Journal*, May 1936, p. 104, June, 1939, p. 56; *AA*, 18 May 1936, p. 44, 27 Feb. 1939, p. 1; *Tr.*, VI, 2 (1940), third cover. All Greyhound histories agree on the importance of the Chicago World's Fair in rescuing Greyhound's ailing business. Schisgall, *The Greyhound Story*, p. 41; Jackson, *Hounds of the Road*, pp. 45–8; Walsh, 'The early growth of long-distance bus transport in the United States', p. 89.

26 *HT*, V, 3 (1933), p. 3, VI, 2 (1934), pp. 34–5, VI, 3 (1934), p. 2, VI, 6 (1935), p. 8, VII, 5 (1935), third cover, XIX, 2 (1947), third cover, XIX, 3 (1947), second cover, XXIII, 2 (1951), fourth cover; *Tr.*, I, 5 (1936), fourth cover, II, 5–6 (1937), fourth cover, II, 7–8 (1937), p. 17, IV, 9 (1938), p. 6, fourth cover, XI, 4 (1947), pp. 1, 28–9, XIII, 4 (1949), p. 23, XV, 1 (1950), third cover; *AA*, 19 Feb. 1940, p. 27, III, Jan. (1955), p. 20; *BT*, XXIV, 9 (1945), p. 63, XXV, 5 (1946), pp. 75–6, XXXIV, 7 (1955), p. 44; *RVM*, XII, 12 (1945), p. 1, XIII, 3 (1946), p. 8, XIII, 8 (1946), p. 3, XVII, 2 (1950), p. 6, XVII, 8 (1950), p. 13; NGLB*TT*, 22 June 1952, fourth cover, 26 Sept. 1954, p. 3, 27 June, 1956, p. 3.

27 *HT*, XXIII, 3 (1951), pp. 21–3, XXV, 3 (1953), pp. 40–1, XXVI, 3 (1954), pp. 36–7; *BT*, XXIX, 2 (1950), p. 60; NGLB*TT*, 28 Oct. 1952, p. 3, 26 Sept. 1954, second cover, 27 June 1956, second cover.

28 Newspapers and magazines have remained popular outlets for advertising. As late as 1982 in the USA, newspapers received 27 per cent of the total advertising expenditure, with television coming second at 22 per cent and direct mail third with 15 per cent; Schudson, *Advertising: the Uneasy Persuasion*, p. 67.

29 'How to increase bus patronage?' Book 2, *Motorbus Transportation* (Scranton, Pa, 1930), pp. 15–45; NAMBO, *Proc.*, IV (1930), pp. 70–5, VI (1932), pp. 42, 45.

30 'Piggybacking' describes the flexible way in which Greyhound could personalise and make every advertisement in the newspapers or on television a local advertisement. E. H. Holzer, 'Greyhound bus line', Ms, Grey Advertising, Chicago, n.d., p. 5.

31 *BT*, III, 3 (1924), pp. 105–8, VI, 12 (1927), p. 673, XV, 3 (1936), pp. 118–20, XIX, 5 (1940), pp. 208–9; *The Greyhound*, I, 1 (1928), p. 4; *The Greyhound Limited*, I, 5 (1929), p. 2; J. B. Walker, 'Advertising the long haul operation', Report of the Committee on Advertising and Publicity, NAMBO, *Proc.*, III (1929), pp. 31–3; 'Plan for newspaper advertising', Report of the Committee on Advertising and Publicity, *NAMBO Proc.*, VI (1932), pp. 41–5; *RVM*, XVII, 8 (1950), p. 6; L. A. Rossman to C. E. Wickman, O. S. Caesar and P. Tibbets, 'Advertising plans for the Northland Greyhound Lines' and 'Advertising problems of the Motor Transit Company and the Greyhound Lines', being part of discussion paper on subjects pertaining to the motor bus industry, 21 Aug. 1929 (L. A. Rossman papers, Grand Rapids, Minn.). Advertisements from the personal files of W. Grosvenor, who worked for Beaumont & Hohman of Cleveland, OH and from Trailways Bus System, East Coast Group, 1951–59, Microfilm AD 70 (JWT Archives).

32 'Advertising budget and revenue quotas . . .', n.p.; untitled piece on advertising, 2p., *c.* 1929, File 3 No. 3 GCR; Fowler, 'Advertising in the motor business', n.p.; *The Greyhound Limited*, I, 6 (1929), p. 2, II, 2 (1929), p. 2; *BT*, III, (1929), p. 144; *SEP*, 23 Feb. 1929, p. 135, 23 Mar. 1929, p. 180, 20 April, 1929, p. 200, 8 June 1929, p. 159, 14 Sept. 1929, p. 244, 9 Nov. 1929, p. 208; *American Magazine*, May 1929, p. 117, July 1929, p. 111, Aug. 1929, p. 125, Oct. 1929, p. 135; Marchand, *Advertising the American Dream*, pp. 5, 7; Presbrey, *The History and Development of Advertising*, pp. 590–7.

33 *AA*, 13 Jan. 1936, p. 30, 10 Jan. 1938, p. 20. The image of long-distance bus transport was not yet perceived as being suitable only for those who could not afford better. This post-war image tends to be projected backwards without any substantive evidence.

34 M. Walsh, '"Serve See America Now": Advertising Bus Travel in the US during the Second World War', *European Journal of Marketing*, XXII (1988) (concurrently with *Journal of Advertising History*, XI (1988), pp. 41–60).

35 *AA*, 9 Mar. 1936, pp. 1 4; NAMBO, *Proc.*, XVI (1942), pp. 135–8; *RVM*, XVII, 8 (1950), pp. 6–7. Greyhound officials estimated that the forty-four periodicals had a total single issue circulation of 83·5 million, and that each copy of the magazine averaged at least two to three readers. No account was taken of how many of these people read more than one magazine and were thus included twice or several times.

36 Information on company newsletters is difficult to locate because relatively few were deposited in libraries. Fowler, 'The why of Greyhound advertising', pp. 26–7; *The Greyhound Limited*, I, 8 (1921), p. 1; *HT*, II, 2 (1930), p. 3, III, 4 (1931), p. 31, XIX, 6 (1947–48), p. 48; *RVM*, X, 1 (1943), p. 1, XIX, 3 (1952).

37 JWT, *Newsletter*, 15 Sept. 1928, pp. 1–2; *Pickwick–Greyhound Highway Log*, I, 8 (1930), p. 3; *BT*, X, 11 (1931), pp. 578–80, XIV, 9 (1935), pp. 347–8, XVII, 4 (1938), p. 178, XIX, 3 (1940), p. 113, XIX, 5 (1940), pp. 208–9; *RVM*, XVII, 8 (1950), pp. 6–7, XVIII, 9 (1951), p. 3, 10; *AA*, 1 Oct. 1951, p. 70; Erik Barnouw, *A Tower in Babel*, I, to 1933, and *The Golden Web*, II, 1933–52 of *A History of Broadcasting in the United Staes* (Oxford and New York, 1966, 1968) and Marchand, *Advertising the American Dream*, pp. 88–110 offer some general insights on radio advertising.

38 *HT*, VI, 1 (1934), pp. 16–17, 38; *RVM*, III (1940), p. 2, VIII, 1 (1941), pp. 16–17, XIII, 4 (1946), p. 7, XVIII, 1 (1951), p. 14, XVIII, 11 (1951), p. 13, XVIII, 12 (1951), p. 9, XIX, 3 (1952), p. 3; *AA*, 28 May 1956, p. 77; Jackson, *Hounds of the Road*, pp. 48–9. For background information on the social impact of films, see Robert Sklar, *Movie-Made America: a Social History of American Movies* (New York, 1975).

39 Fowler, 'Advertising in the motor bus business', n.p.; W. C. Beaumont, 'Selling transportation to the public', NAMBO, *Proc.*, IV (1930), pp. 90–1, 'Advertising as a medium of getting additional revenue', NAMBO, *Proc.*, XX (1949), pp. 171–5; *BT*, IV, 3 (1925), p. 129, IV, 7 (1925), p. 330, V, 1 (1926), p. 18, XVI, 11 (1927), pp. 613–16, XVIII, 3 (1939), pp. 122–6, XVIII, 6 (1939), pp. 294–6, XXV, 11 (1946), pp. 66–9; *RVM*, VIII, 11 (1941), p. 3, VIII, 12 (1941), p. 7, XII, 2 (1945), p. 8, XIII, 7 (1946), p. 6, XIII, 12 (1946), p. 4, XIV, 10 (1947), p. 3, XVI, 5 (1949), p. 2, XVII, 10 (1950), p. 4, XVIII, 12 (1951), p. 9.

40 'Advertising budget . . .', n.p.; NAMBO, *Proc.*, V (1931), pp. 49–50; NAMBO, 'Minutes of the Board of Directors', 26–7 Oct., 1944, pp. 11–12; *AA*, 12 Apr. 1945, p. 22, 3 Oct. 1949, p. 18, 18 Aug. 1950. p. 24.

41 *RVM*, XVII, 12 (1950), p. 4.

42 Schudson, *Advertising: the Uneasy Persuasion*, pp. 85–6.

43 The most frequently cited figures of advertising budgets in the 1920s and 1930s ranged between 2·5 and 5 per cent of gross revenue. Bus operators set aside a specific percentage and then added fixed amounts for particular campaigns. Fowler, 'The why of Greyhound advertising', pp. 26–7; Fowler, 'Advertising in the motor bus business', n.p.; *BT*, X, 8 (1931), pp. 457–9, XVII, 4 (1938), p. 178, XIX, 5 (1940), p. 213; NAMBO, *Proc.*, IV (1930), pp. 74, 91.